JONI MITCHELL

IN HER OWN WORDS

Woodstock

I came upon a child of God
He was walking along the road
And I asked him "Where are you going?"
This he told me
He said "I'm going on down to Yasgur's farm
I'm going to join in a rock 'n' roll band
I'm going to camp out on the land
And try and get my soul free"

    We are stardust
    We are golden
    And we've got to get ourselves
    Back to the garden

"Well can I walk beside you
I have come here to lose the smog
And I feel to be a cog
In something turning
Well maybe it is just the time of year
Or maybe it's the time of man
I don't know who I am
But life is for learning

    We are stardust
    We are golden
    And we've got to get ourselves
    Back to the garden

By the time we got to Woodstock
We were half a million strong
And everywhere there were songs and celebrations
And I dreamed I saw the bombers
Riding shotgun in the sky
And they were turning
Into butterflies
Above our nation

    We are stardust (billion year old carbon)
    We are golden (caught in the devils bargin)
    And we got to get ourselves
    Back to the garden.

JONI MITCHELL

IN HER OWN WORDS

conversations with

MALKA MAROM

ECW PRESS

Editor for the press: Jennifer Knoch
Cover and text design: Tania Craan
Typesetting: Troy Cunningham
Endpapers: © Joni Mitchell
Front cover: Photograph by Jack Robinson,
The Jack Robinson Archive, LLC;
www.robinsonarchive.com
Back cover: © Sherry Rayn Barnett
Author photo: Anne Bayin
All lyrics reprinted with the permission
of Joni Mitchell

Published by ECW Press
2120 Queen Street East, Suite 200
Toronto, Ontario, Canada M4E 1E2
416-694-3348 / info@ecwpress.com

LIBRARY AND ARCHIVES CANADA
CATALOGUING IN PUBLICATION

Marom, Malka, author
Joni Mitchell : in her own words / Malka Marom.

Issued in print and electronic formats.
ISBN 978-1-77041-132-6 (bound)
978-1-77090-580-1 (pdf);
978-1-77090-581-8 (epub)

1. Mitchell, Joni, 1943–. 2. Singers—Canada—
Biography. 3. Composers—Canada—Biography.
I. Title.

ML420.M523M35 2014   782.42164092
C2014-902514-9   C2014-902515-7

Printing: Friesens   5 4 3 2 1
PRINTED AND BOUND IN CANADA

The publication of *Joni Mitchell: In Her Own Words* has been generously supported by the Canada Council
for the Arts which last year invested $157 million to bring the arts to Canadians throughout the country, and
by the Ontario Arts Council (OAC), an agency of the Government of Ontario, which last year funded 1,793
individual artists and 1,076 organizations in 232 communities across Ontario, for a total of $52.1 million.
We also acknowledge the financial support of the Government of Canada through the Canada Book Fund
for our publishing activities, and the contribution of the Government of Ontario through the Ontario Book
Publishing Tax Credit and the Ontario Media Development Corporation.

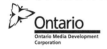
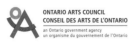

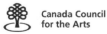

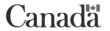

For Joni

In search of love and music
My whole life has been
Illumination
Corruption
And diving, diving, diving, diving,
Diving down to pick up on every shiny thing
Just like that black crow flying
In a blue sky

I looked at the morning
After being up all night
I looked at my haggard face in the bathroom light
I looked out the window
And I saw that ragged soul take flight
I saw a black crow flying
In a blue sky
Oh I'm like a black crow flying
In a blue sky
       ("Black Crow")

One November night in 1966, I was driving in circles, around one block, then another, which was very strange. I always drove with purpose from point A to point B, no meandering, no detours, pressing over the speed limit sometimes — okay, most times. Trying to juggle a big career and a household with two little children and a bad marriage, I was always rushing, yet could never catch up. Why did I deviate from my norm that night? I don't know. Earlier that evening I had been dealt a crucial dilemma, but instead of sleeping on it, as common sense demanded, I was driving on it. Driving from one dark and deserted street to another — they rolled Toronto up for the night very early in those days. It was already winter cold, and the usually humming Yorkville Village was deserted. Even the winos and the flower children had taken shelter. The only light still on was above the entrance to the Riverboat coffeehouse.

I had never gone alone to a club, a bar, or a coffeehouse so late at night. "Only streetwalkers go out alone late at night," my mother had drilled into me ever since I reached puberty. But it was a night like no other night already, and maybe because the street was deserted and no one could see me, I got out of the car and went down the steps into the basement that housed the Riverboat.

Inside, the coffeehouse was a dark hole. After the eyes adjusted, you could see that the place was empty, except at the back — was that two of the staff making out? Long and narrow, the coffeehouse resembled a submarine more than a riverboat and, at a squeeze, could hold 120 people decked out in their fab, groovy, or funky attires. They would fall into a hush as soon as the house lights dimmed, crowding so close to the stage they could almost touch performers like Odetta, Gordon Lightfoot, or Neil Young. But on this November night, bereft of their presence, the place looked forlorn. And devoid of the veil of their cigarette smoke, the naked décor seemed embarrassingly tacky: the blue glass in the portholes windows was too harsh to suggest river or sky, and the brass that ringed each window was Vegas glitzy. But the pine-panelled walls enhanced the acoustics of a sound system so good it lured musicians from all over the continent to perform there. Solid-wood slab tables anchored the booths and lent the place a sense of permanence uncommon to most of the other coffeehouses that were sprouting in Yorkville Village like mushrooms after a summer soak. I slid quietly into the darkest booth nearest to the door.

On the lit-up stage — a platform only a foot, if that, off the floor — stood a girl who must have picked out her miniskirt at the Salvation Army. With her back turned to the empty seats, she seemed totally engrossed in trying to tune her guitar and failing, trying and failing, which gave me the impression that she was one of the waitresses who had nothing better to do than to playact at being the performer.

"Compliments of the house, Malka," whispered a server as he rested a cappuccino in front of me.

"Thank you." My fingers clasped the cup to warm up. I savoured the aroma and sipped the cappuccino slowly, very slowly. I was in no hurry that night. I felt like I was sneaking out of life, and like stolen water it was sweet.

The girl on the stage also seemed to be in no hurry to do anything but tune and retune her guitar, tune and retune. My cappuccino cup stood empty and still she kept turning the knob of one string, then another, this way and that way, a bit higher and just a bit lower — but with such intensity that, like a magnet, it drew you out of yourself. She turned to face the empty seats and, leaning closer to the mike, she strummed a progression of chords with a surprisingly assertive hand. They were unlike any chords I'd heard before. I found myself hanging on every note. And then she started to sing. From verse to verse, her song was like a kaleidoscope that splintered my perception, turned it round and round, then refocused to illuminate a reality I had not dared to see.

> We're captive on the carousel of time
> We can't return, we can only look behind
> From where we came
> And go round and round and round
> In the circle game
> > ("The Circle Game")

> I came to the city
> And lived like an old Crusoe
> On an island of noise
> > ("Song to a Seagull")

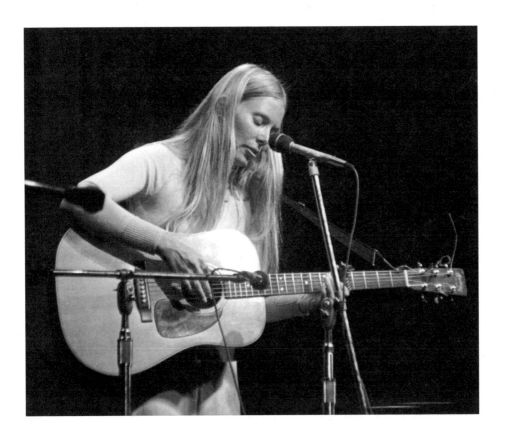

I get the urge for going
But I never seem to go
When the meadow grass was turning brown
Summertime was falling down and winter was closing in

Now the warriors of winter they gave a cold triumphant shout
And all that stays is dying and all that lives is gettin' out
 ("Urge for Going")

Go where you will go to
Know that I will know you
Someday I may know you very well
 ("Michael from Mountains")

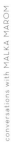

The stranger on the stage knew me very well already. And the more she sang, the more her voice became my own.

> I can't go back there anymore
> You know my keys won't fit the door
> You know my thoughts don't fit the man
> They never can, they never can
> ("I Had a King")

As she sang, I realized there was no more escaping into hope now, into illusions or denial. "I had a king in a salt-rusted carriage / Who carried me off to his country for marriage too soon." My marriage was a bust.

This girl, who looked no older than seventeen or eighteen — twenty at most — portrayed an existential reality with such power, it broke me down even as it lifted my spirits. Whoever she was, her unique gifts generated an extraordinary elation inside me. I applauded till my hands burned, but compared to how I felt, my applause sounded hollow.

The singer nodded her appreciation. She was standing now, almost a little pigeon-toed, her cheap miniskirt askew, and as she inched her way closer to the microphone for the start of her closing song, she let her long blond hair cover her face, almost like she wanted to disappear and just let the songs be who she was.

> I've looked at life from both sides now
> From win and lose and still somehow
> It's life's illusions I recall
> I really don't know life at all
> ("Both Sides Now")

My chest expanded from the sheer beauty of it.

As soon as she stepped off the platform and started to take her guitar strap off, I slid out of my booth and hurried over to her. "What an artist you are! What a musician!" I gushed like a lunatic wildly high. "Where did you find these incredible songs? Don't tell me you composed them — did you compose these songs?"

"Yeah."

"You did? My God, what an enormous talent you are! Immense! And what a range, your voice, four octaves, even five — huge range! And the poetry! What a poet you are, as wonderful as Dylan and Leonard Cohen!"

"Really?" she muttered, astonished.

"Really, really. You're going to be acclaimed the world over, or else this world is a much dumber place than it appeared to be before you sang your songs tonight. Who are you?"

"Joni Mitchell."

"I'm Malka."

"I know who you are."

"Your songs certainly know who I am," I said, hoping that she didn't know of me from the silly TV talk shows, or from the Johnny Carson shows. Even my appearance at Carnegie Hall, the Place des Arts, and all the concert tours felt dwarfed now by that one set of Joni Mitchell.

And yet, "you don't know what you've got / Till it's gone." It was well after my singing partnership with Joso was "gone" that we, Malka & Joso, came to be regarded as a major force in changing the perception that the immigrants of Canada were not aliens but importers of vitality, hope, daring, ancient and avant-garde sophistication, humour, and culture.

Well, to be more exact, for a brief while before it was *gone*, the accomplishments of Malka & Joso were recognized in 1966, the very autumn I first met Joni. It lasted only for the proverbial fifteen minutes, but it was a very big deal back then that the official face and voice of English Canada, the Canadian Broadcasting Corporation, programmed a new weekly show, *A World of Music* starring Malka & Joso, which aired coast to coast in the dream broadcasting slot — following the hockey game on Saturday night.

It was the first time that World music ("Ethnic music," it was called then) was accorded such prominent recognition in English Canada after years, decades really, of being relegated to basements, as if there were something subversive about it. Basements of churches, community centres, the YMHA, as well as those of immigrants from nearly all the continents and many of the islands. And only recently the basements of coffeehouses — out of which trailed long lines awaiting the next set of Malka & Joso.

And yet, the mores of Colonial England in those days were so deeply rooted in Canada that almost as soon as the cultural epicentre of English Canada decided to recognize and promote an expression of the cultures that were now penetrating its

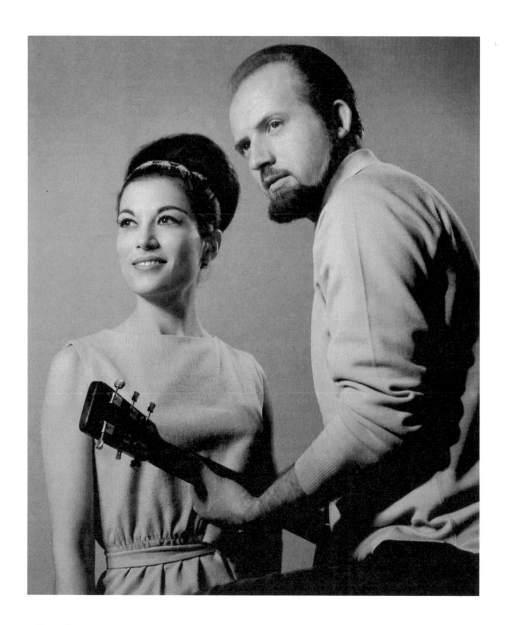

Malka & Joso
Courtesy Malka Marom

boundaries, it started to pull a Pygmalion on us, the ambassadors of those cultures. "Somebody teach Malka and Joso to speak English and to sing in English without their terrible foreign accents, for heaven's sake. And do it fast," decreed CBC management.

Joso was willing to accommodate them. "This CBC is a gold mine," he'd tell me in Italian; he could hardly speak English. But oh, could that man sing! Andrea Bocelli would have nothing on Joso Spralja. There wasn't a song in any language — even English — that Joso couldn't sing divinely, no matter how he mangled the pronunciation of the lyrics. Joso's hearing was so acute, he could learn a harmony the minute he heard it, but when it came to parroting a sentence of even just five words in English, even after he heard it a hundred times from one CBC Professor Higgins or another, there was something that blocked him from doing it. To compensate, Joso agreed to cover his handsome, balding head with a toupee that management "suggested" he don and, just as they suggested, he had a dentist plug the gap between his front two teeth. And above all, or more correctly below, he acquiesced to refrain from jutting out his hips, from moving them in any way that would suggest manhood. He shrugged it off; that's how he expressed his manhood now. And only when he thought I couldn't hear, he'd whisper to his wife, Angiolina, "It takes a crew of dumb-assed no-talent dickheads to turn a beauty that the camera loves as it does Malka into an ugly woman."

"Don't let them get to you," he urged me in Italian. "Bend, bend — a reed that doesn't bend breaks."

I tried, really tried, not to balk at the constant attempts to transform me. The cheques for this gig were not "a gold mine," but I certainly needed them. So I really tried to bend, and to be careful not to bruise anyone's ego up in management whenever I had to bring to their attention "details" like their arrangement of a Greek song requiring a bit of a change because the monotonic oompah-oompah rhythm was not Greek. And still they considered me "arrogant." So I tried my best deferential demeanour when I brought to their attention that their translation of the Italian song was incorrect and, since there's a large Italian community in Canada, it would have to be fixed. Well, they corrected the translation, but they didn't appreciate my "tone." So I tried to tone it down the next few times they butchered a song and/or a translation. But I still got on their nerves and their stiff upper lip went to hell. They deemed me a "stupid bitch" behind my back, "uninformed" to my face. "Broadcasting is a matter of ratings," they went on to explain, as if I were a brainless novice. "The majority of our audience is comprised of 'the little woman in Saskatoon, the little woman in Regina' . . ." (It was never "the little man in . . .")

"These 'little women' loved us in Regina just as we are, and they loved us even more in Saskatoon. That's why you booked us for this TV gig, no?" I blurted, forgetting to tone it down, and by their reaction you'd think I'd dropped the atom bomb.

Joso let me have it later when we were alone. "Are you crazy?! Crazy! Dumb to talk back to them! They'll cancel our show! You'll have no money to get out of your marriage . . . no money to support your two kids if you won't do what they want us to do. And what about *me*? You know I need every penny to support my family. Come on, don't be selfish. Pretend it's a game."

But I couldn't. I couldn't play this game without laughing or crying at how bizarre and sad it was to be selling out, prostituting our gifts, artistry, achievements — our souls, really — and for what?

In my broken Italian, I told Joso, "The glue that bound us was the sheer joy of making music, and where is it now? Remember how good it was to be true to the essence of our music? How good it was to give voice to the voiceless? How well our talents served us — better than this fool's gold."

"Spare me this bullshit. Artistic integrity is for the self-indulgent super-rich English Canadian. Get real!" he responded as I was getting into my car that night in November '66 that led me to Joni Mitchell, a woman who would be no stranger to battles over artistic integrity.

The day after I met Joni, I phoned the A&R guy at my record company and raved about Joni and her songs: "A unique enormous talent; you've got to get down to the Riverboat to see her — you'll be grateful to me for the rest of your life for this tip."

"What's the name of this unique enormous talent?"

"Joni Mitchell."

"Never heard of her."

"That's why you'll have the honour of being the first to discover and record her. Your name will be remembered for that . . ." It took all of my persuasive powers to move that A&R man to the Riverboat.

But once there, he kept drumming his fingers on the table while Joni tuned and retuned her guitar. His impatience plugged his ears to the "chords of inquiry," as Joni called those chords that send you to the edge and keep you hanging there. By the time Joni sang "Night in the City," he had no ears to hear her. "This singer has no stage presence, she'll amount to nothing," he decreed in a whisper, then left in the middle of her set.

I made no mention of him to Joni when I approached her after her last set that night. This time I asked her if it would be alright to sing one or two of her songs, even though my foreign accent wouldn't do them justice.

Right there, Joni scribbled down the lyrics of "I Had a King," "Night in the City," and "The Circle Game" for me.

I sang them at every gig thereafter, and I advised the audience to remember the name Joni Mitchell and her songs, so that they'd be able to boast that they had heard her songs and name *before* she became famous. When that day arrived, I dropped her songs from my repertoire because, alas, I didn't sing them well — to put it kindly.

By then, my singing partner Joso had become my *former* singing partner — partly because of my "stupid integrity." But just as he had predicted, I came out of my marriage penniless with two little children to support.

Yet even he did not foresee the stigma attached to being a divorced single mother in "Toronto the Good," as it was sometimes called in those days. The term "single mother" had yet to be invented, and a divorced woman was regarded not only as a loser, but loose.

Landlord after landlord told me without any compunction that they wouldn't rent the advertised apartment to a divorced single mother of two little children. And the ones who recognised me from TV, live performances, or the papers apologised before informing me that they wouldn't rent me the apartment they'd advertised because "we don't rent to entertainers, you know. Entertainers are always late with the rent, always make noise, trash the place . . ."

Now I discovered that I was no longer a singer, not to mention an artist, but an entertainer. A name that plunged my esteem even lower than "divorced single mother of two" — not only in the eyes of the landlords, but in the opinion of my children's teachers and their friends' parents.

It also relegated me to "fair game," or so it appeared on a night when I had to sing five sets and it was close to 3 a.m. that I headed to my duplex — for which I was charged nearly double the advertised rent. I'd driven less than ten minutes when a policeman stopped me — for speeding, I thought, or failing to come to a complete stop at a stop sign.

"What are you doing so late at night, driving alone?" the policeman inquired. And maybe because of the way he leaned over my window, or because he flashed his flashlight onto my face, or because of the stigma I'd faced lately, I wished I had removed the stage makeup back in the dressing room.

"I've just finished work," I replied.

"What do you do?"

"I'm a singer."

"Ah, an entertainer!" the policeman exclaimed, then added that he'd follow me to make sure I made it home safely.

It did no good to assure him that I'd be alright. His headlights kept blinding me in my rear-view mirror. The longer he tailed me, the more I feared that his intention might not be all that honourable. By then, I knew that no judge would take the word of an "entertainer" over the word of a policeman. I was shaking when I veered into the nearest fire station. And only then did that policeman stop tailing me.

The next night, just in case that policeman was that "one rotten apple in the bushel of 'our finest,'" Gordy Lightfoot insisted he drive behind me. And wouldn't you know, that same "rotten apple" stopped me at the same corner. Before I rolled down my window, Gordy jumped out of his car and said, "I'm with her. What's the problem, Officer?" That's all it took to stop his unwanted attention. Yet I felt defeated — for a woman who liked to think of herself as independent and quite strong, it was sad, humiliating really, that I'd need the protection of a man, be he even a "low down entertainer" like me. And not in a seedy or dangerous part of town, but in one of the safest parts of a city considered to be one of the safest in North America. This was the same Toronto the Good in which, a few years earlier, Joni, as an unwed mother, was subjected to extreme cruelty, abject poverty, and indignity much worse than I ever had to endure.

"The road" was starting to get tiresome. I cut most concert tours and out-of-town gigs as my children approached that age when a parent should stay home to supervise them. Wanting to find a job based in Toronto was altogether different than actually finding one. Frankly I didn't know how or where to begin. Despite my success as a singer, I had no degrees to show prospective employers — no music degree, and no schooling in theatre or TV. I was wracking my brains, as well as my friends', and knocking on doors to no avail. Until one Sunday, while watching *60 Minutes* on TV, it came to me that compared to singing, broadcast journalism was a cinch: just stick a mike in someone's face and ask question after question.

So I put on a suit and started to knock on doors at the CBC. The response wasn't encouraging: "You can't sing and do broadcast journalism. Journalism is a full-time job. Anyway, you're not going to quit singing, not if I can help it." You could have got whiplash from the change at the CBC, where I was now suddenly regarded as God's gift to World music.

They got tired of my pestering, I think, and perhaps to show me that you can't switch from music to broadcast journalism, "just like that, like changing hats," the late Don Cameron assigned me to interview country singer Charley Pride on live TV. "Screw up on this, and you'll be the laughing stock of the whole country," he warned. "Are you sure you still want to do it?"

"Yes, sure." It was probably a first for Charley Pride that a journalist leaned on him, physically, throughout a whole interview. I was so scared. Yet, ironically, they gave me the break I'd been pestering them for, because I had "the nerve to go for it."

One of the very few times in my life that I was right about anything was that night in November '66 when I told Joni that she was an enormous talent bound to be acclaimed the world over.

I had had no contact with Joni since then, except through her songs. Seven years after that night in November, I remarried, purchased a house with a big mortgage, and I was working double shifts at TV studios, recording studios, and editing rooms. One day, I switched on my car radio and I heard Joni singing: "I'm going to make a lot of money / Then I'm going to quit this crazy scene / Oh I wish I had a river / I could skate away on . . ." I laughed, thinking how Joni still understood me.

I'd heard that she had not granted interviews in the past few years; still I decided to give it a try. How to reach her? I had no idea. In '73 there was no Google. I dialled 0 for the operator. Luckily, I got a terrific phone operator who was more than glad to help me find a contact number for Joni Mitchell. She was a fan, and she stayed with me until we found the phone number of Joni's recording company, which shunted us from one person to another, until someone gave us the number of Joni's management company.

"I'd like to speak with Joni Mitchell," I said to the person who picked up the phone.

"Does she know you?"

"I don't know. We met briefly seven years ago."

"Who shall I say wants to speak with her?"

"Malka."

"Who? Can you spell it?"

Later that day, my phone rang. I picked up the receiver and heard, "Malka! It's Joni, how are you? So glad to hear from you!"

I was so excited by her response I could barely muster the voice to ask if I could fly over to interview her for CBC Radio. "Just me and a recording machine," I promised.

"Sure, come over, we are in rehearsals but come over." She gave me her address before she hung up, but when I arrived, I thought I had the wrong place. The house looked like a movie star's — huge pool, manicured garden amid terraces that stretched forever, pillars out of *Gone with the Wind*. It didn't seem like a house that someone like Joni would live in. (Much later I learned that Joni was staying there as a guest of David Geffen, who had rented this house from a movie star.)

Joni invited me to have tea in the kitchen, and that's where most of the '73 interview was conducted. But even before she started to brew the tea, I suggested that we talk only when I was recording. She agreed, and we stuck to this rule through the five days of interviewing. Quite a few portions of that interview were recorded with the preamble "off the record." In one of those moments, Joni told me of her efforts to find the baby girl she had "out of wedlock." I kept that tape in my safe deposit box at the bank for nearly twenty years until it became common knowledge. A while later, when PBS was interviewing me for their program on Joni, the executive producer told me that not many journalists would be that loyal — that foolish, she meant, judging by her expression.

The rehearsals that Joni had mentioned on the phone were in preparation for the tour to launch her new album, *Court and Spark*. No one knew then what a mega hit that album would be. And yet those rehearsals were bubbling with the elation and joy of artists who loved what they were creating, knew that it was truly great, and believed that it would resonate with whoever heard it.

Rehearsal halls look the same the world over, or so it seemed when I walked into this nondescript space. There were musical instruments galore — resting in their cases, open or closed, on any flat surface — and a full set of drums, and then some, at the back. Ashtrays were heaped with cigarettes, their smoke still curling through the air. Most everyone was wearing jeans — expensive jeans, perhaps; most of the musicians worked as studio musicians in Hollywood earning top dollar. But despite their casual attire, they were professional and attentive. No musician laughed or found it strange when Joni asked the band for a bit of yellow here, aquamarine there . . . She was a painter even as she arranged music.

One of Joni's many talents is to surround herself with musicians, like her recording engineer Henry Lewy with whom she recorded and produced thirteen albums, who embrace her originality and spur her on to change and push confidently in new directions.

During a break in rehearsal, when I interviewed Tom Scott and the other musicians of the L.A. Express band, I learned from them just how unique Joni's music was, and how challenging it was to play it and to note it, or "map it," as John Guerin, the drummer/percussionist who put the music to paper, called it. (In a later interview, Joni mentioned that Guerin also inspired the album's title, as he was courting and sparking her at the time.)

Watching those rehearsals, I felt that *Court and Spark* was bound to be a watershed album. Joni's image of the vulnerable sole being on the vast stage changed drastically when she sang with the band. There was a certain power and confidence, and something masculine about it, that was conveyed through the bass and the drums. It was such a dramatic change, it drove me to ask her if she thought that by singing with a band she might lose something, lose that vulnerable image.

"I don't want to be vulnerable," Joni replied, and then laughed — the laughter that I later came to recognize as a sort of editorial laughter.

Joni's candour could be unsettling from the start, and it became even more so as she demanded of herself "a deeper and greater honesty, and more revelation" in her work in order to affect listeners. She wanted to "strike against the very nerves of their life and, in order to do that, you have to strike against the very nerves of your own." Her fearless openness has been described as "the secret to her impossible-to-bottle essence" (*Toronto Star*).

After the '73 interview, we continued to meet as friends, at her house in L.A. and at her place in B.C. — and at mine in Toronto, to visit with my cat, Joni said; she would turn into a kitten when she played with that cat.

Joni could also turn into a trickster, like when she came to Toronto with the Rolling Thunder Revue in 1975 and invited me to keep her company in her dressing room while she waited for her turn to go on stage. It was a long show, four hours give or take, so we had loads of time to catch up on our lives. After the finale, Joni suggested I meet Bob Dylan before he disappeared from his dressing room. She laughed when I told her that I didn't want to meet Bob Dylan in passing, like the groupies; I'd rather she and I went out to Chinatown. "Oh come on, you've got to meet him. Dylan is one of the greatest in our generation," she insisted, and playfully she took hold of my hand and led me through that cavernous backstage, past the scary-looking hefty guys who were securing the "inner sanctum" where Dylan stood half-naked, his shoulder bleeding from the pull of his guitar strap, sweat dripping over his white clown makeup.

"Bobby," Joni said to Dylan, while pulling me to face him. "Bobby, I'd like you to meet the only person I know who doesn't want to meet you."

Though she is as famous as Dylan, I've never seen Joni surrounded by bodyguards. Whenever we went for a walk or to a café or restaurant, most people would respect her privacy; they'd smile or wave hello, a few would come over to thank her for the songs, and then they'd go on with their own lives.

In 1979, just before her *Mingus* record came out, I recorded our second interview, in which Joni told of her encounter with the legendary Charles Mingus, the jazz master, the artist, the man. She recounted how he came to choose her for this record and what a struggle it was for her to come through for him, and how she overcame her writing

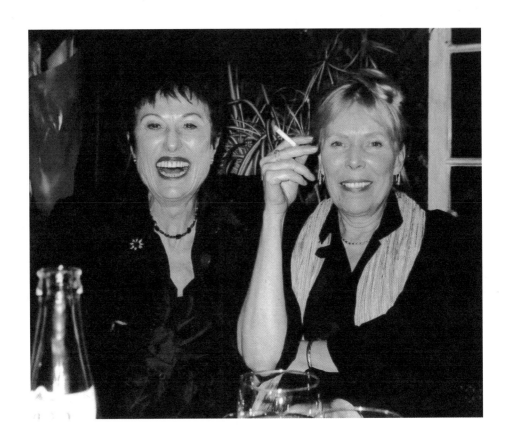

Malka & Joni after the opening reception of Joni's 2006 art exhibition *Green Flag Song / Mixed Media Originals* Courtesy Malka Marom

block. Then she went on to reveal in riveting detail how each song on this album came to her — and how stinging the rejection of records like *The Hissing of Summer Lawns* was for her. And yet it obviously didn't deter her from forging boldly to yet another unexplored direction — aiming higher and further in each of the works she recorded after *Mingus*: *Wild Things Run Fast*, *Dog Eat Dog*, *Chalk Mark in a Rain Storm*, *Night Ride Home*, *Turbulent Indigo*, *Taming the Tiger*, *Both Sides Now*, *Travelogue*, *Shine*.

I was itching to touch on these albums with Joni, especially when I saw how much more profound the first two interviews were on the page than on the air, where they passed by all too quickly. The page, to my amazement, transposed the interviews to the realm beyond time, beyond the personal to the universal.

So in 2012, more than forty years after Joni first came to my life, I recorded the third interview, mostly in her "library," as I call the dining room of her beautiful L.A.

home because of the books heaped on every surface: the dining room table, the sideboard, the side tables, the coffee table, the floor, the windowsills . . . In this interview, Joni, approaching her seventieth birthday, reflected on what it took to create her vast and truly great body of work over more than half a century, as well as on life in the arts and for the arts, over the changing decades.

During the last two decades, I've become a bookworm, and had a novel published in a few countries and translated into different languages. I've come to love words as much as music, and to appreciate one of Joni's earliest songs even more.

> We're captive on the carousel of time
> We can't return, we can only look behind
> From where we came
> And go round and round and round
> In the circle game
> > ("The Circle Game")

When I reread the transcripts of all the interviews that were recorded over the years, I was astonished at the extent to which Joni and I had tried to crack something so mysterious, something that had eluded countless others: the creative process itself, in all its fullness. Joni and I had tried to approach it from every possible angle that might offer a clue: childhood and adulthood, running away from home and yearning to return home, love and loss, working on the road in dives and at huge festivals, poverty and affluence, glamorous triumphs and tragic mistakes.

At the end of our interviews, although the origin of the muse or how to tease her remained elusive, what became very clear is that Joni had the courage to get on that "tightrope walk to keep your heart alive, to keep your art alive, to keep it vital and useful to others. To encounter and in a way, be in touch with the miraculous" (PBS's *American Masters*).

Strangely, although Joni has been accorded recognition and awards of all shapes and kinds in many parts of the world, she mentions the lack of recognition accorded to her music, her songwriting, and her poetry, and she sort of denigrates many of her awards, so as not to sit on her laurels and to remain humble: the stance of a true artist as she continues to lure the muse. Or so it seemed at one moment. But then she goes, "You want me to be humble, but . . . I'm defending my right to arrogance."

"Joni is a different woman every year," Henry Lewy, her recording engineer, explained in the '79 interview. "It's like meeting a different lady every year. Somebody who's grown, who's advanced, and who has something new to share with you."

"I want to be a pioneer, not a traditionalist," said Joni. "It does put you kind of in no man's land. Sometimes you think, 'Geez, look what I've done with my life. Wonder they haven't stoned me to death at this point.' I'm too different in many ways. I've made myself too individuated in a time when individualism is massively discouraged."

Her favourite compliment, she told me, was accorded to her by a black and blind piano player: "Joni, you make genderless, raceless music." Joni noted, "I hadn't set out to make 'genderless, raceless music.' But I *did* want to make music that crossed . . . I never really liked lines, class lines, social structure lines, and I ignored them always."

Yes, Joni is an artist who won't be slotted into any category, and she has always been "going over the edge of the box," as she put it. Yet Joni maintains in her song "Borderline": "All convictions grow along a borderline [. . .] All liberty is laced with / Borderlines."

"All liberty is laced with borderlines?" I asked her during our most recent interview.

"Everything," Joni replied. "If you belong, whatever you belong to has a perimeter. Me, I don't belong to much, so, in a certain way, I'm very free, but when I get into trouble, I have no support system, no allies, no peers. But what cost, liberty? In order to be free, not boxed in . . ."

And what tremendous strength to really believe in something intangible, to live with great respect for this mystery, and with an openness, to invite this mystery — the muse, the creative spring.

On that November night in '66, the vulnerable girl on the stage kept tuning and retuning, one guitar peg then another, and retuning yet again and again, almost as if she knew even then that she was tuning to the key of timelessness.

These interviews have been edited and condensed. The first interview was recorded in '73, the second in '79, and the third in 2012; the latter binds the first two like book covers: at the beginning and at the end.

Brief excerpts of my interviews with Elliot Roberts, Henry Lewy, Tom Scott, John Guerin, Roger Kellaway, and Max Bennett are also included.

The Seamstress, 1983
© Joni Mitchell, photo by Sheila Spence

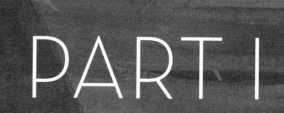

PART I

Malka: I'm intrigued, Joni, with this part of the liner notes to your CD *Dreamland*: "Like her paintings, like her songs, like her life, Joni Mitchell has never settled for the easy answers; it's the big questions that she's still exploring."

What big questions?

Joni: The Garden. Adam and Eve. Original sin. I've been chasing around the story of Adam and Eve and the continuing expulsion from Eden, the planet Eden, earth Eden, which I explored and explored and explored . . .

> And just as Eve succumbed
> To reckless curiosity
> I take my sharpest fingernail
> And slash the globe to see
> Below me
> > ("Paprika Plains")

> They paved paradise
> And put up a parking lot
> > ("Big Yellow Taxi")

> We are stardust,
> We are golden
> And we've got to get ourselves
> Back to the garden
> > ("Woodstock")

M: So let's go back to the Garden, to the early days — where did it all begin for you? When you were little, did you dream of singing on the stage, writing songs, composing music?

J: I always had starry eyes, I think. I mean, I always was interested in the glamour of it. Well, glamour for me then . . .

I lived in the tail end of a horse-drawn culture. We still had our water and the milk delivered by horses, and at Christmas a mound of packages would come on an open

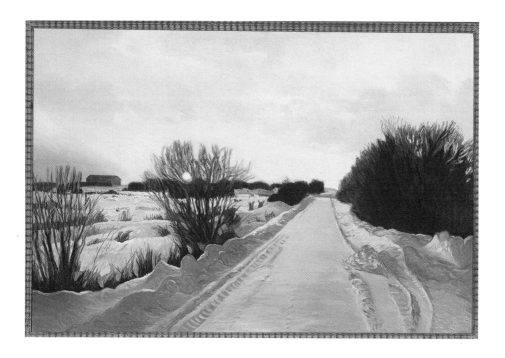

40 Below Zero, 1995
© Joni Mitchell, photo by Sheila Spence

sleigh. There were only two stores in town. My dad ran the grocery store and Marilyn McGee's dad ran the general store. She and I called the Simpsons-Sears catalogue "The Book of Dreams." It was so glamorous when I was a child, four or five. We'd be down on our bellies looking at every page, and she and I would pick out our favourite object from the front page to the back page. We would pick out our favourite matron's girdle and our favourite saw and our favourite hammer. "I like that one best." Every page, "That's my favourite." So in that way you learned to shop before you have money, you learn the addiction of the process of selection.

You could take me anywhere on any budget level and I'll go into "That's a good thing for that much money. That's a beautiful thing."

M: Even today?

J: Yeah. The Book of Dreams, when everybody had read it, because we were on rations, it became toilet paper. Even the mayor, if you could imagine, wiped his ass with the Simpsons-Sears catalogue, glossy coloured paper. We, at grocery stores, would try to save the orange tissue. Oranges used to come wrapped in orange tissue. We tried to stockpile that for toilet paper.

There was no sewage system in this town. It was like the Klondike, wooden sidewalks, electricity, but no running water, cisterns, no flush toilets. So you had to empty them. And next to the toilet can, basically, sat the Simpsons-Sears catalogue — the Book of Dreams. Either you ordered something or you just dreamed on it.

M: Was it that Book of Dreams that triggered in you the desire to draw pictures?

J: No, that was brought on by trauma and anxiety. And the trauma and anxiety was *Bambi*, of all things. The fire scene in *Bambi*, where Bambi's mother gets trapped in the fire, was horrific to me, and I couldn't exorcise the vision. For days, maybe a week afterwards, I was down on the floor drawing fire and deer running, day after day after day.

M: How old were you then?

J: Four or five, or maybe grade one. I'm not sure. I just drew and drew. That trauma and anxiety — the forest burning and the animals getting hurt — sparked an obsessive need to exorcise emotion, by drawing it out, drawing it out.

I think maybe that's the beginning of my contempt for my species and what it does. How ignorant it is of sharing this planet with other creatures. Its lack of native intelligence, common sense, or spirituality addressed to the earth . . .

I couldn't get the image out of my head. I just had to draw deer running out of flames, draw it and draw it. It was very disturbing to me.

M: It reminds me of the drawings at the Altamira caves. You know, tens of thousands of years ago they painted on the walls of that cave the animals that terrified them. Perhaps it's an inborn instinct to exorcise fear. So that's what started you to paint. Did you continue?

J: Yes. One of the [assignments at school] was you had to draw a doghouse. I did the best doghouse in the class. At that moment, I forged my identity as an artist.

M: And did you like it? Was it a good feeling to be regarded as an artist?

J: Well, I wasn't. I was regarded as a dunce. It was either the second or the third grade when [the teacher] graded us and moved us out of our normal spontaneous desk positions into rows. The A students in one row, which she called Bluebirds; the B students in another row, which she called Robins; and C students in another row, which she called Wrens; and the flunkies in another row, which she called Crows. I was in the Wren row, which is like a third-class citizen. I looked at the A row and I thought, "Look at them, they're all so smug." Their little hands would clasp and they looked like they won something. "What is the prize here?" I thought. "All you did was spit back what the teacher told you." I don't remember the language that I thought at this particular time, but I do remember that I had this thought.

From here on in, I'm not interested unless she asks us a question that nobody knows the answer to. I had this need to discover in order to learn. There was this compulsion to originality. That's why I'm self-taught and outside the box in so many ways.

But at that time, I remember that the thing that gave me the strength and the confidence to be basically a sort of dodo bird was that I drew the best doghouse. It was then that I noticed my skill. And I said, "I'm an artist." I forged that identity so that later when they put me in the corner with a dunce cap and tried to ridicule me, I managed to make it into something sort of glamorous. It didn't make me put my tail between my legs. It made me kind of proud.

M: You were courageous already at that young age.

J: Well, I had to be really courageous because the following year I got polio, and when they found out what I had, they shipped me out of town, a hundred miles away.

When it was intimated that I would never walk again — it was never directly said, it was implied by a man who would never walk again, a man in a wheelchair — I couldn't accept that destiny and I said, "I am not a cripple. I am not a cripple."

M: Like a mantra.

J: Out of the question. By God, I was gonna get up and walk. "I am not a cripple . . . not a cripple . . ." I said to a Christmas tree, which my mother had placed in the room

— the only time she came to visit me. She brought me that little Christmas tree and left. My father never came to visit me when I was in the hospital.

In the meantime, I was stuck there with Christmas coming on. Someone sent me a Christmas carol book, a Good King Wenceslas colouring book, which was Dickensian images of carols, for the most part with mutts, you know. No crayons. But I had ulcers in my mouth, which they would paint with Gentian violet, and sometimes they'd leave the swabs behind. So I would colour everything in this colouring book light purple, dark purple, purple dots, purple stripes — to get the different shades. But everything was purple. So it wasn't very exciting, one colour.

I was sharing a room in this trailer annex that was outside the hospital, because we were so contagious, with a six-year-old boy who was very sullen and picked his nose all the time.

On this particular day, they had given me some kind of therapy and left me sitting up at the edge of the bed, all kind of warped with my paralyzed legs dangling over the edge. A nun had rushed in and called me a "shameless hussy," and pushed me back to the back and covered my legs. And I thought, "I'm nine and he's six. What's wrong with my legs?"

Anyway, I'm sitting at the back of the bed and I'm still kind of propped up, and I started singing these Christmas carols, and he picked his nose and told me to shut up.

"SHUT UP!" he kept saying. That was my first audience, right? [laughs]

They let me keep the Christmas tree that my mother brought with some reflectors and a few ornaments. That night or one night near it, after the lights-out, I said to the tree, "I'm not a cripple, I'm gonna get out of here . . . I'm not a cripple, I'm gonna get out of here . . ."

It was a private ritual praying for my legs back. And because I broke with the church the year before — church was interesting, still I broke with it because when I asked questions, they looked at me and their eyes called me a bad girl. "Adam and Eve were the first people on earth, and they had two sons, Cain and Abel, and Cain killed Abel, and Cain got married. Who did he marry? Eve?" "Bad girl." So it wouldn't be Jesus or God [I prayed to].

"I'll make it up to you," I said to someone. I don't know who. Maybe it was the Christmas tree? "I'll make it up to you. Just get me out of here. Give me back my legs."

A year later, I did finally stand up and walk well enough that they let me go back home. I was good to my promise. When they asked me to join the church choir, I said yes. I took the descant part, which most of the kids couldn't follow because it had very radical intervals. It rolled over and under the tighter harmonies, which were easier for kids to learn. I thought descant was quite adventurous, very exciting, and that's probably why it has been a major influence on my melody, why I like odd intervals too.

Well, I'd only been to about three choir practices when a girl bought a package of cigarettes and we all went down to the empty church pond, passed the cigarettes around. One girl threw up. There was a lot of coughing. I took one hit and went, "This is great."

M: You were smoking since then?

J: Yes, since I was nine.

M: Was it at that time that the minister of your church became your hero?

J: Yeah. I was in the fourth grade when my friend, Anne Bayin, and her father, Allen Logie, who was going to be the minister, arrived. He didn't call me a bad child when I asked him questions. He was one of my early heroes. Thank you for respecting my questions.

He told me . . . what was the word he used . . . symbolic. Never heard that word before but I understood it. "Oh, that's just symbolic. Adam and Eve weren't really the first man and woman. It's symbolic." He dared to tell me it was myth.

M: Was it from then that your fascination with the story of the Garden started?

J: Right. This story has been a favourite of mine since I was a child. Adam and Eve were living happily off the land in harmony with nature. So there they are. And, according to the story, what happens is, Eve gets curious, right? And the snake, seeing her curiosity, sticks it to her, so to speak. He says, "Ah, this chick's curious." He makes it even more enticing.

Symbolically, she makes the mistake of eating. She's curious for knowledge. She eats from the tree, but she doesn't eat from the tree of immortality first. There's the curse. If you had the immortality, my interpretation is you would have the foresight. If you had immortality, you would have a God-vision. You would be able to withdraw and see far into the future. But unfortunately, they just chose knowledge and it's a little knowledge in the hands of fools.

Spirit of the water
give us all the courage and the grace
to make genius of this tragedy unfolding
the genius to save this place
("This Place")

J: One time I asked my grandmother why my mother was so pathologically horrified of snakes, horrified. And she said to me, "Oh Joan, ever since Eve was in the garden, women haven't liked the serpent very much." So again, the story comes back to me.

The truth of the matter was that my mother had handled snakes, garter snakes. She was a farm girl and was cool with them. But one day she stepped on one in a dark root cellar with a bare foot, and it freaked her out. I've seen her touch a photograph of a black and white snake going through the encyclopedia, and shudder. The whole experience would come back, horrifying. A movie like *King Solomon's Mines* when the snake would drop out of the tree — in the movie theatre my mother would practically die.

So as I was growing up, I thought if I ever stepped on a snake in my bare feet, I would die. It was like a curse on the family. And I spent many years watching the grass carefully in the country so I wouldn't step on one, being horrified if I even saw one.

Finally, one day in Laurel Canyon, I woke up out of bed, blurry eyed, carrying my nightgown out to the laundry hamper. I stepped on a snake in my bare feet in my living room, of all places. This is when the symbolism began to really pick up.

For a while I bought Freud's thing, the phallicness, it's such an obvious symbol. But I don't see sex as the original sin. To me, that's not it at all. The fact that when they had knowledge they saw that they were naked, they saw their humanness, their vulnerability . . . I've been chasing around that symbol . . .

M: Fire compelled you to paint; was it anything in particular that brought you to music?

J: I had, as a child, I don't remember what age, a hurdy-gurdy that had a rope around the neck. It had circus images and it was made of heavy cardboard and it had a rubber thing that when you wound it, it hit some prongs, which played the melody "London Bridge Is Falling Down."

I used to always play it backwards because backwards it rocked. It had a different rhythm. The melodic intervals were quite surprising. It was really entirely a different piece of music — almost African in its rhythm. Once I played it backwards, playing it forward was kind of corny. Played backwards, it was a much more interesting piece of music, the first piece of music that inspired me.

The second one was when I was in the fourth grade. I had one friend who was a classically trained grade eight piano student, Frankie McKitrick. He let me dream big without any kind of contest. He was the only kid I could kind of play with, and I was exposed to a lot of music and ballet and things like that because of his interests. He was a real musician. I never thought of myself as a musician. He and I went to some pretty far-out movies together. My mother was horrified that the principal, his father, let us play hooky to go and see them. And among them was a movie called *The Story of Three Loves*, which had Rachmaninoff's *Rhapsody on a Theme of Paganini* as a theme song. And that piece of music thrilled me to no end. It was the most beautiful piece of music that I ever heard. I had to hear the record of it. I asked my parents to buy it for me, but it wasn't in the budget. It would be seventy-five cents or something. So I would go down to Grobman's department store, take it out of its brown sleeve, and go in the playback and play it maybe two or three times a week and just swoon.

I saw [the movie] recently. It was really corny, but the piece of music is still stupendous. There isn't another piece of music on the planet that has touched me like that.

When I heard it as a child, that music was like pleading to my mother. "Don't interpret the situation that way. You're breaking my heart. And I'm trying to explain to you . . . I'm not trying to wiggle out of anything. I'm just trying to explain. And you won't let me. You insist on creating this barrier by getting it wrong." There isn't a piece of music that affected me emotionally like that. Then I started to dream that I could play the piano beautifully.

M: To dream or to wish?

J: To dream. In my dreams, my hands would be on the keyboards and I'd be composing these fantastic pieces of music, like *Story of Three Loves*, that I could play and make emotions come out like that.

And I also dreamed I could drive a car. [laughs]

So I told my mother that I wanted a piano, but it wasn't in the budget. I begged, I wheedled, I pleaded, and finally, one winter night, because there was no piano store in North Battleford, this van pulled up with a lot of spinets on the back. Mine was not a good instrument at all.

I began piano lessons from a teacher named Jill Evan, who wore her hair in a bun like a Spanish dancer, and a lot of red lipstick and long, red fingernails. And like all piano teachers at that time, she hit you with a ruler for all kinds of things. But I didn't know that, that corporal punishment was the methodology. I took it personally. I thought she didn't like me and my mother because she had a crush on my dad. Because she and my father used to do these duets, and she also played tennis and so did my dad.

But it was just the way they taught piano in those days.

It took us a year of right-handed, da da da da da da da da scales, and left-hand scales before you got your first two-handed piece, which was written by a nun. It was called "The Little Regret" and it went from major to minor. It was quite a nice little piece of music.

Once I got my first two-handed piece, I wrote my first piece of music, "Robin Walk." I wrote it out in notes. So I'm proud. And I bring in this "Robin Walk" to play it for this teacher — "Look what I've done. I wrote my own song here." And I play it for her. When I'm finished, she says to me, "Why would you want to play [this song] when you could have the masters under your fingers," and she whacked me across the knuckles with a ruler.

I went home and I said, "That's it. I'm not going back there. She hit me." And my mother called me a quitter.

When my mother was in her eighties, one day she said to me, "All that money we spent on your piano lessons and you quit!"

M: By that time you were already . . .

J: Yeah. I had fifteen albums out. It was ridiculous. I played Carnegie Hall! So I laughed . . . She went, "All that money we spent and you quit!" I said to her, "Look, I think you got some bang for your buck."

M: Was she joking?

J: No! She just had a trap mind. I don't know what it is. I lied to her once in my teens. I told her I was going someplace and I went to a public dance, where I wasn't supposed to go. So I was always a liar after that. A liar, a quitter, and a lesbian. She's wrong on all three counts and would not stand corrected. She just got these things fixed and they wouldn't erase.

M: Did you continue to play the piano after you quit those lessons?

J: No. It killed it.

Later I played a little bit of "Moon River," like Henry Mancini. Other than that, my fingers found their own patterns.

I think the fact that I did not have the masters, that I don't have any musical heroes . . . my music is pretty original.

Nearly anyone you talk to in my generation had a hero that they studied and analyzed and strove to be like. They did air guitar in front of the mirror. So it was less "muse" than "ick." [laughs] Music comes from the muse, not from other musicians.

M: And poetry? What sparked the songs, the poetry?

J: The spark for the poetry came and died. I moved from North Battleford to Saskatoon in the sixth grade. Towards the end of the year, we were having a parent-teacher day and I was hanging some drawings of mine for this thing when the new grade seven teacher, Kratsman, came up to me. He said, "You like to paint?" I said, "Yes." He said to me, "If you could paint with a brush, you could paint with words." And I went, "I can?" I took his word for it.

M: You mean the poems came just like that: because he said that you could paint with words?

J: Yeah, the first time we were given an assignment to write a poem, he smothered the board in really interesting topics. I chose to write about a stallion, because I was into horses, because of Roy Rogers and cowboys. I used to play cowboys with the boys. And I used to spend my allowance riding [the pony] at the stockyard on the weekend.

So I wrote a poem about a stallion and how he leads the horse hunters along a precipice and the horse hunters fall off the cliff. It was in sympathy with the horse. There were two words in it that I really stretched for. "Equine" I got from *Reader's Digest*: "it pays to improve your word power." And one I got from my mother, which was a synonym for yellow. She gave me "saffron."

Anyway, I believed the teacher — if I could paint, I could paint with words. So I wrote this very ambitious poem. I thought it was good. And he gave me an A minus, but he passed out A plusses, including an A plus to the "toad stabber" — the kid who sat across from me who kept drawing bleeding toads with daggers through them all over his notebooks.

I stayed after school, and I said, "You told me I could do this. Did you not like my poem." He said, "I thought it was alright." And I said, "Did you think his, the toad stabber's, was better? You gave him an A plus." I don't think I called him the "toad stabber," but whatever his name was, I forget. The teacher said, "No, but that's the best poem he's ever gonna write. This is not the best poem you're ever gonna write."

I took that as an explanation.

He wrote things in the margin, like, I repeated an adjective . . . It was poetic, part of it, but it had a story.

"Softly now, the saffron colours of the day
Fade and are replaced by silver grey
As God prepares his will for night
And high upon a silver shadowed hill
A stallion, white as newly fallen snow" — he circled [it and wrote] *cliché white as newly fallen snow*.

"Stands deathly still" — *deathly* — *better adjective?*

"An equine statue bathed in silver light" — *silver* is circled.

"For on the wind was strong the scent of man
He worried for the safety of his clan
And whinnied, hoping they would hear and heed."

M: You remember the poem. My goodness, Joni . . .

J: Well, first stanza. I remember that much. I remember the criticism, which was valid criticism, good adjudication for a seventh grader. His take was "How many times have you've seen *Black Beauty*? The things you were telling me about what you did over the weekend are more interesting than this." And in a way, that was the encouragement to write more autobiographically.

It's the only thing I learned in the school system. It's the only thing I remember from thirteen years in school really.

M: You dedicated your first album to him.

J: Yes, but in talking to him in later years, he unfortunately resented my success because he taught special kids at special schools and they were supposed to be the most likely to succeed — I was probably the least likely to succeed. I don't think he ever could quite come to grips with that. He didn't really mean what he said. He told me I could paint with words and then he told me I wasn't very good at it. Even though his criticism was valid, his support was not there, as it was initially. So the spark went out, because I felt he lied to me. He let me down. And I never had any support from my family or anything. And at that stage, you need somebody to believe in you.

M: What encouraged you to do it, then? How did the spark come to marry the paintings with the words and the music?

J: It all happened later. High school hit, and I used to do the backdrops for school plays. I did a lot of large paintings — a thirty-six-foot painting for my French teacher as an apology that I was such a shitty French student, because I was just a lousy student. All I was interested in was art. I should have been in a special school, really. I was wasting my time in there, other than socialization.

I lived for dances. My teens were pretty much obsessed with dancing, but I did one good poem in high school about celebrities — feeling sorry for them.

At sixteen, we had to write a blank verse poem, it was on a Friday and I had to get this poem in on Monday. [That weekend] I was gonna be at one of the dances, so I was getting my hair done at a beauty school. A beehive with sparkles. I'm sitting there and stacked around me are *Silver Screen* and all these movie magazines. And on every cover, Sandra Dee is crying. She and Bobby Darin were breaking up and there were all these candid paparazzi shots of her and I thought, "That's horrible. Imagine if you were breaking up with your boyfriend and people are snapping pictures and putting them on the school cover!" I thought that would be unbearable to me — to be looked at like a bug.

That was the spark or the inspiration. Sympathy for Sandra Dee being photographed with her mascara running. It all just poured out this poem I called "The Fishbowl." The fishbowl being Hollywood. I can pretty much remember it, although I did it in high school.

"The fishbowl is a world reversed
Where fishermen with hooks that dangle from the bottom up
Reel down their catch without a fight on gilded bait
Pike, pickerel, bass,
the common fish all go through distorting glass
see only glitter, glamour, gaiety
Fog up the bowl with lusty breath
Lunge towards the bait and miss
And weep for fortune lost
Envy the goldfish?
Why?
His bubbles breaking round the rim
While silly fishes faint for him and say
Oh my God, I think he winked at me"

M: I'm totally amazed that you remember this poem also, especially when you consider the body of work you composed since high school. And it's almost as if you had a premonition that you would be in that same sort of fishbowl.

J: There were things that I worked out at sixteen. Like, I had a column in the school paper called "Fads and Fashion." And I started fads and stopped them. I knew the mechanics of hip. It's hip to wear your father's tie to school. Ugh, it's uncool, we did that last week.

So by the time I was sixteen, I knew that hip was a herd mentality, certain people would do it, they'd follow you, and you could embarrass them easily by saying, "Ewww, that's not hip now." And they would stop.

M: Music-making was dormant in you then?

J: Hitting me with a ruler during those piano lessons sent my love of playing music underground for ten years or so.

When I wanted a guitar, my mother said, "Oh, no, no. You'll buy it and you'll just quit. You're a quitter." I couldn't afford to buy it on my own. So I saved up thirty-six dollars, and on the day when my wisdom teeth were pulled, with bloody sutures in my mouth, I went in and plunked down the thirty-six dollars, bought this ukulele,

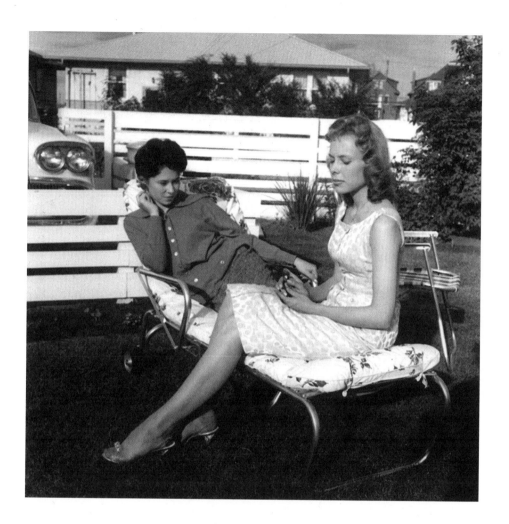

Teenage friends Joni and Anne Bayin (then Anne Logie) swapped clothes for this photo in Joan's backyard in Saskatoon. "Joan was the most original person I knew," says Bayin. Courtesy Anne Bayin

and just hunkered over it everywhere to the point where my friends said to me, "Anderson, if you don't put that goddamn thing down, I'm gonna break it in half." I was just obsessed with it. And in six months, I could play and sing well enough.

Some kids heard me play at the lake and they said, "You're good," and they put me on a late night [TV] show. It replaced a hunting and fishing show. I always think they took off the moose and took me on. [laughs] They gave me half an hour to play these little folk songs — after I had only been playing for only six months.

My mom and dad went to the top floor of the Bessborough, which was the highest building in town, and looked at the snowy image of me in this neighbouring town about a hundred miles away playing.

Anne's mother saw it also. She was in charge of the adjudicated music festivals of the United Church, and she said to Anne, "Joni is pretty good." So that was the beginning. I took it as a hobby at art school. I got into playing just for spending money, for smoking money and movie money. And for fun; it was just fun when you got a room full of people playing, you know. That's the way I started and it really was to be no more than that.

My ambition was to be a painter.

M: How did it switch to music?

J: Well, in Saskatoon there was a coffeehouse, which I was kind of involved with in the beginning. Some friends of mine were doing the carpentry and I was hired initially to be kind of a resident artist. There was some talk of me doing portraits of people as they came in and I ended up waitressing.

I came there with an interest in jazz, which I was starting to get into at that time. Folk music didn't excite me at all.

M: Did someone or something give you the impetus to start performing on stage, or was it an accident, as it was in my case?

J: It was an accident, in a way . . . My mother said to me, before I went to art college, that my stick-to-it-iveness at certain things was never that great. She said, "You're gonna get to art college and you're gonna get distracted." She said this very prophetic thing.

But I said, "Oh, what could possibly detract from my art." This is what I always wanted to do. I doodled through French and history and biology. I'd failed mathematics but I had done drawings of mathematicians for the math room. So finally, here I was in a situation where it was all drawing. But when I got there, the same thing happened to me. A lot of the courses were meaningless to me and not particularly creative.

I had no money, so I thought I could pick up some — to smoke and to bowl and to go to a movie and eat a pizza. So I went and auditioned for the coffeehouse in town. I said, "Look, I play this ukulele . . ."

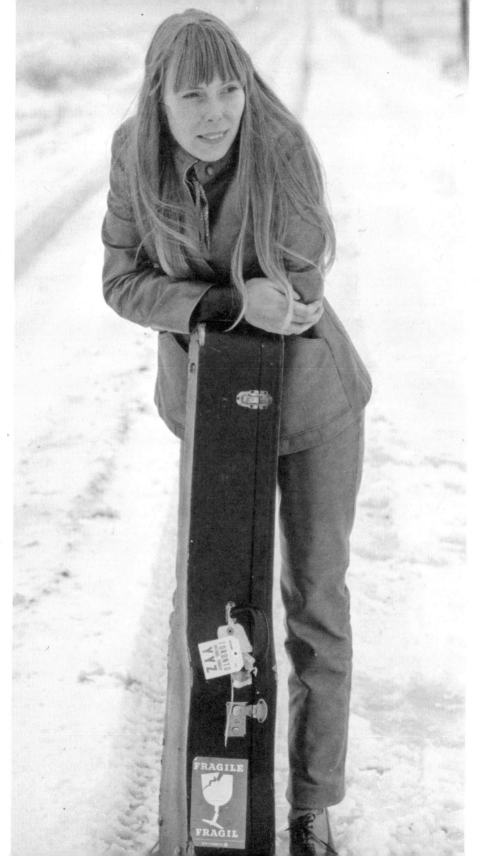

I think I had a guitar at that point. Yes. A Martin tiple, which is a glorified South American ten-string ukulele. It has more sound because of all the strings. It was sort of a novelty item, and I began to sing in this little coffeehouse [in Calgary], called The Depression.

An English kid had gotten there a day before they hired me. He said to me, "What is your repertoire?" I said, "Well, 'Crow on the Cradle.'" "You can't sing that. That's my song." And I named another one. "You can't sing that. That's my song." This is my introduction to territorial songs. I ran into it again in Toronto.

The territorial thing in the folk scene was part of why I began to write my own songs.

In that coffeehouse, and another one in Edmonton . . . I forget the name of it, but they wrote me up in the local newspaper: "two-career girl." When I saw it, I thought, "Two career? I'm a painter. I don't have two careers."

"Winged words fly from her pen," they wrote in the yearbook. So I was acknowledged in high school as a writer, but I never acknowledged myself as a writer. That gift had to be drawn out by tragedy, it seems.

The writing of my own songs came out of the trauma of my being an unwed mother and being destitute. I mean destitute in a strange city and pregnant, and living in a fifteen-dollar-a-week room. It was the attic room, and all the railings . . . there was one left out of every four because last winter, the people burnt them to keep the room warm. It was run by a Chinese guy that they said was waiting for my child to be born and then he'd ship me off to Shanghai or something.

M: I can't imagine writing or painting, or playing guitar and singing in these conditions, but maybe you did.

J: No, no, no. I was in the middle of this trauma.

M: Where did you live?

J: In Toronto, on Huron Street, in a house full of artists, starving artists.

M: Why not in a shelter for unwed mothers?

J: Couldn't get in. They were flooded. I tried to. I tried to spare my parents by going to the anonymity of a large city, under the ruse that I wanted to be a musician. Because my mother already thought I was a quitter, so I thought, "Okay, she thinks I'm a quitter, so she'll believe it." "I want to be a musician." "Oh, I knew you'd be a quitter." That would get me out of town.

And in Toronto I had, I think, sixty dollars, maybe, with me in a town where the cheapest room was fifteen dollars a week. And I had six months ahead of me, no work.

You had to be in the union to work all the clubs. It took 160 dollars to get in [but] I couldn't earn the money to get in. It was a catch-22. You had to work to get the money to get in the union. And you couldn't work until you got in the union. So I worked at a scab club called the Purple Onion till my sixth month. We did good business because I was a good scab act. We drew business until . . . I had to quit because I had to go undercover.

M: Undercover, because you started "to show," as we called it then? What a different world it was [in 1964]. Did any welfare agency help you when you went "undercover," or did you have to rely on the kindness of strangers — not in a sexual way, just, you know, when you were in need of kindness?

J: That's the only thing that impresses me anymore. Kindness. One kind act was Duke Redbird, when I was expecting and I lived in this attic in Toronto. I was living on Ingersoll cheese spread and Hovis loaf because that place was full of starving artists and you couldn't keep anything in the fridge, so my diet was atrocious. And one day Duke Redbird's brother came from the reservation. This big Indian. I'd never even met him. He came to my door. He knocked on the door and he said, "Here." And he shoved me a basket of McIntosh apples. They used to come in those bent-wood baskets. "Here." Very rudely. It's one of the kindest things that ever happened. And he turned on his heels and went away. A total stranger. And I thought, "He must know. Do they know what condition I'm in?"

M: What it took to sustain the child you were carrying and yourself couldn't have left anything to inspire songs, or to paint, I imagine. I never bought the romance of the suffering, starving artist that movies like to sell.

So, when did it happen to you, the turn from the girl occasionally writing to writing obsessively like an artist does? What sparked the transition from the gifted amateur to the professional artist?

J: How did I become a songwriter, how did all this come together . . . after the trauma?

M: Yes.

J: I worked at Simpsons-Sears, and I struggled . . .

M: Simpsons-Sears?! What an ironic twist to the Book of Dreams, the Simpsons-Sears catalogue.

J: Yeah . . .

The following year, I made a bad marriage, in an attempt to keep my child . . . But then I realized that I couldn't bring a child into that marriage, because I grew up with people that shouldn't have been married, really. So there was further trauma.

When Chuck Mitchell — where my name comes from — and I got married, I kind of got sucked into music, compromised music because he wanted us to sing as a duo, and his choice of material would not be mine. It was show tunes. Flanders and Swann, which I kind of sent up. I brought as much comedy as I could to it.

But we played in these places [in Detroit] that would go jazz after hours, and as I began to write, the jazz musicians wrote out my lead sheets and they were quite melodic, the early songs. Better than the lyrics, I think — some really nice melodies. And the jazz musicians would go, "Hmm, this is nice." And they started to incorporate it into the jazz set, and blacks started coming early to catch the last set because they were hearing this music of this girl in the jazz set, so they came out of curiosity. And when I do all this corny stuff with the kazoo and putting a pillow under my dress because I'm the fair hippopotamus and all of this stuff to save face with these songs that I had to sing with Chuck, you'd see these big Cheshire white teeth in the dark room smiling. They tolerated this goofy kazoo playing and everything.

So I ended up in the Motown anthology as a Motowner. In the Motown anthology, the more recent one, it said, "Meanwhile, on the other side of town, Joni Mitchell was making a new kind of folk music." Jazz was originally called Negro folk music, which is ridiculous. Duke Ellington? Negro folk music? That was black classical music. It made classical music just sound square.

That's how I began to write "Circle Game" and "Both Sides Now." I used to go down to the Toddle House and write, until the riots, and the waitress said, "Oh honey, you better not be coming back in here."

We lived in the black neighbourhood. It was cheap housing. After the riots, whites couldn't live in the black neighbourhood. There was real racial tension there.

M: Were you still married to Chuck Mitchell when you wrote these songs?

J: Right.

M: What motivated you to write these songs?

J: It was my version of "I've got a headache coming." [laughs]

M: What a headache!

J: Yeah, I'd just stay up all night and write.
"Come to bed!"
"No, I'm writing."

M: Did you realize then how good the songs are?

J: No. I couldn't really judge them. The best of them, really . . .
Tom Rush would come to our apartment — it was big and low rent, and people would stay with us, and when we travelled we'd stay with them. We couldn't afford hotel rooms at this point. We were making so little money. So people would take you in, and it was nice, the social aspect of it.
Anyway, Tom Rush would come over and he'd ask me if I'd written any songs, and the ones I held back I didn't hold them back perversely.
"Both Sides Now" I held back because Chuck ridiculed me: "Oh, you're only twenty-one. What do you know about life?" Chuck had a BA in literature. I married into a hotbed of teachers and I only had a high school education, and I called children "kiddies," which is an Irish regionalism but it made me seem déclassé and, to him, stupid.
I didn't know what they were talking about, the Mitchells, and at that time I had a bird fetish, I used to paint birds on things — a little dresser that I salvaged out of the garbage and a little vanity with fold-out mirrors on the sides. I did these birds on a wire, sparrows with peacock feathers, one for each of the Mitchell family, and one of

them was hanging upside down. Guess who? That's how I felt. Like a bird on a wire, the one that was upside down.

Chuck called me stupid a lot. He kept trying to get me to read what he read so that we could converse about what he knew. He tried to get me to read *Catcher in the Rye* and a few things. Finally, I did read the Tolkien books. And out of that came my own mythology, "Sisotowbell Lane." It's an anagram — Sisotowbell stood for "Somehow, in spite of troubles, ours will be ever lasting love."

It was my idea of heaven. It just goes to show that while most kids are playing air guitar at this time, and they want to be rich and famous and fabulous and be on the red carpet, I had a fantasy of living rurally with nice neighbours that came over every once in a while, and a son named Noah . . . It was a call for a simple life.

Sisotowbell Lane
Noah is fixing the pump in the rain
He brings us no shame
We always knew that he always knew
Up over the hill
Jovial neighbors come down when they will
With stories to tell
Sometimes they do
Yes sometimes we do
We have a rocking chair
Each of us rocks his share
Eating muffin buns and berries
By the steamy kitchen window
Sometimes we do
Our tongues turn blue

Sisotowbell Lane
Anywhere else now would seem very strange
The seasons are changing
Everyday in everyway
Sometimes it is spring
Sometimes it is not anything
A poet can sing

Sometimes we try
Yes we always try
We have a rocking chair
Somedays we rock and stare
At the woodlands and the grasslands and the badlands 'cross the river
Sometimes we do
We like the view

Sisotowbell Lane
Go to the city you'll come back again
To wade thru the grain
You always do
Yes we always do
Come back to the stars
Sweet well water and pickling jars
We'll lend you the car
We always do
Yes sometimes we do
We have a rocking chair
Someone is always there
Rocking rhythms while they're waiting with the candle in the window
Sometimes we do
We wait for you
                    ("Sisotowbell Lane")

M: Over dinner tonight, Joni, you mentioned that "Both Sides Now" was somehow connected with Saul Bellow.

J: Bellow's *Henderson the Rain King*. That was the inspiration for "Both Sides Now." Chuck must have gotten me to read it . . . I can't really sort this out because I usually didn't travel on planes when I was with him; plane travel was not in our budget. It might have been when I did *Let's Sing Out*. I'm not sure.

I know I wrote "Both Sides Now" while I was with Chuck because he ridiculed me about it. It must have been near the end.

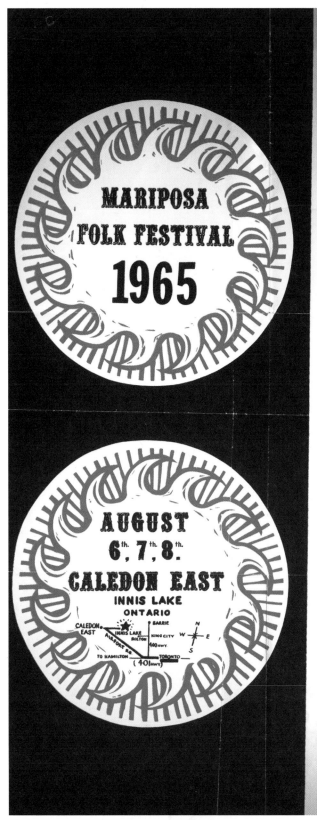

IAN & SYLVIA
PHIL OCHS
GORDON LIGHTFOOT
JOHNNY HAMMOND
THE
COUNTRY GENTLEMEN
'SON' HOUSE
ALLEN-WARD TRIO
THE DIRTY SHAMES
JONI ANDERSON
THE YORK COUNTY BOYS
JERRY GRAY
SHARON TROSTIN
LOTYS & RUSS
DAVID REA
ELYSE WEINBERG
THE COMMON FOLK
OWEN McBRIDE
WADE HEMSWORTH
BILL PRICE
AND MANY OTHERS

CHILDRENS CONCERT
CHILDREN ADMITTED FREE

WORKSHOPS
SEMINARS
MARIPOSA CANOE RACE
HOOTENANNYS
CAMPING
SWIMMING
DANCING

TICKETS
SAM THE RECORD MAN
347 YONGE ST.
TORONTO

NEW GATE OF CLEVE
AVENUE RD. & YORKVILLE
TORONTO
MAIL ORDERS & INFORMATION
MARIPOSA
FOLK FESTIVAL INC.
20 COLLEGE ST.
TORONTO

PRICES
FRIDAY $3.
SATURDAY (DAY) $1.50
SATURDAY NIGHT $3.50
SUNDAY $2.
ALL TICKETS PURCHASED
BEFORE JULY 31st 50¢ LESS
WEEK-END TICKET...$8.
INCLUDES ALL ABOVE
PLUS FREE PARKING & CAMPING

MARIPOSA
FOLK FESTIVAL
1965

AUGUST
6th, 7th, 8th.
CALEDON EAST
INNIS LAKE
ONTARIO

M: Did you write it during a plane ride, or did you just happen to read Saul Bellow?

J: Yeah, I'm trying to think why I was reading the book — the Chuck connection, because I didn't read then. I know I read the Tolkien books at his request. So he must have given me *Henderson the Rain King*.

I got to page . . . That's what would happen when I would read books. I'd get a little ways into it and I'd go, "Bullshit." I could see the thumbs in the lapels. Or it would get great and I would get inspired, like in the case of *Henderson the Rain King*.

It's about escaping a woman. He's married to a woman that he doesn't like who he thinks is gross and sloppy and has bad hygiene. He takes a flight to Africa and he eventually becomes a kind of . . . I don't know what happens.

But I was reading this on a plane — page twenty-eight, I think it is. He's up in a plane, looking down on clouds, and I go, "Huh! I'm up on a plane looking down at clouds." I put down the book, I look out the window, and I start to write. I write the first verse. I think I only wrote the first verse on the plane. It was a catalyst. Other than that, it doesn't really have anything to do with Saul Bellow but it was the point of inspiration.

Also at that time . . . If I'd been raising my daughter . . . "Both Sides Now" was triggered by a broken heart, the loss of my child. In this three-year period of childhood's end. I'd come through such a rough, tormented period as a destitute, unwed mother. It was like you killed somebody, in those times. It was very, very difficult. I ran into people behaving very cruelly, ugly. I saw a lot of ugliness there. They experimented on me in the hospital. No one to protect me. So I had, in fact, seen quite a bit of the "I've looked at life from both sides now." I had some serious battles for a twenty-one-year-old. But I was trying to become a realist in all ways.

"Both Sides Now" was a meditation on fantasy and reality. Half childhood, looking at the clouds with childlike wonder . . . I never felt it was a very successful song because it was such a big meditation. It seemed to just scrape the surface of it. But in retrospect, in its generalness, there was much that people could read into it. It became very profound in its ambiguity to a lot of people.

I know one guy played it for his parents, then sat them down and announced, "I'm gay." It found utility in people's lives. It was a song that I think I had to grow into. I don't think I performed it well until I was in my fifties.

M: I think — I mean, memory is not always reliable but according to what I remember — I heard you performing it when I first met you, Joni, at the Riverboat.

J: As a young girl? You think I could pull it off?

M: Pull it off?! I'll never forget that evening. It moved me to the core, changed me, changed my life. That's how I've remembered it all these years, decades by now. But just in case memory has not served me well, if it wasn't "Both Sides Now," it was one of the songs you sang that night, or all the songs.

J: There is a performance from *The Johnny Cash Show*, the first *Johnny Cash Show* [in 1969] I sang it on, I haven't looked at it in many years. But I know that in that particular case, because Bob [Dylan] was just coming out of what they called a motorcycle accident, which, really, I think was a nervous breakdown of sorts, by the way he behaved. He would introvert [in an] almost catatonic [way] while we were doing that show. And it was like I wasn't even there. That kind of confirmed to me then that the song "Both Sides Now" was meaningless. But people seeing it now on the internet say that it's a good performance. So I don't know.

> Rows and floes of angel hair
> And ice cream castles in the air
> And feather canyons ev'rywhere
> I've looked at clouds that way
>
> But now they only block the sun
> They rain and snow on ev'ryone
> So many things I would have done
> But clouds got in my way
>
> I've looked at clouds from both sides now
> From up and down, and still somehow
> It's cloud illusions I recall
> I really don't know clouds at all
>
> Moons and Junes and Ferris wheels
> The dizzy dancing way you feel
> As ev'ry fairy tale comes real
> I've looked at love that way

But now it's just another show
You leave 'em laughing when you go
And if you care, don't let them know
Don't give yourself away

I've looked at love from both sides now
From give and take, and still somehow
It's love's illusions I recall
I really don't know love at all

Tears and fears and feeling proud
To say "I love you" right out loud
Dreams and schemes and circus crowds
I've looked at life that way

But now old friends are acting strange
They shake their heads, they say I've changed
Well something's lost, but something's gained
In living ev'ry day

I've looked at life from both sides now
From win and lose and still somehow
It's life's illusions I recall
I really don't know life at all

I've looked at life from both sides now
From up and down, and still somehow
It's life's illusions I recall
I really don't know life at all
                    ("Both Sides Now")

J: Chuck and I worked for a couple of years as a duo, and then my work began to mature. I felt that I couldn't grow with him, that we would never grow together. That I had to separate myself from the duo, that I had to become an individual in order to grow. And as soon as the duo dissolved, the marriage dissolved.

I had a king dressed in drip-dry and paisley
Lately he's taken to saying I'm crazy and blind
He lives in another time
Ladies in gingham still blush
While he sings them of wars and wine
But I in my leather and lace
I can never become that kind

I can't go back there anymore
You know my keys won't fit the door
You know my thoughts don't fit the man
They never can they never can

I had a king in a salt-rusted carriage
Who carried me off to his country for marriage too soon
Beware of the power of moons
There's no one to blame
No there's no one to name as a traitor here
The king's on the road
And the queen's in the grove till the end of the year

I can't go back there anymore
You know my keys won't fit the door
("I Had a King")

M: That's the song that changed my life. Did you continue to live in Detroit, or . . . ?

J: I went to New York and I played a lot of coffeehouses. I worked the bulk of the year, in club dates. North Carolina, South Carolina, Philadelphia. I booked myself. I worked very hard. I had no manager. And then I met Elliot Roberts, who became my manager.

In Kalamazoo, that was the first time I travelled with Elliot and, for the first time in my life, there sat someone who was proud of me. I never had anyone in my corner, never. Not a parent or really . . . occasionally a boyfriend, moment to moment, here and there.

I was [Elliot Roberts'] first act and later on he took on Crosby, Still, Nash & Young, and it continued to expand, so we all grew together.

Elliot Roberts: It was 1967 that I first went down to see Joan in the Village. I was working with comedians then. I was managing a comedian named Jackie Mason and a comedian named Jackie Vernon, and a duo called Stiller and Meara. I was more into that scene. I was into clubs and I would hang out with a Scotch and soda. I hadn't really been managing folk singers or working with musical artists before I went into Café au Go Go that night, which was a little folk club in New York City in Greenwich Village.

Buffy Sainte-Marie told me that Joan had just come from Toronto and that she was really marvellous, and to go down to this Café au Go Go and see her. I went down that night. She was opening up a show for Richie Havens, and she had all those songs then. She did "The Circle Game" and "Urge for Going" and "Marcie" and "Cactus Tree," "Pirate of Penance" . . . I was overwhelmed. I had never heard such fine songs from someone who I had never heard of and no one knew who she was. But yet she had all of those incredible songs.

I went backstage after the performance and I told her that I was a manager and I would like to work with her. I'd give anything to work with her.

She told me that she was leaving the next day, she was starting a road tour, and she was going to a club called the Chessmate in Detroit. She said, "Well, if you want to go with me, you can come with me and we'll see what happens."

I said, "Oh great." I went home and packed, and I picked Joan up that morning.

We did a month tour, and at the end of the tour Joan told me that yeah, she'd like to work with me.

I said, "Gee Joan," because she was just so marvellous. It was such a pleasure working with her. I left working with all these great comedians to work with Joan. And it really literally changed everything that I was doing.

We were both new then. I made a lot of mistakes in the beginning with Joan that Joan was totally aware of. We both grew together that way.

I remember once I had Joan audition for *The Mike Douglas Show*. I had this flash and I said, "Joan, we must do TV. When America sees you doing these songs . . . We've got to get a TV show. The only other show is the Johnny Carson show and that's a little too far out." We went down to the Mike Douglas show and had to audition. She did "Both Sides Now" and "Urge for Going" at the audition. The guy came

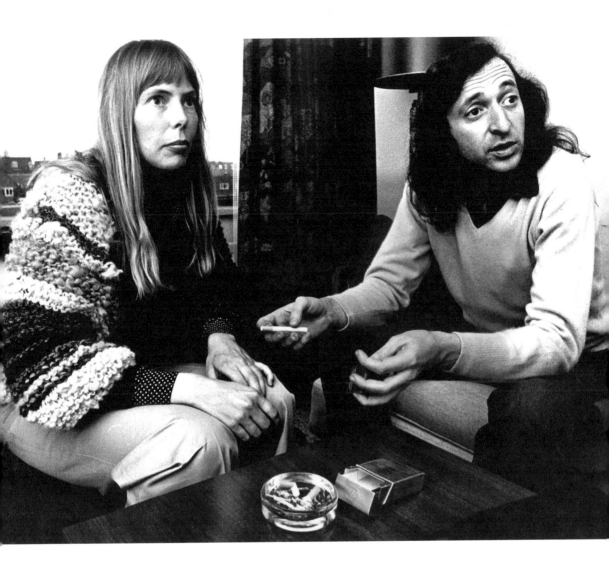

Joni and Elliot Roberts in Amsterdam in 1972

© Gijsbert Hanekroot/Redferns

over to me afterwards and he says, "We just don't have a place right now for a folk singer, but if we do, I'll give you a call." It was right then that I realized that that was not the direction to take with Joan. I mean, it wasn't a question of TV exposure, of being Vikki Carr or Teresa Brewer, I mean, Joan was much more than that. We didn't do any television after that.

J: The first time I took Elliot on the road, I took him on a trial basis. I said, "You know, you pay your own way." "Why should I cut you in?" was my thing. The bottom's gonna fall out of this. I'm doing fine. I can just keep rebooking myself. What could you possibly do for me? It's gonna collapse. The folk movement is dead. I'll never be able to get money ahead again working as a salesperson, which is all my education made me suitable for. I'll have to go back to that. But this way, I'll have a little nest egg. So it was like "reap while ye may" and then get out.

M: Once you've known poverty, it digs into you no matter how successful . . .

J: Yeah, I was suspicious of wealth.

M: I wonder if you could recall the feelings and thoughts that went through you in those years of paying dues. I remember certain occurrences myself, but it seems that the further I'm removed from that time, the more I seem to forget the hardship of that period. I wonder if it's the same with you?

J: Yeah. You do forget it. Or else a lot of things become comical to you. Or magical, mystical. For instance this concert [at the Sippin' Lizard in Michigan] . . . it was one of the most mystical concerts of my entire career, and there have been a few that things got kind of occult. But this particular night was the first time that I was getting a piece of the door instead of a salary and, wouldn't you know it, there was a tornado going through the town. My guitar got smashed on the airline. I had to borrow a guitar I wasn't familiar with. I'd been exposed to hepatitis and I'd had a gamma globulin shot in one arm and it was numb. Everything was against me.

Now, I get to this club and the people who congregated there in that bad weather were about fourteen blind children and their teacher who had come from the north, and there was an Anglican minister with his collar, there was a motorcycle gang drinking wine out of a squirt thing, and then there were a few normal people. But it was a very small crowd. And the club had a bay window for a stage with black burlap over it.

Well, as the storm progressed, it came down right on top of us. A lot of thunder, on top of us, in the middle of a song called "Songs to Aging Children Come" — "Some come dark and strange like dying." And right about that point, the thunder blew the power out. What I didn't know was that the thunder was eating my sound because there was no mike. I kept playing in the dark, and when the lightning was right on top of us, it was backlighting me. So I was this silhouette.

Half the audience is blind, so they're missing this, but they're not missing the sound effects. The ones with eyes are getting a whole show and it was really surreal. There was a point where the thunder rolled so much that I added a couple of bars to dig myself out from underneath it, and it would go, "Songs to aging children come" [thunder sound]. It would come in right after that. "Aging children, I am one" [thunder sound]. It almost orchestrated itself. Well, at the end, I stopped playing and there was no applause. I thought everybody left. It was dark.

I groped my way to the edge of the stage, and in the meantime, Charlie Latimer, my Chessmate [friend who] had travelled up to see me, he had lit a candle in the backroom, so when I opened the side door there was light in there.

I went in. I kicked off my shoe, I was so pissed off, stepped on a cigarette — mine, I guess, that had fallen out of an ashtray onto the ground. "OWWW!" I'm jumping around with this hot foot, and I burst into tears. "You always sleep through your own magic," Charlie said to me. And he played me back [on his tape recorder] this thing with the thunder and I couldn't believe it.

I played it once for Judy Collins and that's the last I saw of that tape. It just disappeared.

> Through the windless wells of wonder
> By the throbbing light machine
> In a tea leaf trance or under
> Orders from the king and queen
>
> Songs to aging children come
> Aging children, I am one
> People hurry by so quickly
> Don't they hear the melodies
> In the chiming and the clicking
> And the laughing harmonies
>
> Songs to aging children come
> Aging children, I am one

Some come dark and strange like dying
Crows and ravens whistling
Lines of weeping, strings of crying
So much said in listening

Songs to aging children come
Aging children, I am one

Does the moon play only silver
When it strums the galaxy
Dying roses will they will their
Perfumed rhapsodies to me

Songs to aging children come
This is one
("Songs to Aging Children Come")

J: Another gig, there was nothing mystical or magical about that one in Charleston, which is a naval town, and there were two clubs. One was in Fayetteville and one was in Charleston. So you're playing army and navy, right?

The gig came with accommodation, and the place that they accommodated me [laughs] was over an all-night greasy spoon with a jukebox that came up through the floorboards. I think mine was the only room in the building which wasn't . . . It was a whorehouse, that place. So I'm alone [with] drunken sailors banging at my door for Gladys. And the floors had been sprayed with kerosene for cockroaches. They call them Palmetto beetles, which is sort of polite, but they're these huge cockroaches. The room smelled of kerosene, or some sort of black, slick grease that went all up the baseboards, and I can remember being afraid in that room. Very lonely and afraid.

It was down near the slave quarters in the city and there was something at the same time that was very romantic about it to me. I guess it went along with my idea of the struggle, but finally I said, "I don't like to stay there." They moved me into the slave quarters where the shower curtains were all covered with that green moss that accumulates in the South on shower curtains.

The thing that seemed ironic to me was that with the same repertoire of songs, only a few months after, I was the opening act there on a triple billing and people talked all the way through the show — and only a few months transpired from the time that I made my record, which was a sort of an establishing point. I would play in the same areas, with the same songs and the same delivery, but the reaction would be different.

I realized then that the bulk of the people, the mass of the people, really, cannot formulate their own opinion. A few people can, and those little clubs that I played where I had a consistent following, where they even liked the fact that I was undiscovered and they had discovered my work, seemed to keep it in balance, so I wasn't totally frustrated.

M: Rumour has it that you auditioned for a coffeehouse in Toronto and the owner said, "Well, you can wash the dishes here."

J: Oh that's [Bernie Fiedler]. That's another story. The first time I met Bernie, I was playing at a place called Half Beat in Toronto. And he and his wife had a club up the street called The Mouse Hole. They came in one night, sort of snooping. And Bernie's got this great kind of dry wit. We're friends now, but at that time I didn't really understand him. He came up to me and he said, "Oh, very nice. Trying to achieve the Bayou sound, are you?" [laughs] That was my introduction to him. Later, as I could feel my growth almost prematurely — I could feel that I had potential, before it really showed — I'd play at his hoots and there'd be a little bit of response and I would come to him and I would say, "Bernie, you know . . ."

Well, obviously, from a business point of view, I was not a draw. So he'd say, "Darling, don't bother me, I don't like to associate with failures." That was one of the things he said. "Yes, I'll call you when I need a good dishwasher." It was all like his sense of humour, but there was a certain amount of seriousness to it. He wasn't interested. I wasn't going to make him any money.

M: How did it affect you? Did it affect you personally when you were rejected professionally?

J: I was very angry with Bernie, those two times. I could remember really burning over those things. I was insulted. [laughs] I really was. Now, Bernie, he takes credit for giving me the tailwind that drove me to success. [laughs]

M: What is it that gave you the confidence — way back when you were rejected — the confidence that you would succeed?

M: Oh God, I don't know. I've never thought of that. I guess the only thing was being witness to my own growth. You know, I would suddenly see that, yes, the music was getting better, and the words were getting better. Just my own sense of creative growth kept me going, I guess.

M: And what was actually the turning point?

J: Turning point? I don't see it as a turning point. I see it as a long, very slow gradual spectrum. Like, at first I had trouble just getting club work because even the clubs wanted a recording artist.

Tom Rush recorded some of my songs; Judy Collins recorded some of my songs. I guess if there was a turning point that would be it. Because they were established and hearing an established person doing songs created some interest, opened up a curiosity as to "Author! Author!" So I was able to play in some of the clubs where Tom Rush worked. And Judy's recording of my songs, since she had a bigger audience than Tom, was like a further stepping stone.

M: How did you feel when Judy Collins had a hit with your "Both Sides Now," even before you recorded it?

J: I think I probably would have liked to have had it myself. But at the same time, it was so successful, the song was picked up by so many different artists that it was only good. I mean it only did me good. But I remember thinking, "Yes, I would like to have sung it."

M: How did you get Judy Collins interested in your work?

J: I'm not sure where Judy heard the songs first. I remember I had this song "Michael from Mountains," and at that time, Judy Collins was going with a man named Michael, and a friend of hers and mine, a mutual friend, said, "Oh, wait till she hears that. She'll love it. She'll relate to it completely." I think that's how that began. And when she heard that song, she asked for more material. So I showed her some things. That's really how it went down. Judy Collins also gave Leonard Cohen a greater audience.

J: [pointing to a photo of Leonard and Joni that Malka rested on the table] This picture of us hugging at the Newport Folk Festival . . . Leonard did "Suzanne." I'd met him and I went, "I love that song. What a great song." Really. "Suzanne" was one of the greatest songs I ever heard. So I was proud to meet an artist.

He made me feel humble, because I looked at that song and I went, "Woah. All my songs seem so naïve by comparison." It raised the standard of what I wanted to write.

M: And what were *you* doing in that same Newport Folk Festival?

J: I was performing also.

M: Yet you looked up to him, rather than seeing him as an equal?

J: Yeah, oh definitely. I thought he was much more sophisticated. It made me feel like, "Oh Jesus, my songs are kind of naïve. Stupid." My "Both Sides Now" took such ridicule from Chuck, I came out of the marriage with a chip.

So when I met Leonard, I said to him, "I need to read some books," and he said, "What kind of books?"

"Well, I hear people talking about books, and I got a kind of a chip out of my marriage that I'm stupid because everybody's read a lot of books that I haven't read. Give me a reading list."

He said, "Well, you're writing quite well for someone who hasn't read anything. Maybe you shouldn't read anything."

He gave me his reading list, wonderful books: Camus, *The Stranger*; the *I Ching*, which I've used all my life; *Magister Ludi*; *Siddhartha*. A wonderful reading list.

But, unfortunately, in the Camus, I found he lifted lines. "Walk me to the corner, our steps will always . . ." That's literally a Camus line. So I thought that's like Bob Dylan.

M: I once asked Dylan when did he know that the work on a song is completed. He said when it felt that he didn't write it. That somebody else wrote it. That it was outside of him already.

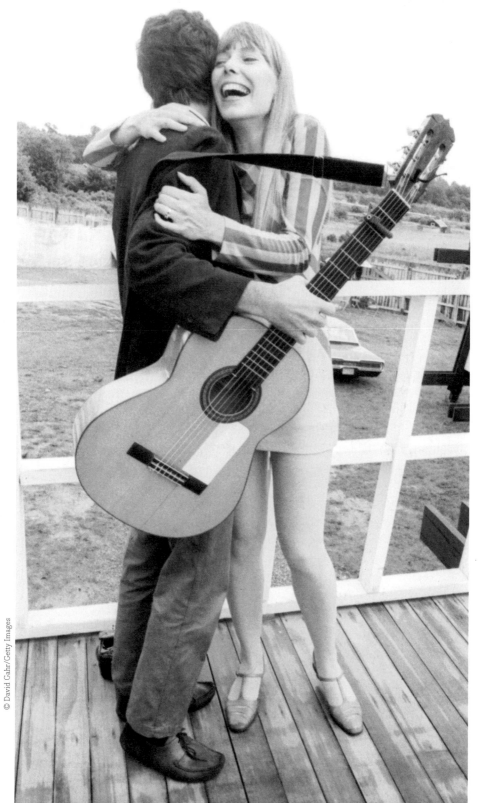

Leonard Cohen and Joni at the 1967 Newport Folk Festival

© David Gahr/Getty Images

J: That's because somebody else did write most of it? [laughs] When I realized that Bob and Leonard were lifting lines, I was very disappointed. And then I thought that there's this kind of a self-righteous quality about — you're a plagiarist and I'm not. So I plagiarized from Camus in "Come In from the Cold" intentionally. I forget which verse it is, but when I put the single out, I edited that verse out. I just took it out.

Leonard got mad at me actually, because I put a line of his, a line that he said, in one of my songs. To me, that's not plagiarism. You either steal from life or you steal from books. Life is fair game, but books are not. That's my personal opinion. Don't steal from somebody else's art, that's cheating. Steal from life — it's up for grabs, right?

So I put something that he said in one of my songs and he got real irritable, [saying], "I'm glad I wrote that."

M: I read somewhere that Leonard Cohen's "Suzanne" inspired you to write "Marcie."

J: No. "Marcie" was complete fiction. At that point, I was writing mostly fiction.

M: Do you find it easier to write fiction than autobiographical material?

J: That's how I started. Everything I wrote was fiction. I had a better imagination then. I can't write fiction anymore. I killed it intentionally.

M: Why?

J: Because I wanted to be a realist. So I killed my fantasy head and I was unable to write fiction after that. All I could write then was from personal experience.

I even would be punished by circumstance if I didn't write from my own blood. It was almost a divine or cultish thing that would happen if I wrote some things that were outside my experience — then it would descend on me eventually with a vengeance. I talked to Bob [Dylan] about that and he said that he too had to be very careful not to write about things that he didn't experience.

But even the fiction, I understood enough about the Marcie character, living alone in New York, to write it. Everything she does is pretty mundane. She washes her curtains, I recall. She arranges his fruit in a bowl.

Still no letter at her door
So she'll wash her flower curtains
Hang them in the wind to dry
Dust her tables with his shirt and
Wave another day goodbye

Marcie's faucet needs a plumber
Marcie's sorrow needs a man
Red is autumn green is summer
Greens are turning and the sand
All along the ocean beaches
Stares up empty at the sky
Marcie buys a bag of peaches
Stops a postman passing by
And summer goes
Falls to the sidewalk like string and brown paper
Winter blows
Up from the river there's no one to take her
To the sea

Marcie dresses warm it's snowing
Takes a yellow cab uptown
Red is stop and green's for going
Sees a show and rides back down
Down along the Hudson River
Past the shipyards in the cold
Still no letter's been delivered
Still the winter days unfold
Like magazines
Fading in dusty grey attics and cellars
Make a dream
Dream back to summer and hear how he tells her
Wait for me

Marcie leaves and doesn't tell us
Where or why she moved away
Red is angry green is jealous
That was all she had to say
Someone thought they saw her Sunday
Window shopping in the rain
Someone heard she bought a one-way ticket
And went west again.
         ("Marcie")

M: So "Marcie" has no connection to Leonard. What about "The Gallery"?

J: Yeah, Leonard is an influence on that song.

When I first saw your gallery
I liked the ones of ladies
Then you began to hang up me
You studied to portray me
In ice and greens
And old blue jeans
And naked in the roses
Then you got into funny scenes
That all your work discloses

"Lady, don't love me now I am dead
I am a saint, turn down your bed
I have no heart," that's what you said
You said, "I can be cruel
But let me be gentle with you"

Somewhere in a magazine
I found a page about you
I see that now it's Josephine
Who cannot be without you
I keep your house in fit repair

I dust the portraits daily
Your mail comes here from everywhere
The writing looks like ladies'

"Lady, please love me now, I am dead
I am a saint, turn down your bed
I have no heart," that's what you said
You said, "I can be cruel
But let me be gentle with you"

I gave you all my pretty years
Then we began to weather
And I was left to winter here
While you went west for pleasure
And now you're flying back this way
Like some lost homing pigeon
They've monitored your brain, you say
And changed you with religion

"Lady, please love me now, I was dead
I am no saint, turn down your bed
Lady, have you no heart," that's what you said
Well, I can be cruel
But let me be gentle with you

When I first saw your gallery
I liked the ones of ladies
But now their faces follow me
And all their eyes look shady
                    ("The Gallery")

J: Some of them are very unflattering portraits. They scared me. He could be so harsh on women.

M: Harsh in what way?

J: In the songs. "Your thighs are a ruin, you want too much / let's say you came back some time too soon." That's harsh. I countered it with thinking of the pleasure I'm gonna have watching your hairline recede, which is a similar line. I think both of those things are mean.

But Leonard gets funny. When you take him seriously, eventually, you start to . . .

M: Yes, he's got this ironic twist in him that I like. I heard that your song "Rainy Night House" was a farewell to Leonard Cohen. Is it?

J: Yeah. I went one time to his home and I fell asleep in his old room and he sat up and watched me sleep. He sat up all the night and he watched me to see who in the world I could be.

> It was a rainy night
> We took a taxi to your mother's home
> She went to Florida and left you
> With your father's gun, alone
> Upon her small white bed
> I fell into a dream
> You sat up all the night and watched me
> To see, who in the world I might be.
>   ("Rainy Night House")

M: I love those lyrics: "I am from the Sunday school / I sing Soprano"

J: "In the upstairs choir"

M: "You are a holy man
    On the FM radio
    I sat up all the night and watched thee
    To see, who in the world you might be."

J: There's some poetic liberty with those two lines; actually it's "you sat up all night and watched me to see who in the world . . ." I turned it around.

You called me beautiful
You called your mother — she was very tanned
So you packed your tent and you went
To live out in the Arizona sand
You are a refugee
From a wealthy family
You gave up all the golden factories
To see, who in the world you might be.
                    ("Rainy Night House")

J: Leonard was in a lot of pain. Hungry ghosts is what it's called in Buddhism. I am even lower. Five steps down.

M: Some time ago, I bumped into this quote, but I don't recall if it's you or Leonard who said, "What do you talk about with an old lover?"

J: That's what Leonard said to me. I went out to dinner with him one time. He was always hard to talk to. We were briefly romantically involved, but he was so distant, and so hard to communicate with. There wasn't much relationship other than the boudoir.

I thought there had to be more than that. So I asked a lot of questions of him, trying to get to the heart of it. I remember him saying, "Oh Joni, you ask such beautiful questions," but he evaded the questions.

We still became friends and he would stop to see me in Laurel Canyon from time to time. But years went by and I saw him less and less, and one night we went out to dinner and he hardly spoke to me. I felt uncomfortable. It felt unfriendly for the first time, and I said, "Do you like me?"

And he said, "Well, what is there to say to an old lover?"

I said, "Well, that's kind of a shame. There should be many things."

He said, "Well, you like ideas."

And I said, "Well, you can hardly open your mouth without an idea popping out of it."

So after that, all he'd say to me [was] "Joni, they'll never get us." That's all he'd ever say, "Joni, they'll never get us."

J: Leonard and his friend, Rosengarten, the artist, we were in New York and I was doing all that Aubrey Beardsley kind of naïve drawing at that time. I was contemplating fantasy, all these cartoony birds, you know, it was the end of childhood. And I said to Rosengarten, "I don't like my work."

He said, "What don't you like about it?"

I said, "It's too naïve and it's too ornate."

He said, "Okay."

We went to Washington Square and he said, "Draw me and don't look at the paper." It was a very liberating exercise. It enabled me to make a transition to a different style of drawing, which was more realistic and more immediate and more modern.

And once that aesthetic shift took place in the visual, it seemed to shift internally in the music as well — more rhythmic, less classical, more rocky jazz, because the chords were wider than rock chords. They were more polyphonic, but rhythmically they were four on the floor basically, Chuck Berry–ish. That was a big kind of breakthrough, heading towards *Court and Spark*.

M: *Court and Spark* seems like quite a departure: almost a new Joni Mitchell for 1973. A Joni Mitchell with a band. There is something masculine about it, I feel, a certain power and confidence that is conveyed through the bass and drums. But part of the image and the appeal of Joni Mitchell is that vulnerability that results from that lonely person on the stage. Do you think that singing with the L.A. Express band now, you might lose something by losing that vulnerable image?

J: I don't want to be vulnerable. [laughs]

Elliot Roberts: Joan likes to rock, as they say. She likes to party. She's a girl wine drinker, and she likes to have a good time. I don't think that Joan has to live up to an image of being vulnerable.

J: Sometimes I feel vulnerable, and when I do, the song that I write in that space projects that feeling. Sometimes I feel haughty and some of the music expresses that. So hopefully, the tour's concerts will be planned so they'll show a spectrum of a person's feelings, as opposed to locking into one facet.

That's another thing that I have always struggled with in my personal life, as

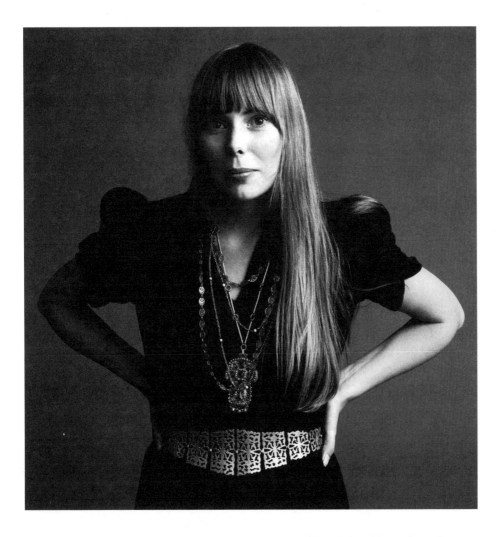

Photograph by Jack Robinson, The Jack Robinson Archive, LLC; www.robinsonarchive.com

well as in my art form: being stereotyped as a magic princess that I got earlier in my career. You know, the sort of "twinkle, twinkle little star" kind of attitude. I didn't like that feeling when it was returning to me. And no, I think that the band will only show that there's another side to the music. I think that it's a good expansion.

M: What happens to you when you go on stage, Joni? What happens inside your body, inside your head, when you perform?

J: I always get nervous before I go on. Once I'm out there, one of the things that I have had to battle is an almost euphoric feeling. If the show is going well, and I'm feeling the music, and I'm into it, sometimes, in certain situations, the audience almost feeds you too much.

I've had a feeling, and I've heard my voice on tapes almost come to a giddiness. There's a thrill. It's a power that you have to learn how to handle. It can be almost like eating too much chocolate cake, like a chocolate cake binge where you feel like you're gonna break out in zits at any moment. I've come to a point in a concert where I've had so much applause and been fed so much enthusiasm and so much love that I've suddenly felt like I was . . . um . . . I don't know how to say this delicately — full of shit. [laughs] Do you know what I mean?

Like all of a sudden, it's not as . . . I was gonna say undeserving, but that's not what it is. It's like out of proportion and yet I would stand aside and see how much I was enjoying it, that it was totally unrealistic, but it was feeding me.

There are moments in shows when I have felt as comfortable with 4,000 people as with talking to one new friend. I felt mass warmth that I could translate to one-to-one. You know, I like these people, as you would say: I like this person, so I will open up to them and be as much myself within the framework of my own theatre. But sometimes I have felt out of control with it, where I no longer was myself, but I was transported. I suppose it's not such an ugly thing. I just would think that there would be somebody out there, maybe one person, maybe ten, maybe half the audience who was thinking, "C'mon." [laughs] Do you know what I mean? Do you ever feel those things yourself on stage?

M: Yes.

J: Because it's an artificial situation. There you are, you have all the power. You have the microphone. You're up there alone and you're receiving all this mass adoration, and you're liking it.

If you don't like it, if you're suddenly up there and you say, "Wow! This is really strange," then that's when your nerve goes, your confidence goes. When you bust yourself. I've had that happen to me. I had to quit performing for a while because of that. I took a leave of absence because it became a very confusing position for me to be in.

I had always thought I was a natural performer. I always thought that I wanted to give people pleasure, to amuse them, to entertain them. Especially to make them laugh. I love to see a large group of people get off and if I'm the instigator, great.

But sometimes, in spite of the fact that I worked a lot of noisy bars under unappreciated kind of circumstances, I found that I became . . . I guess you'd call it temperamental. I got to a place where if anything happened in the room, if there was flutter or something, it would be a distraction to me, and I might lose my place.

I had to deal with that several times. I've gotten halfway through songs and been unable to finish them, simply because I wasn't into them. I just said, "I can't play this. I can't complete this, so I'll play you something else." One time I left the stage.

M: What gave you "courage of conviction," the integrity to say, "Well, listen, I don't feel it, I don't want to continue to sing." Did you see somebody do it?

J: No but, see, I've had the freedom to do that. I think it was an almost self-indulgent thing, another luxury that was provided me simply by being up there by myself and totally in control of my own decisions.

In the wings, Elliot, my manager, might be freaking [laughs], but . . .

Elliot: Yes, sometimes Joan would start and when she didn't feel it, she would just stop in the middle, and the audiences would wonder what was going on. That's how Joan is, that's how she performs. That's why she works so infrequently. It used to drive me crazy.

Once at the Atlanta Pop Festival, it was an outdoor day gig and people were milling around. She just couldn't handle it and walked. She did two, three songs and just walked off stage. "Elliot, let's go," she said to me, "I can't play for these people. They don't want to really hear my music."

They did. There could be 150,000 people, and if two, three people would yell, it will bother her.

J: Finally, I was confronted with it for, I think, the last time. I drew on an experience that I had had in Huntsville, in Hopi land. I saw a Hopi snake dance. It was a rain dance. Really, it was to bring rain to the mesa, and in the course of the dance, a rattler got loose in the audience, and the audience panicked and began to fan out. I mean that was a really genuine disturbance.

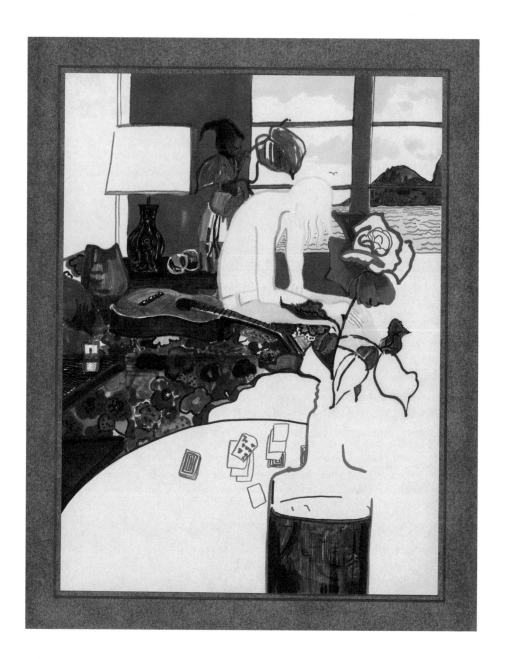

Untitled Iris print on paper

But those old guys didn't lose a beat. They never opened their eyes. They stayed right into the chant. They never lost anything because it was so important and so sacred, and their faith was so deep.

M: There's a deep discipline to being on the stage, like "The show must go on," and the audience paid money to see you and to park the car and maybe to pay for a babysitter.

J: Yeah, I know, and I've seen people go crazy for bad shows simply because they were devoted to the artist, either because the artist was number one on the hit parade, or for whatever reason. But although logically I know that you could go out and do a horrendously bad show and people will jump up and down, emotionally, if the song isn't going well, if all of a sudden I'm playing it like on automatic pilot, and I'm thinking about a hundred other things, I get the feeling that I'm transparent, and that everybody else knows that I'm not into it. So I would stop.

And there have been times where I have over-felt certain songs. I mean, I don't know why "Woodstock" was so moving to me. The two or three times that I first performed it, I had to stop. I would get so caught up in the emotion. I guess it's because I didn't go to Woodstock but I watched it on television, and it seemed like an amazing thing to me, that under the circumstances that many people helped each other out. They delivered babies in the mud, they shared their food, and there was, like, so much brotherhood. It was only one day but still it was symbolic to me of some idealism.

So whenever I would start into that song, and that one more than other songs, which were much more personal — "Woodstock" was almost like a news report — but it really moved me.

> I came upon a child of God
> He was walking along the road
> And I asked him, where are you going
> And this he told me
> I'm going on down to Yasgurs' farm
> I'm going to join in a rock 'n' roll band
> I'm going to camp out on the land
> And try an' get my soul free

We are stardust
We are golden
And we've got to get ourselves
Back to the garden

Then can I walk beside you
I have come here to lose the smog
And I feel to be a cog in something turning
Well maybe it is just the time of year
Or maybe it's the time of man
I don't know who I am
But life is for learning

We are stardust
We are golden
And we've got to get ourselves
Back to the garden

By the time we got to Woodstock
We were half a million strong
And everywhere there was song and celebration
And I dreamed I saw the bombers
Riding shotgun in the sky
And they were turning into butterflies
Above our nation

We are stardust
We are golden
And we've got to get ourselves
Back to the garden
　　　("Woodstock")

M: Your name has been linked to some powerful people in this business — James Taylor; Crosby, Stills, Nash & Young. Do you think your connection with them helped your career?

J: At the time that James [Taylor] and I were spending time together, he was a total unknown. Maybe I helped his career. [laughs] Crosby, Stills, and Nash. They met in my house and they became a band. I introduced them here. But, yeah, at that time, we were all writing new songs.

The rock 'n' roll industry is very incestuous, you know. We have all interacted and been the source of many songs for one another. James has written songs for me, I've written songs for him. Graham and I have written songs for one another.

Like Paris was to the Impressionists and the post-Impressionists, L.A. was the hotbed of all musical activity. The greatest musicians in the world either live here or pass through here regularly. I think that a lot of beautiful music came from it, and a lot of beautiful times came through that mutual understanding. A lot of pain came from it too, because inevitably different relationships broke up and it gets complicated.

Rolling Stone did a really horrible, sort of catty thing, where they showed broken hearts and arrows to try and chain this complex organism altogether. I don't like that sensationalistic kind of publicity. I don't like it when *Rolling Stone* does those numbers on me.

M: Aren't you creating your own world when you surround yourself with musicians, troubadours, doing the same kind of work that you are doing, with almost the same outlook on life — a world not so open to what is happening outside your sphere, in the rest of the world?

J: A friend of mine criticized me for that. He was someone in another field. He said that my work was becoming very inside. It was making reference to roadies and rock 'n' rollers, and that's the very thing that I told you that I didn't want to happen; why I like to take a lot of time off in the course of a year to travel someplace else. To travel someplace that's foreign enough, where I have my anonymity and I can have that day-to-day encounter with other walks of life, you know.

M: Still, many of your songs are autobiographical — your lifestyle, your affluent lifestyle must have affected your songs, no?

J: I don't know. I had difficulty at one point accepting my affluence, and my success, even the expression of it seemed to me distasteful at one time, like to suddenly be driving a fancy car. I had a lot of soul searching to do. I felt that living in elegance and

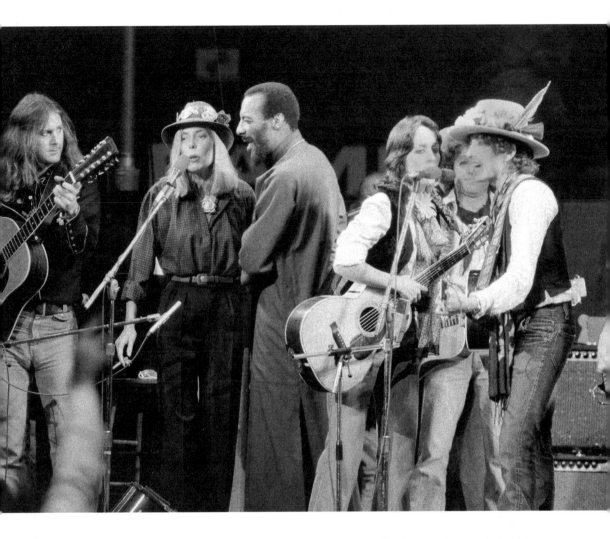

Roger McGuinn, Joni Mitchell, Richie Havens, Joan Baez, and Bob Dylan perform the finale of the the Rolling Thunder Revue in December 1975 AP Photo

luxury cancelled creativity, or even some of that sort of Sunday school philosophy that luxury comes as a guest and then becomes the master. That was a philosophy that I held onto. I still had that stereotyped idea that success would deter it, that luxury would make you too comfortable and complacent and that the gift would suffer from it.

But I found that I was able to express it in the work, even at the time when it was distasteful to me. Like "I slept last night in a good hotel / I went shopping today for jewels." The only way that I could reconcile with myself and my art was to say, "This is what I'm going through now; my life is changing. I show up at the gig in a big limousine and that's a fact of life."

I'm an extremist as far as lifestyle goes. I need to live simply and primitively sometimes, at least for short periods of the year, in order to keep in touch with something more basic. But I have come to be able to finally enjoy my success, and to use it as a form of self-expression.

Leonard Cohen has a line that says, "Do not dress in those rags for me, / I know you are not poor." When I heard that line, I thought to myself that I had been denying, which was hypocritical. I had been denying, just as that line in that song, I had played down my wealth.

Many people in the rock business [have] their patched jeans and their Levi jackets, which is a comfortable way to dress, but also it's a way of keeping yourself aligned with your audience. For instance, if you were to show up at a rock and roll concert dressed in gold lamé and all of your audience was in Salvation Army discards, you would feel like a person apart.

That's what it was. I began to feel too separate from my audience and from my times, separated by affluence and convenience from the pulse of my times. I wanted to hitchhike and scuffle. I felt that I hadn't done enough scuffling. Although my success was very gradual, I felt that I had been deprived of a lot of the experience of people who broke away and tried alternate lifestyles, communal living and that kind of experimentation, which, if I hadn't been successful, I would have been more a part of.

> I slept last night in a good hotel
> I went shopping today for jewels
> The wind rushed around in the dirty town
> And the children let out from the schools
> I was standing on a noisy corner
> Waiting for the walking green
> Across the street he stood
> And he played real good
> On his clarinet, for free.
>
> Now me I play for fortune
> And those velvet curtain calls
> I've got a black limousine

And two gentlemen
Escorting me to the halls
And I play if you have the money
Or if you're a friend to me
But the one man band
By the quick lunch stand
He was playing real good, for free.

Nobody stopped to hear him
Though he played so sweet and high
They knew he had never
Been on their TV
So they passed his music by
I meant to go over and ask for a song
Maybe put on a harmony . . .
I heard his refrain
As the signal changed
He was playing real good, for free.
                    ("For Free")

M: Was it only in your songs that as soon as you were lauded and applauded, accorded curtain calls, fame, fortune, and limousines, that you decided, "I'm going to quit this crazy scene"? Did it also happen in real life?

J: Yeah, I quit. I quit for two years. That was at the time when, like I told you, money and success, somehow or other, seemed distasteful to me. It seemed out of proportion to what I had done. Although sometimes I felt I deserved every bit of it. I mean, this wasn't just one attitude. I go from one extreme to the other. Hopefully, eventually, like a pendulum comes to rest in the middle . . . But I remember being incredibly grateful when people wanted to talk to me, or to tell me that they liked my music. Later on, I didn't want to hear it, and I didn't want praise or criticism. I couldn't handle either one of them. [laughs]

M: How old were you then?

J: Twenty-seven. During that time, right before I bought my land in Canada, the world, the vision of the world in its tendencies, was too much with me.

I hadn't cried for years, but at that time I cried all the time. They walked on the moon, I cried. Everything made me cry. Going to see Elvis . . . I went with David Geffen and Elliot Roberts. It was at that time where [Elvis had] been in Vegas for a while and he'd gotten kind of stout. He had a cold that night. He's very playful, Elvis. That's one of the things I liked about him. He's making fun of himself, about this cold, like a little boy. Coughing into the microphone and laughing at himself. It was a throwaway, childish, boyish behaviour, but it was okay. I like boys. I don't mind boyish behaviour, goofiness. Geffen and Elliot, as I recall, wished he wouldn't do that, but I found it kind of endearing.

Afterwards, Geffen disappeared. He's got the Midas touch. He went out and made himself quite a bit of money. I don't know on what table.

I took a Styrofoam cup full of dimes and went to [one of] the one-armed bandits, gave it a few pulls. I looked down the line and there were all of these geriatric women from old age homes. They send buses to the geriatric homes when their pension cheques arrive. With gloves on, they were pulling on the lever and feeding it and pulling on the lever and feeding it. And I'm looking at these women, pulling on these things, and I felt so bad that they were being exploited, that buses were picking them up and draining them of their pension in this way. And they were like hypnotized chickens, and I go, "Oh my God, this is the way of the world." It horrified me. I burst into tears. Abandoned my cupful of dimes. Ran out into the lobby.

There was a bad dress shop with bad lingerie, like Frederick's of Hollywood kind of junk. In the window display, there were European antiques, and among them was this Salvation Army portable organ with gold letters on it that said, "Seek Ye The Lord While Ye May" in English script. I rushed into the store and, with tears in my eyes, I said, "I have to buy this organ."

"Oh, it's not for sale, dear," she said. "It's window dressing."

I said, "You don't understand. I have to buy this organ."

She refused me again. I burst into tears. I sobbed, "But you don't understand . . . I have to . . ." She finally took pity on me and sold me the goddamn thing.

That was the year I burst into tears. I cried all the time.

M: So this is when you quit, when you were twenty-seven years old?

J: Yes. When I was looking and looking for my land. I looked at all the islands all around. Every place they showed me, I burst into tears, beyond consolation. Imagine, trying to take a client around parcels of land in British Columbia and she's crying every time they showed me something. I was a basket case. A guy would have taken the bulldozer and pushed the land over and chopped down trees and there were stumps all over the place. I just burst into tears.

One time I had to pull over, what made me cry was the telephone poles were going . . . telephone lines made me cry. Everything made me cry. And I started having visions. About the destruction of the earth.

Another day, I came upon a boat being pulled by a car crossing under the telephone lines as they went across the road. The name of the boat was *The Wife's Mink Coat*. And I burst into tears. It had two motors and I just saw all the disruption those egg beaters were making in the water, and I felt sorry for the fish. I had to pull over to the side of the road. I was weeping about that.

M: How long did it take you to find the land?

J: I spent part of the year, I looked and looked. A lot of disappointments.

M: That in itself can be depressing.

J: This land is going to be my companion for the rest of my life.

M: At such a young age to think like that, my God.

J: I lost my daughter. I made a bad marriage. I made a couple of bad relationships after that. And then I got this illness — crying all the time. My mother thought I was being a wimp, and she was giving me buck-up advice. Later in life, she was walking through the supermarket and started crying for no reason. She also had it, milder than this. She called me up and apologized.

It also simultaneously appeared when my insights became keener, so I could see painfully — things about people I didn't want to know. I'd just look at a person and I'd know too much about them that I didn't want to know. And because everything was becoming transparent, I felt I must be transparent, and I cried.

I dreamed I was a plastic bag sitting on an auditorium chair watching a big fat women's tuba band. Women with big horns and rolled down nylons in house dresses playing tuba and big horn music, and I was a plastic bag with all my organs exposed, sobbing on an auditorium chair at that time. That's how I felt. Like my guts were on the outside. I wrote *Blue* in that condition.

M: What a price to pay . . . for art.

> Born with the moon in Cancer
> Choose her a name she will answer to
> Call her green and the winters cannot fade her
> Call her green for the children who've made her
> Little green, be a gypsy dancer
>
> He went to California
> Hearing that everything's warmer there
> So you write him a letter and say, "Her eyes are blue"
> He sends you a poem and she's lost to you
> Little green, he's a non-conformer
>
> Just a little green
> Like the colour when the spring is born
> There'll be crocuses to bring to school tomorrow
> Just a little green
> Like the nights when the Northern lights perform
> There'll be icicles and birthday clothes
> And sometimes there'll be sorrow
>
> Child with a child pretending
> Weary of lies you are sending home
> So you sign all the papers in the family name
> You're sad and you're sorry, but you're not ashamed
> Little green, have a happy ending

Just a little green
Like the colour when the spring is born
There'll be crocuses to bring to school tomorrow
Just a little green
Like the nights when the Northern lights perform
There'll be icicles and birthday clothes
And sometimes there'll be sorrow
("Little Green")

J: When I listen to *Blue* now it is still very . . . People were shocked by it at the time. It doesn't seem so shocking or even so bare bones now. The next [album] is even more bare bones.

M: Which is?

J: *For the Roses.*

There comes a point where you just kind of bleed onto the pages. Many artists end up going there. It's like in Job, when God says to Job, "Have you seen . . . ? Have you seen the janitors of Shadowland?" The artist has to see the janitors of Shadowland at some point. You could call it teenage angst. Maybe it's best to face your inner self in your teens when your body's strong. You need to face that when you're young and strong.

In other cultures, that would be called a shamanic conversion. In this culture, it would be called a nervous breakdown. Your nerves are on fire. Since we're not a shamanic people, we don't realize that sharper senses are coming in. I think it's the sixth sense, which is the coordination of all the other five; it comes from sharpening the five. It's the sense that directs the dogs and horses to run for the hills when the tsunami is coming. They could hear it, they could smell it.

It sharpened my vision, as a painter. Sharpened my hearing as a musician. Sharpened my sense of language. Sharpened the speed of my eye. I could see a fleeting expression on a face, like a thirty-third of a second. And in that thirty-third of a second, a lot of times, much is revealed.

Lesson in Survival

Spinning out on turns

That get you tough

Guru books — the Bible

Only a reminder

That you're just not good enough

You need to believe in something

Once I could in our love

Black road

Double yellow line

Friends and kin

Campers in the kitchen

That's fine sometimes

But I know my needs

My sweet tumbleweed

I need more quiet times

By a river flowing

You and me

Deep kisses

And the sun going down

Maybe it's paranoia

Maybe it's sensitivity

Your friends protect you

Scrutinize me

I get so damn timid

Not at all the spirit

That's inside of me

Oh baby I can't seem to make it

With you socially

There's this reef around me

I'm looking way out at the ocean

Love to see that green water in motion

I'm going to get a boat

And we can row it

If you ever get the notion

To be needed by me

Fresh salmon frying

And the tide rolling in

I went to see a friend tonight

'Was very late when I walked in

My talking as it rambled

Revealed suspicious reasoning

The visit seemed to darken him

I came in as bright

As a neon light

And I burned out

Right there before him

I told him these things

I'm telling you now

Watched them buckle up

In his brow

When you dig down deep

You lose good sleep

And it makes you

Heavy company

I will always love you

Hands alike

Magnet and iron

The souls

("Lesson in Survival")

J: I intended to become a hermit when I bought my land in Canada.

M: When was that, in relation to your work?

J: That was after I wrote "Big Yellow Taxi." I bought the land a year or two after that. I was never going to come back. I was just going to live up there. I thought, "I will never get bored on this piece of land."

It's magical. It really is. The mundane aspects of it are magical and then there are two or three things every year that are spectacular — pink rainbow, comets streaking through the clouds, low to the ground. Amazing things. Not to mention I've got a blue heron that I have a relationship with, that lives in my bay — big bird. A robin followed me around one year. Everywhere I went, he was hopping around behind me.

I dragged a stack of books up to British Columbia to figure out what was happening, because something was biochemically off then. I couldn't be around people because everything made me weep. And the desire to study the self became acute.

I read all of these books. Leonard's reading list was part of it. The *I Ching* became part of it. The works of Freud and Jung. And also contemporary self-help psychology books, which were a bunch of junk, sounding intelligent but really not having much to say at all, especially from the perspective of someone who's on the bottom.

"Have you seen the janitors of Shadowland?" From that perspective, you really see what's meaningful and what has the thumbs in the lapel. Most of it is men showing off for an inner group of academics. It's a lot of blah, blah, blah. A lot of the books just kept hitting the wall like that. But Nietzsche made me laugh. Nietzsche . . . I found great humour in his writing. The audacity of the amount of truth he was able to face.

M: Even though Nietzsche said of poets, "The poet is the vainest of the vain, the peacock of the peacocks."

J: "He muddies his waters so that they might appear deep.
Even before the ugliest of water buffalo death, he found his tail.
I have looked among them for an honest man
and all I've dredged up are old gods' heads
and the poets are bad learners too.
And they like what women say,

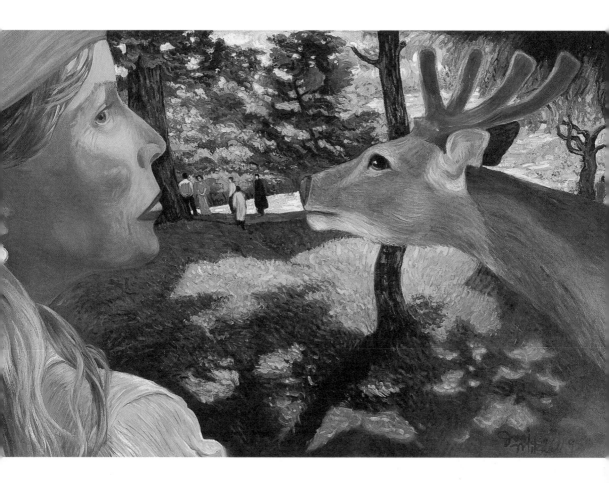

In the Park of the Golden Buddha, 1995
© Joni Mitchell, photo by Sheila Spence

especially late at night,
especially the old women.
He thinks that all of nature is whispering just to him.
But Zarathustra, how can you say these terrible things about the poet?
Is Zarathustra not also a poet?
Of course he is. How else would he know these things?
But I see a new poet on the horizon.
He is the uberman.
He writes in his own blood.
He is the penitent of spirit.

He writes in his own blood."

Nietzsche found poetry vacuous and vain, for the most part. I could always see in most poems the thumbs in the lapels, somebody playing the poet: "Oh, this is poetic." It's all about getting laid, right?

In that encounter with Browning, when she's lying on the couch and he comes to visit for the first time, there's a line in his poem that she can't figure out, and she says to him, "Explain this line," and he laughs and he says, "When I wrote it, only God and I knew what it meant. Now only God knows." He muddies his waters that he might appear deep.

To me, the way I write, that would be irresponsible. I really try, even though it's cryptic. Like somebody said, "What's a sunset pig?" and I said, "A cop on Sunset Boulevard." So it isn't muddy water but it is cryptic. Or "the carbon ribbon rides." That's the carriage being thrown on the typewriter.

And there is some surrealism as well in the writing from time to time. "Beauty parlour blonds with credit card eyes." "A country road came off the wall / And swooped down on the crowd at the bar." It's kind of like a painting, a road and a painting on the wall becomes active. It's not real, it's surreal. But it also works.

M: What about women writers? Simone de Beauvoir, Germaine Greer, for example. Did you have a go at them at that time when "the desire to study the self became acute"?

J: I was never a feminist. I was in argument with them. They were so down on the domestic female, the family, and it was breaking down. And even though my problems were somewhat female, they were of no help to mine. I was already past that. I don't want to get a posse against guys. The men need correcting. The feminists were emulating them.

The things of all of these books, the only things that held up to me, that were working with the problem as a holistic problem, were Carl Jung's, because he had had access to the medicine wheel, this mandala, this concept of a chief's wheel, or a wheel of becoming.

I disagreed with Jung because he relabelled north, which the Natives called "wisdom," to "intellect." And I think that intellect is very limited. Wisdom is really the pulling of heart and mind together. It isn't just pure intellect.

And sensitivity, Jung called it "sensation." I had a problem with that. Because sensitivity is a big thing, but culturally it's very unacceptable. "Oh, you're too sensitive," my mother used to say. "You're too emotional, you've got to learn to control your emotions."

Well, obviously, I studied my emotions. There's quite an emotional spectrum to my work. And sensitivity I found is a good thing in that you notice a lot of details, especially in nature.

One of the bad things about it is that you tend to tread [in place] because sensitivity lacks clarity. You'll get a problem you don't know the answer to and you'll go over and over it, spin your wheels, tread it to death. However, by treading over and over and over, there is a deepening process so in that way you do come to, hopefully, occasionally, some hidden truths, because . . . sensitivity is the setting sun, it's the gateway to the look-within place, it's the deepening place. It's what depression is for. It's to drive you in to face yourself and correct yourself.

People usually try to avoid their depression because it's looked on as so ugly. It makes you look like a loser in America, which is the worst thing you can be, right? But depression is like a great opportunity to figure it out for yourself. "Huh? I have to figure it out for myself? No way!" They go to a movie. They'll just ostrich out all they can. As a result, they miss their opportunity to grow.

I mean, I feel every bit of trouble I went through. I'm grateful for it, you know. [laughs] Really, Malka.

M: What kind of trouble are you referring to?

J: Just woe. Woe is me, trouble on me. A broken heart. A broken body. Little tricks of fate. Bummers. [laughs]

In retrospect, a lot of the bummers change the course of my destiny. I wouldn't have pursued music but for trouble. Fortune changed the course of my destiny. I became a musician.

In retrospect, I've learned that depression is necessary for growth. It gives you an inkling that you're an asshole, but you don't quite know why. If you take a medicine and you don't get to the "why," you're gonna remain an asshole on drugs. You're never gonna get to the bottom or the turning point or the revelation.

You couldn't be a novelist without sensitivity, without a sense of detail. And you can't be deep without sensitivity. And emotionality, God, without emotionality in the arts, it's merely intellectual. It's boring, except to an intellectual. If you're trying to make a whole art, you really need all of those things.

A lot of my work, my complex chords contain emotional nuances that are forbidden within the laws of music. But craving freshness and also craving to express my emotions — and not knowing the rule — I bypassed them, broke the rules. Because I'm abundantly sensitive, I worked and worked and worked to be able to achieve clarity.

But even though I'm ultra-sensitive, it doesn't mean that I'm just always wounded and bleeding but that I'm perceiving things that other people might not.

M: It must make you very lonely.

J: Marilyn Monroe says in *The Misfits*, "If I have to feel lonely, I'd rather be alone." [laughs] It's a great line, isn't it?

> I am on a lonely road and I am travelling
> looking for the key to set me free
> Oh the jealousy, the greed is the unravelling
> It's the unravelling
> and it undoes all the joy that could be
> I want to have fun, I want to shine like the sun
> I want to be the one that you want to see
> I want to knit you a sweater
> want to write you a love letter
> I want to make you feel better
> I want to make you feel free
> want to make you feel free
> ("All I Want")

M: What had moved you to quit your "retirement" in the seclusion of your land in British Columbia?

J: It's like that very beautiful story about the clown. Do you know it?

M: No. I don't think so.

J: He was the greatest clown in the world. One day he went into the arena and something was on his mind. So right at the most tense moment in his bit, where his timing was very important, he locked, couldn't remember what he was supposed to do. And there was a tension created. The audience leaned forward in their seats. Then just at the moment when people would have been embarrassed for him, he regained it, they all heaved this great sigh of relief, and they went to that place which is the highest comedy, where there's pathos and amusement at the same time. They were relieved for him, and they laughed this great laugh of relief.

So he incorporated it into his act. And he did it night after night, he'd come out there and he'd forget, he'd lose it for a minute, it would get awkward. Then he'd regain it and they'd all go, "Oh bravo, you regained it!"

Finally, one day, he couldn't live with the fact that they couldn't tell the difference between the genuine time that it went down and this falsification of it. He left the circus and he wandered around for a long time. But in his soul, he knew he was a clown, and that's all he could do. So eventually, he drifted back. Found a circus playing on the outskirts of a small town, and he was hired to water the elephants and shovel hay.

One night, one of the old clowns took sick. Well, our clown had been watching everybody's part in the show for weeks and weeks by now. So he said to the old man who was sick, he said, "Listen. I think I know your routine. I could do it for you."

The old man was very grateful and said, "Oh wonderful. The show must go on."

So our clown went out into the arena and he did the old man's show. Only he did it so much better that the old man lying in his sick bed, when that old man heard the applause like he'd never heard it for himself, it broke his heart and he died.

When the clown came out of the arena and saw what he had created by trying to do this old man a service, he was really saddened by it, and he wandered off. For years and years, he just wandered around odd jobbing. And one day he was in a park. He was himself an old man at that time and he saw a cop coming towards him. So, he got up and he went into his old routine, his greatest clown on earth routine. And he got to that moment where he loses it, and he regained it, his timing was perfect, and the cop broke into a laugh and applauded him and applauded him. But just then the clown died.

It's a tragic ending, but I think that if we can't help but look at the illusion, the illusion breaks down. You know that you're creating an illusion, no matter how honest you try to be.

But with my new material [*Court and Spark*] I could probably get into the songs pretty consistently, and genuinely feel them. And like that clown, who just recognized that that was his calling, and he had no choice really about it.

And I also . . . I didn't know what to do with myself. I was too young to be retired. What was I gonna do?

I painted for a while, and I did a lot of writing at that time, but it was the public thing which I was quitting. That's the wonderful thing about being a successful playwright or an author, you still maintain your anonymity, which is very important in order to be somewhat of a voyeur, to collect your observations for your material. But to suddenly be in a lot of situations, the centre of attention . . . it threatened the writer in me. The performer threatened the writer.

When I did come back, I came back "like a red hot mama with a band," Eric [Andersen] says. I started writing more fun-loving things and having more fun on stage. Less burdenment — that went out of the Nordic angst thing, which I had explored enough anyway. I did outgrow it.

M: Before I flew here, we were listening at home to your records, and my son asked me, "How does a person create a song?"

J: How does a person create a song? A lot of it is being open, I think, to encounter and to, in a way, be in touch with the miraculous.

I'll tell you about the way one song was written, because it has a song within a song. I had a line which went "three waitresses all wearing black diamond earrings, talking about zombies and Singapore slings." Well, the song can be taken on a couple of levels.

Symbolically, to me, it represents the trinity in a way, the three waitresses. It's like a religious parody. Making Mecca, or making the shrine or the church Bar 'n' Grill.

I had two verses written to it, and I didn't know how it should end. I didn't know what kind of point I was trying to make or anything. And one night, I pulled into a gas station at four o'clock in the morning. There was an old man there. There was no one else around. And the old man said to me, "What are you doing out so late?"

I said, "Well, I've just come from this recording studio down the street."

He said, "Oh, you sing!" Then he asked me to sing him a song.

But I couldn't. I was tired, and I was impatient. I really wanted him to just put the gas in the car and let me go home.

"Well, listen," he said, "if you're not gonna sing a song, I'll sing you a song. You know, I could sing just like Nat King Cole," he said. And he burst into two verses of "Merry Christmas." Just exactly like Nat King Cole.

All this time, he still hasn't put the gas in the car, and I'm feeling this incredible tiredness and impatience to go home, but he's being amazing.

"You know," he said, "you can write a song about anything," he said. "Why, I could make up a song about this car," he said. And he started singing this song about my car having nice tires and white walls and windshields and different things just around the gas station. He was so amazing.

The thing that came to me, and the thing that I used in writing my song in the last verse, was just that common thing that's bandied around now about being in the here and now. It was like I suddenly recognized my impatience to get home was spoiling my absorption of how beautiful this incident that I was in the middle of was.

So that became the last verse of the song. It went, "He makes up his own tune / Right on the spot / About whitewalls and windshields / And this job he's got / And you want to get moving / And you want to stand still / But caught up in the moment / Some longing gets filled / And you even forget to ask / 'Hey, where's Barangrill?'" — Barangrill being whatever it is you're seeking for.

Three waitresses all wearing
Black diamond earrings
Talking about zombies
And Singapore slings
No trouble in their faces
Not one anxious voice
None of the crazy you get
From too much choice
The thumb and the satchel
Or the rented Rolls-Royce
And you think she knows something
By the second refill
You think she's enlightened
As she totals your bill
You say "Show me the way
To Barangrill"

Well some say it's in service
They say "Humble Makes Pure"
You're hoping it's near Folly
'Cause you're headed that way for sure
And you just have to laugh
'Cause it's all so crazy
Ah, her mind's on her boyfriend
And eggs over easy
It's just a trick on you
Her mirrors and your will
So you ask the truck driver
On the way to the till
But he's just a slave
To Barangrill

The guy at the gaspumps
He's got a lot of soul
He sings Merry Christmas for you
Just like Nat King Cole
And he makes up his own tune
Right on the spot
About whitewalls and windshields
And this job he's got
And you want to get moving
And you want to stay still
But lost in the moment
Some longing gets filled
And you even forget to ask
"Hey, Where's Barangrill?"
    ("Barangrill")

J: That's how he finished my song for me. So a lot of it is being open, because the muse, or the giving up of songs, from wherever they come, they just pass through you, as you allow yourself to experience.

M: Do you have the audience in mind, "the popular song," when you write?

J: It depends on the song. For the most part, I write . . . Sometimes I think it would be better if I just sent a letter. I do write often to individuals. Sometimes, I write just to think clearly, to clear up some vagueness in my own mind — almost like a meditation.

But one song I wrote out of blatant commercialism. [laughs] It's called "You Turn Me On, I'm a Radio." I thought it would have a certain amount of disc jockey appeal, since it was full of things, like "the recording tower" and "call me at the station." It was just my own peculiar warped sense of humour, so I decided to make an attempt, almost like you go to the races and you play a horse.

Well, the charts, the top 100, are very much like a race track. If it gets on the charts, say you come on at seventy-seven with a bullet, that means that your horse is racing up the charts and has a chance of making it. So just to follow it, like a racing sheet, is kind of a good game.

If you're driving into town
With a dark cloud above you
Dial in the number
Who's bound to love you

Oh honey, you turn me on
I'm a radio
I'm a country station
I'm a little bit corny
I'm a wildwood flower
Waving for you
Broadcasting tower
Waving for you
And I'm sending you out
This signal here
I hope you can pick it up
Loud and clear

I know you don't like weak women
You get bored so quick
And you don't like strong women
'Cause they're hip to your tricks
It's been dirty for dirty
Down the line
But you know I come when you whistle
When you're loving and kind

But if you've got too many doubts
If there's no good reception for me
Then tune me out
'Cause honey who needs the static
It hurts the head
And you wind up cracking
And the day goes dismal
From "Breakfast Barney"
To the sign-off prayer
What a sorry face you get to wear
I'm going to tell you again now
If you're still listening there

If you're driving into town
With a dark cloud above you
Dial in the number
Who's bound to love you
If you're lying on the beach
With the transistor going
Kick off the sandflies, honey
The love's still flowing
If your head says "forget it"
But your heart's still smoking
Call me at the station
The lines are open . . .
                    ("You Turn Me On, I'm a Radio")

M: What about the music part of the songs?

J: The music? The only time I really play an instrument is to explore it. Sometimes I have to play an instrument in order to rehearse material for a tour. That's drudgery to me. That's work. That's the piano lessons as a child, that's hammer and saw. Practice. Practice. Practice.

    The time that I enjoy playing the most is when I'll sit down late at night and tune my guitar into a tuning which I'm unfamiliar with, so I have the unknown in front of

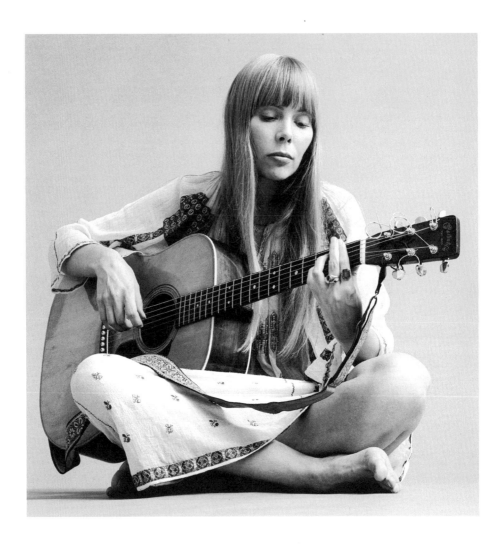

Photograph by Jack Robinson, The Jack Robinson Archive, LLC; www.robinsonarchive.com

me, a combination of chords in front of me, a combination of strings, which I'm unfamiliar with the fingering. Then I would just pass my fingers, in sort of a mathematical fashion, fifth to the seventh, maybe back to the third, you know, to the eleventh, to get a really sort of strange colour in there. And just mess around with it, and then gradually introduce liaisons — the things that smooth from chord to chord, and then it gradually takes shape, and that . . . that's also a magical process and sort of trance-like, takes total preoccupation with it. But that comes easier to me than words do. I think that you keep your writing muse alive as long as you're open enough so that experience seems amazing to you and things continue to be magical. [But] the musical muse, in my particular case, is easier to keep alive, since it's abstract emotion. It's feeling and it's the colours which transport certain feelings into you or out of you.

I seem to be more prolific musically than I [am] lyrically.

M: And yet so many people seem to appreciate your lyrics more than the music.

J: Hmm.

M: As a matter of fact, I read a review of the record *For the Roses*, and it said, "*For the Roses* should convince anyone that this lady never has been a folk singer. She's a poet who embellishes her poetry with music."

I heard it in the wind last night
It sounded like applause
Did you get a round resounding for you
Way up here
It seems like many dim years ago
Since I heard that face to face
Or seen you face to face
Though tonight I can feel you here
I get these notes
On butterflies and lilac sprays
From girls who just have to tell me
They saw you somewhere

In some office sits a poet
And he trembles as he sings
And he asks some guy
To circulate his soul around
On your mark red ribbon runner
The caressing rev of motors
Finely tuned like fancy women
In thirties evening gowns

Up the charts
Off to the airport —
Your name's in the news
Everything's first class —
The lights go down —
And it's just you up there
Getting them to feel like that

Remember the days when you used to sit
And make up your tunes for love
And pour your simple sorrow
To the soundhole and your knee
And now you're seen
On giant screens
And at parties for the press
And for people who have slices of you
From the company
They toss around your latest golden egg
Speculation — well, who's to know
If the next one in the nest
Will glitter for them so

I guess I seem ungrateful
With my teeth sunk in the hand
That brings me things
I really can't give up just yet
Now I sit up here
The critic!
And they introduce some band
But they seem so much confetti
Looking at them on my TV set
Oh the power and the glory
Just when you're getting a taste for
worship
They start bringing out the hammers
And the boards
And the nails

I heard it in the wind last night
It sounded like applause
Chilly now
End of summer
No more shiny hot nights
It was just the arbutus rustling
And the bumping of the logs
And the moon swept down black water
Like an empty spotlight
            ("For the Roses")

M: Let me show you another photo, this one is of you and Eric Clapton.

J: Eric Clapton is watching my hands, his mouth is gaping open because he couldn't figure out what I was doing: "What is she doing? How is she getting those sounds?"

People would comment on my hands from the start, like when Chuck Mitchell and his partner then, Lauren James, went to see me. Lauren James went, "Look at her right hand," and Chuck went, "Hell, look at her legs." [laughs]

What it was, I guess, I had a classical arch. I didn't study classical guitar from anybody but, practically speaking, you find that if you want to get the notes to bark, if you want to get the control where you touch variation, that's the best way to get it, because *bam!* you could snap the strings and make strong, powerful notes and also you're in a position for the delicacy.

In order to get the emotional variation out of it, that's the logical position, so it's just common sense, which happens to be not what is taught. I find it very strange.

M: Strange that superb guitarists try to figure out how you do it?

J: It just looked crazy to them. Plus I was coming over the top of the bar, barring over the top. They're going, "What the hell is she doing?" And yet, it was all logical.

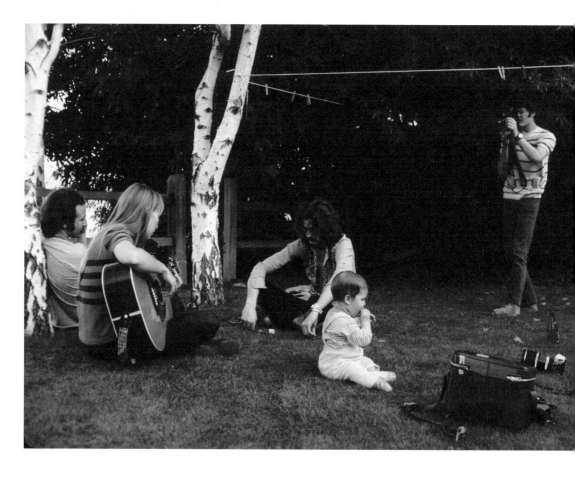

Joni playing, David Crosby (left) and Eric Clapton (right) look on as Micky Dolenz takes pictures

© Henry Diltz

M: Logical to you.

J: To the ear. It was musical, but looking at the hands, they never saw hands that were doing those things, I guess.

My guitar playing was never like anybody else's. For a moment, I sounded a little bit like Joan Baez. An influence snuck in but when I started to write, it disappeared. And I never, from then on, wanted to sound like anybody else. Do you know what I mean?

M: Yes. [laughs] Were you self-taught on the guitar?

J: The only instruction I had on the guitar was I bought a Pete Seeger Folkways album [on] how to play folk-style guitar. It's very simple. It starts out with a first band: "Now we will tune the guitar." Then you learn maybe two or three basic chords. And it has a book accompanying it with tablature, which is a simplified kind of form. It shows you what string your thumb should be plucking. He does the pattern very slowly and then he speeds it up. I got about three bands into it, although it was a beautifully presented album and a great instructor, and you can take your own time with it and start the band over again and over again, I lost interest with it. I was impatient. I don't learn anything well by instruction.

And then Eric Andersen showed me one open tuning. Eric showed me open G tuning, which is banjo tuning. That's the tuning that Keith Richards uses, and the old black blues guys used, because they had played banjos. When they got a guitar, they didn't know Spanish tuning, so they tuned it like a banjo.

"Circle Game" was written in it. I wrote a lot of stuff in open G. I began to play with that, and I discovered a lot of my own tunings, so that now I can't play standard tuning at all.

Nearly all the Rolling Stones' music was written in open G, at least the ones that Keith Richards created. Most of it, he plays only in open G, so it has a different sound.

M: Did you take to the open G right away?

J: Well, I only wrote two songs in standard tuning. "Urge for Going," which was one of the very first ones, if not the first one I wrote — the first one that I considered successful anyway. I never wrote and played in standard tuning again, because everything sounded like it was mined out. No matter how well you played in it, it just seemed like a tired and worn-out road. Everything sounded derivative.

I was trying to get at something that would excite me, a fresher thing. Before I began my own tunings, which a lot of them are tuned to sus chords . . .

M: Sus chords?

J: Well, I used to call them, not knowing what a sus chord was myself, I called them chords of inquiry. They have a question mark in them. They're sustained. Men don't like them because they like resolution, just like they do in life.

Wayne Shorter said to me, "What are these chords? These are not guitar chords and these are not piano chords. What are these chords?" And then he said, "You realize some of them are sus chords." And he went, "They create suspense. They're suspensions. They're unresolved, like a major is a positive statement. A minor is a tragic chord, right? The seventh is a kind of a bluesy chord. But a sus chord has a question mark in it. It lacks resolution."

So the law, according to Wayne Shorter, who studied music and had a degree from Berklee College of Music, he said, "We were taught to never stay on a sus chord too long. Never ever go from a sus chord to a sus chord."

I stay on sus chords a long time and go from sus chord to sus chord, and then by building that, because it builds tension, when you drop into a major chord, it's like the major chord was never more major. It's like a complementary colour — the sky just opens up.

I don't really know the neck comprehensively, but as far as composing and finding unusual chordal colours and combinations, my system works for me very well. Except that when it comes to sitting down and playing with someone else and following their music, I'm handicapped in communicating with other musicians. I have to just play it, and they'll say, "Oh yeah, now she's going to a C. Here's she's going to a such and such."

M: Your first five records, mostly voice and guitar, were so successful; why the change to a band for *Court and Spark*, and a jazz band, yet?

J: Well, my first five records, it's basically me and my overdubs. There's a few guests on there but they're used very minimally, like maybe the drums coming in on the last verse of the tag out. There isn't very much because I really didn't like the sound of the drums and the bass.

The drums were dead [then] and they had a little flat sound, and I like a resonant slack tom like Gene Krupa. I like a bass that you could hear three blocks away. When you're approaching the Avenue A swimming pool, you get off the bus and you're walking across the lawn. It's three blocks and the jukebox is playing in the distance. All you hear is the bass line. It's an acoustic upright bass, and it's resonating blocks away.

By the time I got to making records, the bass players used dead strings. Flat, toneless. The drummer stuck a pillow in their kit drum and they had their snare drum really tight. Everything was dry and small and lacking in resonance. So I would be saying, "Would you please take that pillow out of your kit drum? Would you please slack up your snare and give me a little more resonance?" And they'd be saying, "That's not hip." I'm saying, "If this is the hip new sound, I don't care for it." And now I've offended them.

I couldn't get anybody to explain how this got to be hip because it wasn't as good as the sound that went before, and people were saying, "Oh, you like that old sound." They're trying to make you square. And I'm going, "Yeah, I like that old sound. It was a better sound than this. That's the sound I want." Couldn't get them. The bass player would say, "You're trying to tell me how to play my axe."

Also, because I started in the middle — voice and guitar, in the mid-range, the bass being below it — I started stacking up with the voice, going higher and higher and higher, once I learned you can overdub. Ray Charles had done that.

Ray Charles was the first rock concert I went to, but I heard that he was the Raelettes on his records because he could do it faster. That knowledge gave me the courage to . . . oh, as fast as I can think up background parts, I'll come up with a family blend, like the Andrews Sisters or the Everly Brothers. So I put on my own background.

When you're building up above the melody, you could keep going, first harmony, second harmony, third harmony. If you want to get into dissonance, you can go four harmonies, but then you start to repeat. You end up with an octave. So theoretically, why couldn't you do the same thing going down?

But I would be asking the bass player to play notes and they would say, "I'm not playing that note."

"Why not?"

"Well, it's not the root of the chord."

"So?"

"Well, the bass always plays the root of the chord."

"Why? You can play any note you want on top. Why can't you play any note you want on the bottom?"

"Because it'll change the key."

"So? You set the staff up again — what's the difference?"

Suddenly, by changing the root of the chord, you've indicated that there's been a key change there. What's wrong with that?

And they would get exasperated, like I was ignorant. They didn't know what I was talking about. "I played with James Brown." They start running their credentials.

We bogged down and I wouldn't put a bass or drums on it.

This went on and on and on for five, six years, until one guy said to me, "Joni, you're gonna have to play with jazz musicians."

So I started going to the jazz clubs and I found Tom Scott and the L.A. Express, and that's how I came to them on *Court and Spark*.

Love came to my door
With a sleeping roll
And a madman's soul
He thought for sure I'd seen him
Dancing up a river in the dark
Looking for a woman
To court and spark

He was playing on the sidewalk
For passing change
When something strange happened
Glory train passed through him
So he buried the coins he made
In People's Park
And went looking for a woman
To court and spark

It seemed like he read my mind
He saw me mistrusting him
And still acting kind
He saw how I worried sometimes
I worry sometimes

"All the guilty people," he said
They've all seen the stain —
On their daily bread
On their Christian names
I cleared myself
I sacrificed my blues
And you could complete me
I'd complete you

His eyes were the colour of the sand
And the sea
And the more he talked to me
The more he reached me
But I couldn't let go of L.A.
City of the fallen angels
("Court and Spark")

J: It took me six years to find a band that inflamed me to that degree that I wanted to be part of them in a project, and that already had a working relationship member to member, in which I could just sort of fit into and where I felt that they would be sensitive to my music. It just happened to be that timing. That's following the path of the heart.

But even with that band, Max [Bennett] is a great bass player, but still, he had dead strings, John [Guerin] had a pillow in his kit drum, and I wanted a more resonant sound and I couldn't get them to do it.

What I found out after the fact was that when you went from 45s to 33 1/3 albums, you could only get on an album between eighteen and twenty-two minutes to a side. So I could get from forty to approximately forty-four to forty-eight minutes on both sides.

Well, I had long songs. And the record company wanted ten songs. So what happened on the 33 1/3 album was, the treble is a skinnier groove, but the bass is a big fat groove and it takes up more space, so the bigger the bass sound, the less time you can get on the side. And so, in order to accommodate that, the style developed that you deaden the sound of the percussion. Nobody told me that. If they told me that, that's rational, that's logical. Okay.

Why did the Beatles' records have the voices way up front and the rhythm section telescoped back in? I would think, "Why? Why not like a Chuck Berry song?" The reason was the format. In order to get time on a side, you had to diminish your rhythm section. Once we went to CD, and you could get seventy-five or eighty minutes, you could bring the bottom end up. But not knowing this . . .

I knew that Stevie Wonder was using Moog and stuff. Henry [Lewy, her recording engineer] would not let me do it, but he couldn't tell me why. So I took him to a Stevie Wonder session. And I said, "You see? Listen to this. The bass, the bottom end is getting fatter. Why can't we do it?" Still, no reason.

Same thing with violas. When I hired this one arranger, Dale Oehler. I forget now which song it was. He had done some nice arrangements for Marvin Gaye and I said, "I want to use violas."

"I love violas. You want to use violas?"

"Yeah," I said.

"Nobody uses violas."

"Why is that?"

He told me how they got such a bad rep. You'd see bumper stickers around L.A.: "Kill a Viola Player."

Viola's a beautiful rich sound. But here in Hollywood, the orchestras, because they are mostly composing for movies, and the spoken word, like the viola falls in the mid-range of the orchestra. Violas were left out to accommodate the spoken word in the film. And then they forgot why they took the violas out. So they were all out of viola players. There's this funny technical phenomenon and laws develop, but everybody forgets why the laws developed. And then the laws don't make sense without that.

M: When I phoned you from Toronto, before I flew here to record our interview [in '73], you mentioned that you were looking forward to your first tour with a band, because you're not going to be so lonely this time.

J: Oh, that's the loneliness of the stage. Even in the mass applause, there comes a loneliness because it sets you apart in your specialness. And now being on the stage with a group of musicians who will also be receiving the roses, I can go back and I can say, "Weren't we great" if we were, or "Ewww, weren't we awful" if we were. There's a sharing thing. So it's not such a lonely thing.

M: Loneliness — when I listen to your songs I notice that there are certain themes that keep appearing. One is loneliness.

J: I suppose people have always been lonely, but this, I think, is an especially lonely time to live in. So many people are valueless or confused. I know a lot of people who are living a kind of free life who don't really believe that what they're doing is right, and somewhere deep in them they're confused. And things change so rapidly. Relationships don't seem to have any longevity. Occasionally you see people who have been together for six or seven, maybe twelve years, but for the most part, people drift in and out of relationships continually. There isn't a commitment to anything really.

It's a disposable society. Cars are disposable. Everything can be replaced.

And [there's] loneliness because of the transiency of things. I mean, you may live in an apartment building for two years, go away for a year, when you come back it's torn down.

M: What about loneliness in a personal way?

J: Loneliness in a personal way?

M: I mean in your personal life.

J: Well, I think I've covered a lot of that on my records. I mean, I have expressed it almost like open letters. The areas of the relationship which were not complete, you know, that feeling of lack of fulfillment with another person. Can two very different people come together and maintain their individuality? Can you give somebody the generosity of approval of their self-expression continually or does it eventually come down to incompatibility of moods, of temperament?

I need a lot of time, solitary time. Ideally I would like to be able to withdraw into a corner in a room full of people and work. I love the bustle of a room of people interacting where perhaps I am apart but busy on my own project.

But I've been in the company of people and felt amazingly lonely. Maybe they're a group of people that you've just met and they're all interacting about a mutual friend and you're not inside enough to know who that is. Maybe they do an hour and a half on it and you're sitting there and now, if you were to take out — which in my case would be a defence — a pencil and paper and say, "Well, they've been doing this for an hour and a half and there's no way that I can enter into this conversation so I'm going to disappear now into my own head." But if you sit down and start writing, they say, "Are you taking notes? Are you copying our dialogue? Are you from *Rolling Stone* magazine?" What can you do in defence of it? That's a form of loneliness that I've experienced.

There are other kinds of loneliness which are very beautiful. Like sometimes I go up to my land in British Columbia and spend time alone in the country surrounded by the beauty of natural things. There's a romance which accompanies it, so you generally don't feel self-pity.

In the city, when you're surrounded by people who are continually interacting, the loneliness makes you feel like you've sinned, as Leonard Cohen said. All around you see lovers or families and you're alone and you think, "Why? What did I do to deserve this?" That's why I think the cities are much lonelier than the country.

> . . . you know the grind
> Is so ungrateful
> Racing cars, whisky bars
> No one cares who you really are
> ("The Arrangement")

Oh it gets so lonely
When you're walking
And the streets are full of strangers
All the news of home you read
More about the war
And the bloody changes
Oh will you take me as I am?
Will you take me as I am?
Will you?

       ("California")

In the morning there are lovers in the street
They look so high
You brush against a stranger
And you both apologize
Old friends seem indifferent
You must have brought that on
Old bonds have broken down
Love is gone

       ("Down to You")

Oh I am a lonely painter
I live in a box of paints
I'm frightened by the devil
And I'm drawn to those ones that ain't afraid

       ("A Case of You")

M: Another theme I found predominant in your songs is love.

J: Love . . . yeah. One of my main interests in life is human relationships and human interaction and the exchange of feelings, person to person, on a one-to-one basis, or on a larger basis projecting to an audience.

I really believe that individuality, the maintenance of individuality, is so necessary to what we would call a true or lasting love; that people who say "I love you"

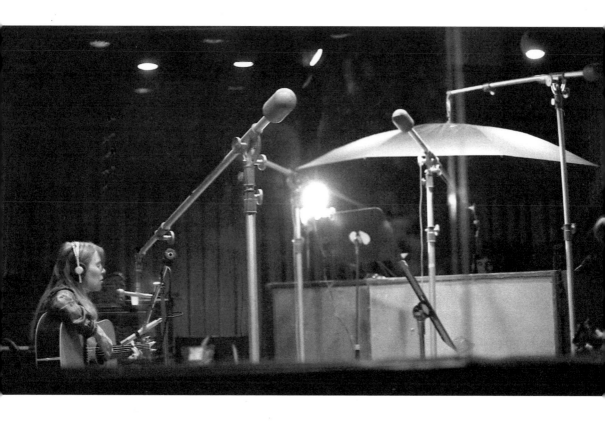

Joni at the recording session for *Court and Spark*

© Sherry Rayn Barnett

and then begin to do a *Pygmalion* number on you are wrong, you know. Love has to encompass all of the things that a person is.

Love is a very hard feeling to keep alive. It's a very fragile plant, you know. Love is a peculiar feeling, because it's subject to so much change. The way love feels at the beginning of a relationship and the changes that it goes through. I keep asking myself, "What is it?" [laughs] Such a powerful force, talk about power. It's a favourite game — it comes to be a game.

"I love you" — these words seemed like a commitment to me. When you said to somebody "I love you," or if they said that to you, it meant that you were there for them and that you could trust them. But knowing from myself that I have said that and then reneged on it — in the supportive, in the physical sense — that I was no longer there side by side with that person. So I say, well, does that cancel that feeling out? Did I really love? Or, what is it?

At one time, I was very into Nietzschean philosophy, which is the philosophy of a loner. Well, the way that I could tell the weakness of that philosophy was that when I was feeling alone and isolated, it was clear and beautiful and perfectly true to me, but when I was feeling warm, goodwill towards men and arms around a group of people, it had no place for that feeling. It totally excluded that feeling, which is a marvellous feeling, a very humanitarian feeling. There's no place for it in there, so I couldn't completely go along with it, although there's a lot of truth in it. There wasn't really a place for love. It's like you didn't have that much love, because love was the idea of surpassing oneself.

But . . . I really feel disillusioned with people and knowledge and where it has led us, you know.

> Sometimes I think love is just mythical
> Up there's a heaven
> Down there's a town
> Blackness everywhere and little lights shine
> Oh, blackness, blackness dragging me down
> Come on light the candle in this poor heart of mine
> > ("This Flight Tonight")

> He's my sunshine in the morning
> He's my fireworks at the end of the day
> He's the warmest chord I ever heard
> Play that warm chord, play and stay baby
> We don't need no piece of paper
> From the city hall
> Keeping us tied and true
> My old man
> Keeping away my blues

> But when he's gone
> Me and them lonesome blues collide
> The bed's too big
> The frying pan's too wide
> > ("My Old Man")

This jealous lovin's bound to make me
Crazy
I can't find my goodness
I lost my heart
Oh sour grapes
Because I lost my heart
      ("Just Like This Train")

I asked myself when you said you loved me
"Do you think this can be real?"
      ("The Same Situation")

You think I'm like your mother
Or another lover or your sister
Or the queen of your dreams
Or just another silly girl
When love makes a fool of me
After the rush when you come back down
You're always disappointed
Nothing seems to keep you high
      ("Woman of Heart and Mind")

Oh I love you when I forget about me
I want to be strong I want to laugh along
I want to belong to the living
Alive, alive, I want to get up and jive
I want to wreck my stockings in some juke box dive
Do you want — do you want — do you want
to dance with me baby
Do you want to take a chance
on maybe finding some sweet romance with me baby
Well, come on

All I really really want our love to do
Is to bring out the best in me and in you too

all I really really want our love to do
is to bring out the best in me and in you
I want to talk to you, I want to shampoo you
I want to renew you again and again
Applause, applause — Life is our cause
When I think of your kisses
my mind see-saws
Do you see — do you see — do you see
how you hurt me baby
so I hurt you too
then we both get so blue.

   ("All I Want")

I remember that time you told me, you said,
"Love is touching souls"
Surely you touched mine
'Cause part of you pours out of me
In these lines from time to time
Oh, you're in my blood like holy wine
You taste so bitter and so sweet
Oh I could drink a case of you, darling
And I would still be on my feet
I would still be on my feet

   ("A Case of You")

Help me
I think I'm falling
In love again
When I get that crazy feeling, I know
I'm in trouble again
I'm in trouble
'Cause you're a rambler and a gambler
And a sweet-talking ladies man
And you love your lovin'
But not like you love your freedom

Help me
I think I'm falling
In love too fast
It's got me hoping for the future
And worrying about the past
'Cause I've seen some hot hot blazes
Come down to smoke and ash
We love our lovin'
But not like we love our freedom
("Help Me")

M: What is your idea of happiness, Joni?

J: Oh my God. [laughs] She's getting heavy on me. What is my idea of happiness? I don't know. I can't answer that. That's really a hard question. It's funny, because I never could describe my joy as well as I could my . . .

To me, happiness is expressed in the hands and in the face and in the light in the eyes. You know what I mean? I can't express it verbally as well as I can my dissatis- faction or my anguish. I have more vocabulary for those things.

M: And for guilt as well. I'd almost expect guilt to be inherent throughout the work of an artist exploring the story of the Garden, Adam and Eve, original sin . . .

Here, this evening, you and the band were rehearsing your latest, "Court and Spark": "'All the guilty people,' he said / They've all seen the stain / On their daily bread / On their Christian names / I cleared myself / I sacrificed my blues." And the other day you mentioned that you fear a child would have to suffer guilt. What's so bad about guilt? Guilt is a strong force in creativity.

J: Well, it's not a very pleasant thing to live with. [laughs] I don't like it. [laughs] Oh God. I don't know.

I'm your average guilt-ridden person. I mean, I'm a worrywart. And always I'm having these moral conflicts, continual battles of what is right, what is good. Am I a rotten person? Guilt as to . . . my running off at the mouth here. Guilt as to my vulner- ability even, which you tried to make a nice quality of. Like guilt that I'm too weak, or guilt that I'm too strong, or guilt that I went out of line here, was too loud here, or too quiet here. Just your general guilt for any occasion, you know. [laughs] I don't think it's necessary to have that much guilt.

Guilt is like conscience. And I guess in its own way sometimes it teaches you that you've gone off the path, but the path is something that has been taught to you early in your life.

There's a story by Hermann Hesse called *Narcissus and Goldmund*. It's really a beautiful story of the Dionysian and the Apollonian kind of attitude, consciousness. At first, in opposition to one another, and then at the end of the story, coming together, and looking each other in the eyes and recognizing that, although they have led entirely different lives. One a monastic life of service and deprival, feeding the mind and not the belly, you know, that kind of thing — and the other fellow who leaves the monastery and leads a life of abandon, becomes a womanizer and a transient. And all this time, not knowing exactly why, he discovers that he wants to be a sculptor and he becomes a very fine sculptor. But he's never felt totally fulfilled because he wants to make a piece which is a madonna, which encompasses all of the expressions that he has ever seen on the faces of women, a vague memory of his mother, who was very wild and abandoned him as a child, and women giving birth, women crying, women in the plague with death on their face. All these expressions he wants to mould into one look for his madonna. And he never completes the piece but he always felt inferior to this aesthetic.

Well, I really feel those things too within myself.

It's like when I left my house in Laurel Canyon, which seemed too soft and too comfortable, too dimly lit, too much red upholstery. I mean, figuratively speaking, it just seemed too comfortable. And the place that I built up on my land in British Columbia was almost like a monastery. The guy, the builder kept saying to me, "Oh, you don't want to put in that window. It already looks like a church." Stone and hardwood floors and hardwood benches. Everything that would be corrective. No mirrors. Like fighting for all of the good virtue that might be in me somewhere, you know. It's really ridiculous. I mean, I just went totally to another extreme, and I made this place very uncomfortable, like a corrective shoe.

I think the artist has always been in conflict, maybe because he has time on his hands to think with a lot of high ideals and values, and he's got to recognize their beauty. And at the same time, the flesh is weak and has too many appetites, so you're in that continual conflict with yourself, you know. You can express these really high and beautiful thoughts but your life may not back them up.

Then he took his contradictions out
And he splashed them on my brow
So which words was I then to doubt
When choosing what to vow
Should I choose them all — should I make them mine
The sermons, the hymns and the valentines
He asked for truth and he asked for time
And he asked for only now.
                ("The Priest")

M: Travelling is another topic that recurs in your songs. "Travelling, travelling, travel-ling . . ." You've been wandering a lot.

J: Yes, it's a nomadic life, isn't it? I guess I have become a gypsy. [laughs] It's hard for me to put down roots, even the idea . . . I like this transient way of being. It's almost like I'm hot on the trail of the song. I like my freedom to wander.

M: Freedom, I was just going to ask you about that. Freedom recurs in your songs, and in particular the word *free*.

There's a man who's climbed a mountain
And he's calling out her name
And he hopes her heart can hear three thousand miles
He calls again
He can think her there beside him
He can miss her just the same
He has missed her in the forest
While he showed her all the flowers
And the branches sang the chorus
As he climbed the scaley towers
Of a forest tree
While she was somewhere being free

There's a man who's sent a letter
And he's waiting for reply

He has asked her of her travels
Since the day they said goodbye
He writes "Wish you were beside me
We can make it if we try"
He has seen her at the office
With her name on all his papers
Thru the sharing of the profits
He will find it hard to shake her
From his memory
And she's so busy being free

There's a lady in the city
And she thinks she loves them all
There's the one who's thinking of her
There's the one who sometimes calls
There's the one who writes her letters
With his facts and figures scrawl
She has brought them to her senses
They have laughed inside her laughter
Now she rallies her defences
For she fears that one will ask her
For eternity
And she's so busy being free
                    ("Cactus Tree")

J: Freedom to me is a luxury of being able to follow the path of the heart, to keep the magic in your life. Freedom is necessary for me in order to create, and if I cannot create I don't feel alive.

M: Did you ever experience the fear that the creative well might dry up?

J: Well, every year I've said, "That's it." I feel often that it's run dry, and all of sudden things just come pouring out. This is a feeling that increases as you get older. I don't know. The creative process is a mystery. Inspiration is a mystery.

I have a fear that I might become a tunesmith, having developed a craft, that I would be able to write songs, but not poetry. That's what happened to Dylan, you know. His work became more and more diluted. Well, he comes from Duluth, so what can you . . . It's a terrible pun, but he's writing again well now. [laughs]

I think that as long as you still have questions, the child questions, the muse has got to be there. You throw a question up to the muse and maybe they drop something back on you.

M: How do you keep that child quality alive, the child questions that you consider so essential in writing? Is it a matter of determination? Or is it a subconscious thing brought on by how an artist conducts her life?

J: I really don't know. The questions get more and more like a catch-22. I think, as I grow older, I realize more and more that there are no answers, so the questions become even more futile than they were when I was in my early twenties. The questions I pose, because a lot of my music is music of inquiry. It doesn't tell anything so much as it asks, you know.

I'm working on a song now and it's very difficult to finish. It's questions of love, trying to keep yourself open in a relationship, and what exactly that entails. I know how important [it is] that individuality be maintained in order to give a relationship longevity. So you're with someone and there are bound to be areas where it isn't even disapproval.

I mean, as a teenage kid you might be turned off because the guy is wearing some kind of funny shoes that you don't think are hip. His shoes stereotype him on a really superficial level. A lot of those things get carried into adulthood and I feel that they shouldn't be important, that as an adult, appearances shouldn't be that important. If you want to dress up in a big frilly hat and your old man looks like he just stepped out of a Western movie, he shouldn't be offended by your self-expression nor you by his.

M: You didn't really answer my question, Joni.

J: [laughs] Ask me your question again.

M: Do you fear that the creative well might . . .

J: The well might run dry, that's what you're asking, is it?

M: Yes.

J: I don't know. I always think the well is gonna dry. Maybe that's why it hasn't dried up. Maybe if I just presume that it's gonna dry up at any moment, it'll keep going. Maybe as soon as the thought enters my mind that, "Oh, it's gonna go on forever" — *bam!* That's it. I'm not sure how you treat a muse. It's been pretty good to me so far.

M: I'd like to clarify something I'd heard you say: "I have a painter's mentality, rather than a musician's or a poet's." What do you mean by that?

J: Okay. The creative process of a painter is absolute solitude. No one's gonna come in and say, "Don't put that blue stroke there. Put an orange stroke there." It's just inappropriate. And it doesn't mean you're controlling. I had a lot of "Joni, you're so controlling."

Yes, I am controlling and so it should be. I should be in control of my art. I'm within my rights to control my own art. You should not be trying to direct it.

In painting, you have to be very decisive. Once you paint over it, it's gone, whereas in songwriting, in music, you can usually get back, if you decide, "Oops, it was better the way it was before," you can get back.

I think that's why I'm able to produce my own records. You have to be able to switch from sensual, sensitive, emotional to [the] adjudicative mind, which is intellectual clarity.

You paint . . . it has to be emotional and sensitive to get the good line, but then when you stand back, you engage intellect and clarity to adjudicate it, so you're your own producer. You have access to those heads and you can shift quickly from one [to] another. You can be very hard on yourself without bruising yourself. And you can be accurate; you can go right to the heart of the trouble. You don't have to tippy-toe around somebody's ego and praise them and stroke them, and then get to the problem and waste an hour like that . . . the delicate problem of addressing someone's ego.

M: Is it a conscious decision: that's a take, or scrap it? Or does it happen organically?

J: Both. Intellectually you go, "This doesn't sound finished." Intellectually you may not know what you want but you know what you don't want. "That's not it, that's not it. Ah! We're getting there. We're getting there." So intellect being basically your data bank — what you know already. But you don't know what you want because you want something fresh, so how do you describe something fresh?

You're going to have to stumble on it. You have to set up a climate, so that you'd be able to stumble on it.

M: How do you do that?

J: Make accidents occur. Drive the operators crazy because they think you lost your marbles. Some of the things that you do to get the quirk going . . . trying to think in other ways. Improvisation — with Henry . . . Henry Lewy never thought that anything I was doing was crazy unless I asked him to do something that was gonna make him look bad technically. He just believed in me.

Henry Lewy and I have had a working relationship made in heaven, where there's no ego in play and it's just pure joyous child's play, mutually supportive, each holding up their end, and not trying to dominate because there's no need for it if you each hold up your own end.

M: They say that a prophet needs only one believer, and it seems that in Henry Lewy you have that believer. Does he give you the added confidence to be your own producer?

J: A record producer is completely unnecessary. It's a babysitter, it's an interior decorator. If you know what you're doing, you have an engineer. You go in, you have the vision, he makes the sound, he has his knowledge, you have yours, and you interact.

Henry and I, our conversation became kind of cryptic. Like, I'd go, "Put a little Elvis on it." And people in the room would go, "You know what she's talking about?" and Henry would smile and go, "Yes."

I never call things by their right name. I had to give everything nicknames because I don't store proper nouns very well, names of places, anything with capital letters. My father's the same way. Any names of cities, streets, people, proper nouns, capitalized words, abstract, and I can't really memorize them or store them. So I give things nicknames. "Put a little Elvis on it" means put a little bit of reverb, a certain kind of echo, just the right amount. A little dab'll do you. [laughs]

M: Do you prefer recording to performing, Joni?

J: They're very different. Recording is more creative or it has been. Performing to me has been very repetitive. Occasionally I would sing a vocal differently or I would change the sequencing of the set, but there isn't that much to discover. Whereas in the recording studio, you're building and you're changing and you're colouring and there are new ideas coming to you all the time. I think performing is my least favourite end of it. It seems to me the most uncreative.

M: How do you go about making a record?

J: In the course of a year, I usually have ten to fourteen songs. So, probably three of them are weaker. Either that, or they don't pertain to some sort of story continuity. Because the album, I feel, hopefully in the course of a year, is more than just a collection of songs. It has some sort of continuity or thread to it. I like to think that it's almost like a novel, and I try as much as possible to link up the songs so that there's a musical connection, one to the other, and also a thematic connection.

For me, the one that worked the best that way was the first album, because, when I recorded it, I had sixty songs or so to choose from. So I could choose songs thematically. I came to the city, out of the city, and down to the seaside theme. That's why songs like "Both Sides Now" that people thought were stronger were left off of that. It was an attempt to make a novelette in music. And on every album there's usually one or two tunes, maybe only one, that's a forerunner of the next:

M: Which are the forerunners in this new album, *Court and Spark*?

J: Well, I think the last song on the album is sort of an oddball. It's not my own song. It's that Annie Ross song, "Twisted." It's an old jazz song but it's in a feel, a rhythmic feel, which is new for me.

M: Why did you decide to record something that is not of your own?

J: Because I love that song. I always have loved it. And I went through analysis for a while this year, and since it's a song about analysis, I figured I earned the right to sing it. It's a funny song, a naturally funny song, whether you sing it straight or add comedy to comedy, it doesn't matter. It's just something that I always wanted to do. I tried to put it on the last record, but it was totally inappropriate. It had nothing to do with that time period. And some of my friends feel it has nothing to do with this album either. It's added like an encore.

M: I hope I'm not encroaching on your privacy, Joni, but why the analysis now?

J: Well, because I felt I wanted to talk to someone about confusion, which we all have. Everyone has confusion. I wanted to talk to someone and I was willing to pay for his discretion. It proved effective because simply by confronting paradoxes or difficulties within your life, designating a time to confront them several times a week, they seem to be not so important as they do when they're weighing on your mind in the middle of the night, by yourself, with no one to talk to, or someone to talk to who probably will tell another friend who will tell another friend. As friends do, people talk, you know.

I went through a lot of changes about [analysis]. It's like driving out your devils — do you drive out your angels as well, you know, that whole thing about the creative process. An artist needs a certain amount of turmoil and confusion, and I've created out of that. It's been part of the creative force. I mean, even out of severe depression there comes insight, if you meditate on it. It's sort of masochistic to dwell on it, but you do gain understanding.

So, instead of meditating and exploring these questions that I had, 'cause that's mostly what it was, questions about myself and the way I was conducting my life and what were my values in this time . . . What aren't values in this time? Everything is so temporal.

Most of it was moral confusion, and some people maybe would turn to a priest, you know. I didn't want to be read any religious rhetoric. I combed religions for certain answers. Found them to be, for the most part, too idealistic for me to put into my everyday life, except for some of the broader religions, which include the yin-yang principle, which give you a broader pendulum swing.

I think it did me a lot of good. I think that self-confrontation is a good thing, whether you do it by yourself in solitude, or whether you do it in the presence of another person. He turned out to be particularly sensitive to me and able to make light of a lot of things that seemed heavy to me, which is just really a good friend, even though he's getting paid.

M: Most people who view your life would find it incredible that with your success

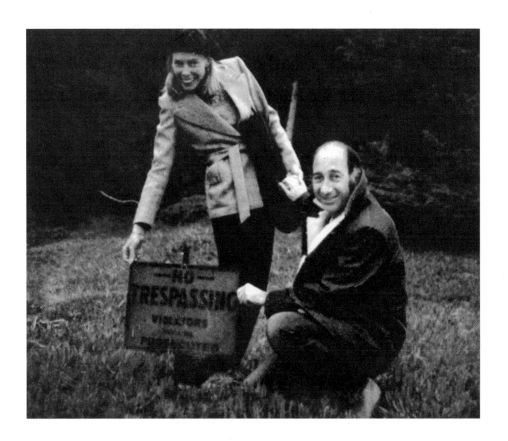

Joni with Henry Lewy
© Malka Marom

and high acclaim, bordering on adulation, bestowed on you, you'd need to pay money to have a friend.

J: Oh, friends all have problems, and at this particular time, all of my friends had so many problems, why should you lay yours on them. I mean, I know that within myself, if somebody who I really liked would come to me, "Oh God . . ." I didn't want to hear it and it would make me feel terrible, because I'm so close to that space too, I don't want to go there, you know. [laughs]

M: Joni, last night you mentioned that you might re-record some of your old songs on this tour with the L.A. Express. Why?

J: Well, the tour is going to be recorded at a few sites.

Let me reiterate that, *s'il vous plaît*.

The label that I used to record for wants to release a greatest hits album. I would prefer, rather than having a collection of songs drawn from the six albums I've already made, I would like a chance to redevelop some of the old songs which I feel were never recorded properly, never given the life they deserve. So hopefully some of the songs will be rehearsed and worked up for the concert tour, and since some of the concerts will be recorded, we'll be able to draw enough material to make a strong live album which will be, in some ways, what they call "the greatest hits" or "the best of" kind of album, because it will be a collection of old songs and new songs, but with the revamping that I think some of them need.

M: How do you feel when you listen to your old records? They're not really old, but, as you said, things move so fast . . .

J: I don't enjoy some of the old records. I see too much of my growing stages, you know. And I find in listening to some early material, qualities in my voice, things which I picked up, which seemed to me to be stylistic affectations. I think we all in the pop field are guilty of this to a certain degree.

I'm very open to almost subconscious mimicry. So if I'm in the South for a while or if I'm in England for a while, or if I'm in France for a while, I find that I'm drawn to the musical inflection of the area where I am. And when I look back over my old records, I see the tracings of what I've been listening to. For instance, in "Real Good for Free," I don't know why I did this, but I said, "I went shopping today for jeee-weeewels / and the wind swept in through the dirty town / and the children let out from schooeewels." Why I did that I don't know. Obviously it didn't seem peculiar to me at the time, but it does to me now. It bothers me when I hear it. I think, "Ewww. Jeeeweeewels and schooeewels. Alright." [laughs]

And in a lot of cases, although I know that I delivered it on the record with sincerity, in looking back on it, I feel again a certain amount of jiveness to my own work.

There's hardly an artist that I know who hasn't gone through these changes.

At one point, maybe you become aware of your style, and you stylize your style so that you become a caricature of yourself. Dylan did that with himself. He began with an affectation of Woody Guthrie's style of singing, Woody Guthrie as taught to him through Ramblin' Jack Elliott. I can listen to Dylan and hear all of his kind of affected manner that he has of delivering and yet forgive him for it. I consider it theatre. It's like he found it necessary somehow to age his voice to deliver his message. He had to sound like he was left over from the Depression; he'd been riding boxcars all his life. He even fabricated his history. Part of his magic was his Hobokenonism, you know, Hoboken . . . [laughs] I don't imagine that it gives him pain to listen to his old things. I don't know, maybe he hates everything he ever did.

I guess it's part of that quest, searching more and more for reality. Will the real me please stand up, you know. I feel sometimes like I'm a multiphrenic person. Like, inside my head, there's this whole boarding house full of people, and some of the people who live there are authoritarian. Like, maybe there's one who has the loudest voice and the clearest voice, [who] assumes leadership in a classically good way. And then there's this other really lazy one. There's one that tells me, "Quit smoking," and tells me very clearly and emphatically why I should quit smoking. And I say, "Oh yes, yes." And I wake up in the morning, and he's moved out. [laughs]

M: Which of your songs have withstood all these changes — if any?

J: Well, on the *Ladies of the Canyon* album, there's a song called "The Arrangement" which seemed to have more musical sophistication than anything else on the album and even the delivery . . . I can listen to that one band on the album with a certain amount of satisfaction.

> You could have been more
> Than a name on the door
> On the thirty-third floor in the air
> More than a credit card
> Swimming pool in the backyard
>
> While you still have the time
> You could get away and find
> A better life, you know the grind
> Is so ungrateful
> Racing cars, whisky bars
> No one cares who you really are

You're the keeper of the cards
Yes I know it gets hard
Keeping the wheels turning
And the wife she keeps the keys
She is so pleased to be
A part of the arrangement

You could have been more
Than a name on the door
On the thirty-third floor in the air
More than a consumer
Lying in some room trying to die
More than a credit card
Swimming pool in the backyard

You could have been more
You could have been more
You could have been more
You could have been more
("The Arrangement")

J: The *Blue* album, for the most part, holds up for me. At that point, I feel that I'm beginning to strip off a lot of influences, country, rock and roll influences, from hanging around with people who were singing in trios, singing so that they could harmonize tightly. I picked up on some of that, which I think interfered with my interpretation as a solo artist. It's like I took liberties with it almost as if I was unaware of it. I think that more and more I will find my way to a more sensitive interpretation of my own material.

Blue, songs are like tattoos
You know I've been to sea before
Crown and anchor me
Or let me sail away
Hey Blue, here is a song for you
Ink on a pin

Underneath the skin
An empty space to fill in
Well there're so many sinking now
You've got to keep thinking
You can make it thru these waves
Acid, booze, and ass
Needles, guns, and grass
Lots of laughs, lots of laughs
Everybody's saying that hell's the hippest way to go
Well I don't think so
But I'm gonna take a look around it though
Blue, I love you

Blue, here is a shell for you
Inside you'll hear a sigh
A foggy lullaby
There is your song from me
                    ("Blue")

J: My twenties were too full of questioning because of being hurdled into the spotlight without any childhood preparation for it. I think they were probably my richest but also my toughest time. So now, it's almost like complacency might even set in. I might just enjoy myself and never write again. [laughs]

Elliot: Joni's been an important artist for about five, six years now and will continue to be as long as she wants to be. She's just an important writer as Dylan is. He's already made his mark, as has Joni. There are certain people who have made their mark. If they never did anything else, they will have influenced a great many people.

M: What are the influences that affect your work?

J: Oh, along the way, there've been a lot of people who have influenced me.
    Anything which moves me influences me. I'm influenced, at this point, by Stevie Wonder, because I think that he's a musical genius. And I love the quality of his singing. Now, at this time in my life, I'm going through a strong musical change from

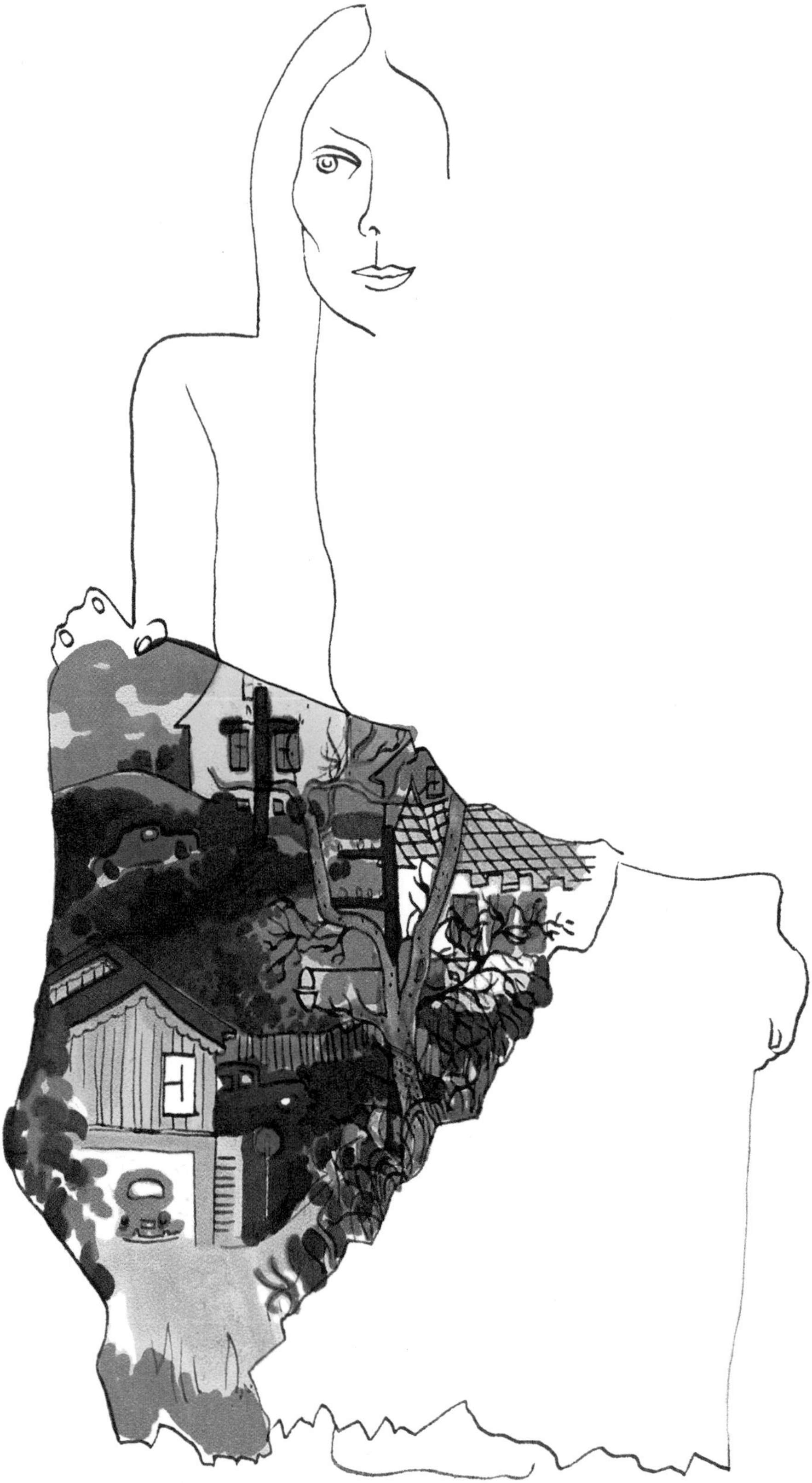

1969 © Joni Mitchell, photo by Sheila Spence

playing with this band whose chordal sense comes predominantly from jazz. Already I'm beginning to think in terms of playing with them, and some of that is creeping in. I wrote something in a rhythmic feel, which is definitely their influence. Lyrically, there's no one at this time who is thrilling me with their words, so I find myself uninfluenced.

I had hoped to hear Bob Dylan's new album, [on] which he would come back and say things as he did in 1966 and '67, which were like "Oh, I wish I had said that" kind of things. It inspired me with the idea of the personal narrative. He would speak as if to one person in a song. Like "you got a lot of nerve to say you are my friend." I mean, nobody had ever written anything like that in song form. Such a personal, strong statement. There was something about the negativity of some of his expressions which even appealed to me. Everybody has that need for negative expression, in spite of Jesus and be good to everybody, you know. And the fact that he had the nerve to come out in music and to speak his mind so openly, it seemed to me he went out on a limb a great deal, and I think that his influence was to personalize my work. I feel this towards you, for you, or from you. Or because of you I feel this.

M: You mentioned the other day that you're a painter derailed by circumstances.

J: Yeah, in order to prevent the derailing entirely, I started to do my own album covers. Usually they say, "Oh, don't put art on it. They want to see your face. Your photo on the cover sells more albums."

Geffen was so exasperated by people fussing over their album covers that he just wanted to say, "This year you get the red cover, next year you get the black cover" to cut it all out.

M: So how did it happen that you got to paint your album covers?

J: They insisted on a photo on the first one, so I put a photo and a fish eye in the middle of this drawing. The second one they insisted had to have my face on it, so I did that self-portrait on *Clouds*, staring right at the thing. "Okay, you want my face? Here I am, looking at you." Then after that because they had no money invested in me, I was under the antennas and could do almost what I want. As long as I brought the records in dirt cheap, which Henry Lewy and I did, and the records sold, they recouped really fast. I was not important because they didn't pay much for me. The disrespect and the underestimation worked for me. They left me alone.

At a certain point, I knew it was a dog race, so I thought, "Why do I want to be part of a dog race? If I want to be in this race, I'm gonna be the rabbit." [laughs] I don't want to be a winner or a loser. I just want to be the rabbit. I just want to always be there, a doer.

I kind of intuited that it was gonna take a long time to develop, to synthesize these diverse interests into something unique, original.

M: Are music and art overlapping for you or contradicting?

J: Art meaning painting?

M: Yes.

J: I use them as crop rotation in my career. Like a farmer. So when the words dried up, rather than go, "Ahh, I'm in the middle of a writer's block," I just paint. You paint your way through it. You let the song rest.

It was very good to be able to keep the creative juices going by switching crops and keep the soil fertile, without the panic of a dry up. Just a farmer's trick. I come from farmers. [laughs]

M: Henry, I heard from Joni that you never thought that anything she did was crazy, even purposely invited glitches and accidents. Can you give me an example of your dynamic in the studio?

Henry Lewy (her recording engineer): That little laugh at the end of "Big Yellow Taxi." Joni wasn't sure what she was gonna do. It was a new song and it was a run-through. She didn't know that I was taking it, but I was. I was very sneaky. I pushed the record button and took it anyway. And, at the end of it, she looked at me and I looked at her and she just broke up laughing. And I said, "That's so good, let's keep it." We kept it, and to me it's one of the most charming parts of that record, just that happy infectious laughter at the end.

I've never met anybody like her. She's a complete original. Everything that she does is uniquely hers, and she's not afraid to do it. And if people say, "Well, you can't do it," she says, "Why not?" I love that spirit. I think that she's a genius.

M: Tom, thanks for letting me steal a bit of your rehearsal break. How did it happen that you and the band got involved with Joni?"

Tom Scott (saxophonist/composer/bandleader of L.A. Express): I was first involved with Joni on the album *For the Roses*, and when I first came into the studio and I heard the tracks that I was to play on, I was literally stunned by the combination of musicality and the lyrics.

[Later] Joni came to hear our band at the Baked Potato. After hearing us, she asked me very, very shyly, "Do you think the guys might want to play a couple of tunes on my new album?"

"Oh, I think they might want to, yeah," I said, and naturally they came in.

I had a vision of what would happen. I was pretty sure that it would be more than two tunes and, sure enough, it turned out to be practically the whole album. So I was absolutely thrilled.

I consider Joni one of the great American poets, in addition to her musical talents. I'm in love with her music. And so to bring her and the band that I love more than anything together was just a total thrill for me.

M: You know, most people, when they comment on Joni's songs, they emphasize the lyrics more than the music.

J: Guerin never listens to the words really.

John Guerin (drums and percussion): No, it's something that [Joni] brought to my attention. When we started to work on her album, the lyrics are so important and they need shading, highs and lows and louds and softs. There's multi-feels in this music, and those different feels dictate different ways of playing. A lot of that is dictated by the words. It's an interesting enlightenment, so to speak. Well, I mean, for me, as a drummer, I'm not lyric oriented.

Elliot Roberts: Most of the people in the band are very well-paid studio players in

Los Angeles. Normally, they would never go on the road. It's a new experience for them, so there's a certain spark on their part.

John Guerin: Joni's writing and her lyricism and her structure are original. I've never heard anybody else do it quite like that. There was a piece we worked on, it's in 4/4 time, and out of the blue come some odd time signatures, like 5/8 and 4/8. So in order to play the tune, musicians have to have knowledge of those time signatures. And if musicians keep on top of it and they're good, then they can put it right into the feeling without sounding stilted so that it continues its flow.

M: Joni, did you realize that your writing has such intricate rhythms?

J: No, I don't really know to count off time. Being self-taught, I'm sort of illiterate in that way. I just play intuitively what feels good. For a long time I've been playing in sort of straight rhythms. But now, in order to sophisticate my music to my own taste, I guess I push it into odd places, places that feel a little unusual to me, so that I feel I'm stretching out. But I can't count them. John sits down and counts them. I don't know what he's . . .

John Guerin: That's a method of transcription. In order for the songs to be transcribed, we have to know, as players, what Joni plays and invents. The best way to do that is write out a map, so to speak, a chart, and then we can get right into it and know where the beats fall.

She does that all naturally. We just put the musical notation to it.

You have to be a very good musician to play her tunes.

Tom Scott: It's fascinating to play her songs because you get involved in that suspension that you've heard and now we're beginning to find out what makes up that suspension.

Roger Kellaway (piano): [Joni's music] has subtle aspects to it. And when you relax yourself to the point where you expand that sense of the space of the music and you begin to get into it, there's a wonderful area that happens, a magic. That's what I like about it.

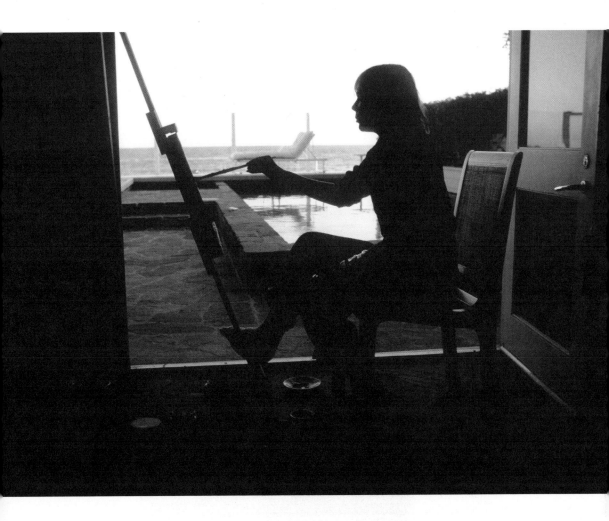

Joni in a waterfront studio, 1984

© Henry Diltz

M: Joni, before I heard these musicians rehearse your songs today, I thought your songs were somewhat delicate and fragile, and a band would sort of break them, but these musicians are amazing.

J: Well, a lot of the guys were dyed-in-the-wool beboppers before we worked together. It was Tommy's enthusiasm that made them look at the music.

But they have more sophisticated rhythmic and chordal sense, and when they first heard my tapes, I don't think that all of the band members felt the same enthusiasm. They were afraid of it. They were afraid that anything added to it would break it, like it was bone china or something and you didn't put nails in the cup, you know. [laughs]

And they also . . . well, jazz bands, for the most part, have kind of an attitude about vocalists. They think that the vocalist is sort of the lowest. They don't believe that the vocalist knows that much about music. So if the vocalist offers an opinion, they're almost ready immediately to reject it. They have sort of a prima donna attitude: I'm talking, I'm a bebopper. So when I did make suggestions for change, when I was dissatisfied a couple of times when I thought that they were not sensitive to the lyrics, there were a few things to be overcome. These are not lyric-oriented people.

For me, I hear the high harmony, the high melodic line and the words first. The rhythm section is the last thing I hear. For them, that's generally the first, and the lyrics the last. So we're coming from polar opposite ends. They're not paying any attention to the words, and suddenly we've got this really good track and it's cooking like crazy but when I sing the lyrics to it . . .

For instance, I'm singing a song about someone who really needs to be in love, needs to make some sort of contact: "Advice and religion — you can't take it / You can't seem to believe it." You really need love now, but in this condition you can't really give it. That's sort of the theme of the song. It's talking about tremendous aloneness, people passing through your life like a river, you know, a river of changing faces looking for an ocean: "They trickle through your leaky plans."

Now, to sing this thing too upbeat, it's like stomping on somebody that's suffering, you know. It's got to be sung sensual and slow. But we made this incredible track. The band loved it. They thought it was great. And three days later, I said, "Listen, fellows, we're gonna have to do this over again." Well, there was no open groaning but it was like me, the vocalist, pulling a number on the band and they weren't sure that I knew what I was doing.

But we slowed it down a lot and we finally got a groove in a slower feel, put the vocal on it again, and they saw the difference; they saw that it was alright. So I gained their respect there.

So what are you going to do about it
You can't live life and you can't leave it
Advice and religion — you can't take it
You can't seem to believe it
The peacock is afraid to parade
You're under the thumb of the maid
You really can't give love in this condition
Still you know how you need it

They open and close you
Then they talk like they know you
They don't know you
They're friends and they're foes too
Trouble child
Breaking like the waves at Malibu

So why does it come as such a shock
To know you really have no one
Only a river of changing faces
Looking for an ocean
They trickle through your leaky plans
Another dream over the dam
And you're lying in some room
Feeling like your right to be human
Is going over too

Well some are going to knock you
And some'll try an' clock you
You know it's really hard
To talk sense to you
Trouble child
Breaking like the waves at Malibu
           ("Trouble Child")

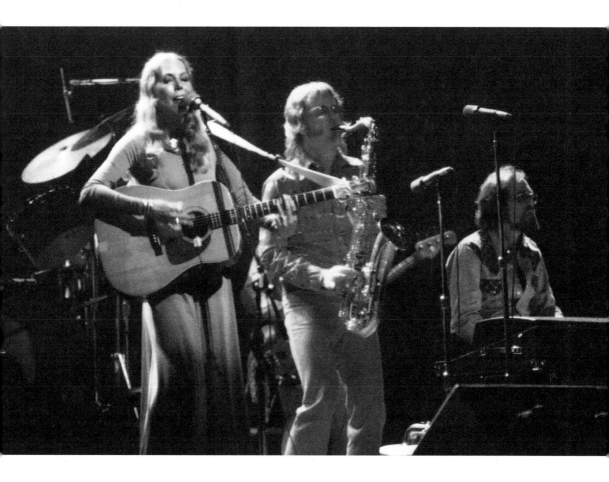

Joni performing with the L.A. Express in London, 1974

J: I made a few changes in the course of the project, but I could sense that by making these changes I was creating a tension which made me feel terrible and inferior — and unsure that my change was right, although at home late at night, listening to the tape we had made, I knew we had to change it.

When I would have to confront [the band], I would be uncertain because I thought they were so much more musically knowledgeable and that maybe my idea was not correct. But finally, as it all came out in the end, they agreed that the changes were right and that my added sensitivity to the words was usually what was creating the change and they gave that to me. So now I think that we work together coming from common ground.

M: Did these arrangements just happen to come together during rehearsals, or do you write them?

J: Well, I have as much control as I am able to understand. The rhythm section is all their own doing because I don't understand the bass and the drums well enough to suggest changes. But the horn lines, which is high melody, which is my realm, I have a lot of control and I arranged a lot of them. Tommy Scott and I, we really fed off of each other. Like, I would say, "Okay, here's a pressure point in the music. It needs a tension line, a drone. It needs a horn line coming out of here and it should begin to break here, right?"

Well, he says, "Alright, that's bar 16." He's got the mathematics and the theory of it. He knows. I just have to point it out as it's going by on the tape. And then I'll say, "Okay, when it begins to bend right here, let's make it a three-part harmony."

And I'll hum him some chords and maybe he'll say, "And what if we add this note to it?" And I'll say, "Great. And what if we take it . . ." So it's really a partnership. Sometimes they're all his ideas, sometimes they're all mine. We work very closely and we work well together.

And the same in the mixing. In the course of producing five of my own records, I've become more and more familiar with the mixing board. I describe the sound I want and we toy with it until we get it. I use Henry's technological head for the information. He'll give me choices — A, B, and C. And I'll say, "This is the one." And then I'll say, "How did you do that?" And he'll tell me and I'll forget it immediately because it's almost like information I don't want to absorb, or I can't retain it because I don't understand it enough.

Even tonight, coming into this session, I feel a little odd-man-out because I don't know. Somebody says to me, "What key is that?" and I don't know something as simple as that.

Tom Scott: Joni can't talk to us in technical musical terms, but that only intimidates us when someone who doesn't know what they're talking about tries to make comments.

Joni's comments, whether they're in the language of a painter or the poet, her thoughts are clear. And if she says, "A little more yellow here," we'll try to work it out because we respect her talent, her ability.

Joni (to the band): I like really long kind of drawn-out bending notes, like dolphin kind of notes that leap out of the water at you, you know? [laughs]

Max Bennett (bass): When talking about Joni not being able to communicate musical ideas like, "What is the chord?" well . . . There's one thing that separates exceptional musicians from just regular musicians, and that's musical intuition. That's where Joni is coming from. Intuition. The biggest role in a band of musicians is intuition. Having a feeling for what someone is gonna say, and Joni can convey it intuitively. We can pick it up intuitively.

M: Elliot, I've been talking to nearly everyone here during rehearsal breaks, and I didn't hear anything other than total love and adulation towards Joni. They're putting her on a pedestal and since you are the one who has known Joni for a very long time, is it true that she's an angel?

Elliot: She's actually a rotten . . . [laughs] She's human, you know. She's a terrible driver. She has all other human frailties that we all have. She loses her temper and she's cranky sometimes, you know; she's a very, very human woman. I think that's why people love her.

M: Joni, when a young person starting on a career, a songwriter, a young troubadour comes to you and says, "Could you advise me how should I go about making it?" what do you say?

J: Well, that's happened to me a lot and I have to think back to my own experience. I once approached Gordon Lightfoot, thinking that he was more successful — he was working a lot of clubs, he had a recording contract, he had a source of publishing his material — and he really could do nothing for me but I felt somehow or other let down by his attitude that he couldn't give me any advice.

Later on when I was in that same position and people came to me and asked me, as they do, for some sort of formula or direction, and there isn't any, you know, I suddenly realized the position that I had put him in, almost as if somehow or other he could open some door for me.

There is no way really, and the times are continually changing, you know, the way that I became successful was the way that I became successful between 1965 and 1973, that was the way that was available. It meant a lot of working in front of audiences. I continually performed, so that's something I say to people.

But there aren't that many places for people to perform, and most of the kids

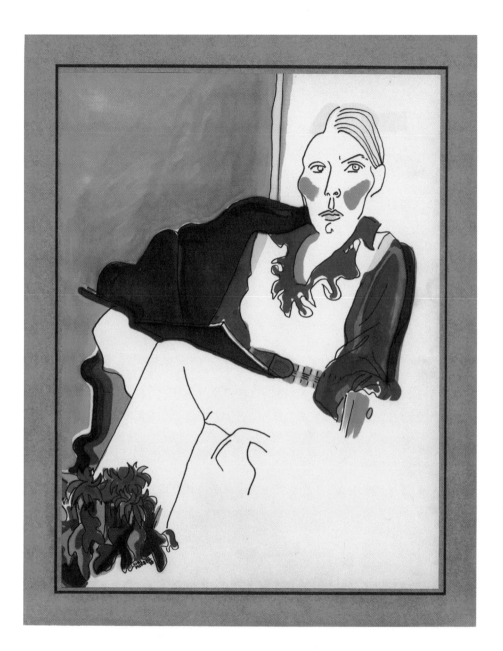

Untitled Iris print on paper
© Joni Mitchell, photo by Sheila Spence

that I come in contact with feel that they have already evolved to a point where they should immediately have a recording contract. A lot of them don't want to go through that work pattern, especially kids that live around this dream town, where things happen overnight.

I don't know. There is no formula.

That always stumps me and there's usually nothing that I can say except that if you are really good, like a lot of kids come who believe that they are good and in their high school they were good, but on the world market . . . I feel if you are great, you will be found out. I think it would be more difficult for people who are only good.

M: Genius has a way of asserting itself — that's what [Pablo] Casals told me when I interviewed him.

J: Right. It finds its way to its audience.

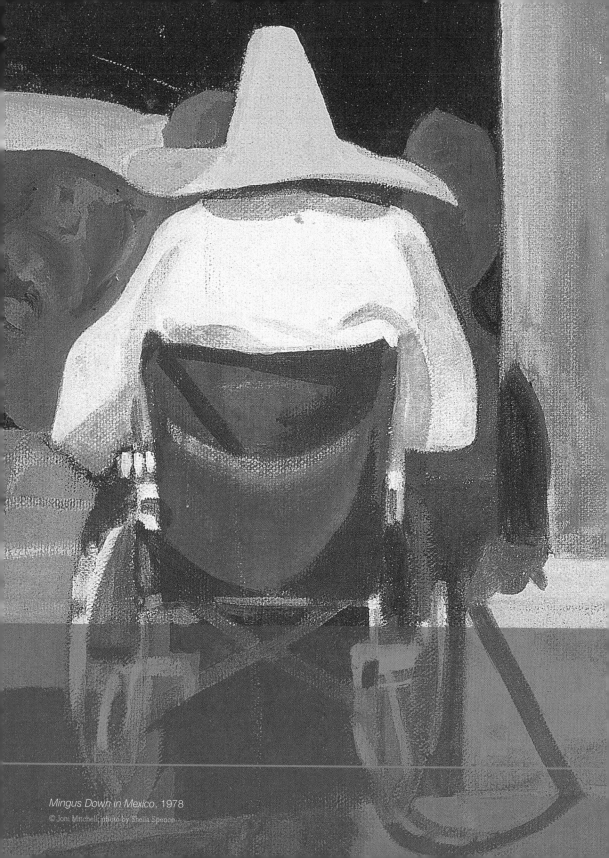

Mingus Down in Mexico, 1978

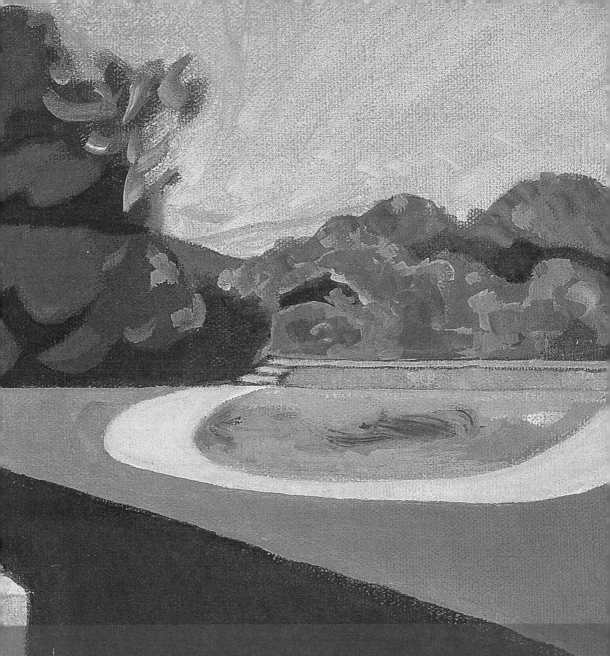

PART II

M: During the five years that passed since we recorded our first conversation in '73, you released four albums: *The Hissing of Summer Lawns*, *Hejira*, *Don Juan's Reckless Daughter*, and *Mingus*, but not one hit among them, not a hit since *Court and Spark*. Does this drought of hits bother you? Do you want to have a hit?

J: A hit would be fun to have, but I would rather come to it accidentally than formalistically. I really don't like formula hits. If I had a hit, it would be a long shot. I would love for a long shot to come in, but that's not really too important to me. *Court and Spark* was a successful album commercially. It had several singles.

Henry Lewy: We found a framework for success in the commercial and pop field. And the record company says, "Oh great, we can just put out album after album like *Court and Spark* and it'll be great. But you know Joni. She changes. And her tastes change, and so when *The Hissing of Summer Lawns* came out, a lot of people really put us down.

J: *Hissing of Summer Lawns* had been critically castrated. It was going further away from rock and roll, going away from contemporary sound. I think it's a much better album than the critics realized at the time. Eventually some of them came past that barrier. But in the meantime, people really couldn't relate to it.

Women found it very confronting. Women suddenly didn't like me very much — for a very simple reason. Prior to that, most of the songs had been sung in first person, and they were a description of my own personal struggle, so that if they could relate to that struggle, they would relate to it, but they also had a way of keeping it at arm's-length.

In *Hissing*, some women didn't like the mirror that it held up. A lot of it was the description of the trapped housewife. "The Hissing of Summer Lawns" meaning, late in the afternoon in the summer when everybody on nice neat streets has their sprinklers going.

But the journalists, the critics . . . I bring them up because they're a public voice. They see me as getting sadder and sadder and sadder, and more depressed, whereas, in fact, I was definitely on an up road. And there was more and more satire in the work, which seemed to go unnoticed because it wasn't leaned on. It was sung with that melancholy tone that comes out of me. So a lot of it was missed.

He bought her a diamond for her throat
He put her in a ranch house on a hill
She could see the valley barbeques
From her window sill
See the blue pools in the squinting sun
And hear the hissing of summer lawns

He put up a barbed wire fence
To keep out the unknown
And on every metal thorn
Just a little blood of his own
She patrols that fence of his
To a latin drum
And the hissing of summer lawns
Darkness
Wonder makes it easy
Darkness
With a joyful mask
Darkness
Tube's gone, darkness, darkness,
    darkness
No colour no contrast

A diamond dog
Carrying a cup and a cane
Looking through a double glass
Looking at too much pride and too much
    shame
There's a black fly buzzing
There's a heat wave burning in her
    master's voice
Hissing of summer lawns

He gave her his darkness to regret
And good reason to quit him
He gave her a roomful of Chippendale
That nobody sits in
Still she stays with a love of some kind
It's the lady's choice
The hissing of summer lawns
                ("The Hissing of Summer Lawns")

J: *Hejira* was more accessible. People seemed to like that album better. Once again, the story was back on me, which seemed to make most of my audience more comfortable. They'd rather hear about my trials than be confronted with their own. Again, people live vicariously. They don't want to really identify with it. [laughs]

M: I love *Hejira*. It has a track, a song — a poem, really — that moved me more than most. A poem that is really like a novel by itself, "Song for Sharon." I feel it's about the price that an artist, a woman artist, had to pay for her gifts and the path that you chose to serve your gifts best.

I went to Staten Island, Sharon
To buy myself a mandolin
And I saw the long white dress of love
On a storefront mannequin
Big boat chuggin' back with a belly full of
    cars . . .
All for something lacy
Some girl's going to see that dress
And crave that day like crazy

Little Indian kids on a bridge up in Canada
They can balance and they can climb
Like their fathers before them
They'll walk the girders of the Manhattan
    skyline
Shine your light on me Miss Liberty
Because as soon as this ferry boat docks
I'm headed to the church
To play Bingo
Fleece me with the gamblers' flocks

I can keep my cool at poker
But I'm a fool when love's at stake
Because I can't conceal emotion
What I'm feeling's always written on my
    face
There's a gypsy down on Bleecker Street
I went in to see her as a kind of joke
And she lit a candle for my love luck
And eighteen bucks went up in smoke

Sharon, I left my man
At a North Dakota junction
And I came out to the "Big Apple" here
To face the dream's malfunction

Love's a repetitious danger
You'd think I'd be accustomed to
Well, I do accept the changes
At least better than I used to do

A woman I knew just drowned herself
The well was deep and muddy
She was just shaking off futility
Or punishing somebody
My friends were calling up all day
    yesterday
All emotions and abstractions
It seems we all live so close to that line
and so far from satisfaction

Dora says, "Have children!"
Mama and Betsy say — "Find yourself a
    charity.
Help the needy and the crippled
Or put some time into Ecology."
Well, there's a wide wide world of noble
    causes ·
And lovely landscapes to discover
But all I really want to do, right now
Is . . . find another lover!

When we were kids in Maidstone, Sharon
I went to every wedding in that little town
To see the tears and the kisses
And the pretty lady in the white lace
    wedding gown
And walking home on the railroad tracks
Or swinging on the playground swing
Love stimulated my illusions
More than anything

And when I went skating after Golden
   Reggie
You know it was white lace I was chasing
Chasing dreams
Mama's nylons underneath my cowgirl
   jeans
He showed me first you get the kisses
And then you get the tears
But the ceremony of the bells and lace
Still veils this reckless fool here

Now there are 29 skaters on Wollman rink
Circling in singles and in pairs
In this vigorous anonymity
A blank face at the window stares and
   stares

and stares and stares
And the power of reason
And the flowers of deep feeling
Seem to serve me
Only to deceive me

Sharon you've got a husband
And a family and a farm
I've got the apple of temptation
And a diamond snake around my arm
But you still have your music
And I've still got my eyes on the land and
   the sky
You sing for your friends and your family
I'll walk green pastures by and by
      ("Song for Sharon")

Henry Lewy: And the year after *Hejira*, we did *Don Juan's Reckless Daughter*. We left in there an eight-minute percussion cut, and a lot of people really didn't like it. They said Joni was a little self-indulgent in that album.

J: They always say it's self-indulgent when they can't get into it.

But there was so much enthusiasm, and they played that piece of music for me as a gift. Something that has that much energy on the spot would communicate to a few people, even if it was only the Puerto Rican drummers somewhere in some tiny club in New York that eventually I would meet and want to play with, so, you know, it would be like a herald for a later encounter.

Henry Lewy: But it was a double album and it didn't do too well. Relatively. I mean it shipped gold, it didn't sell gold.

M: What do you mean it shipped gold?

Henry Lewy: Well, shipping gold, they ship because of a previous reputation. They ship over 500,000 to the dealers. So, you say, "Oh yeah, we shipped gold," and all of a sudden six months later, you get 200,000 records back. And so you only sell 300,000, which . . . it happens in record companies, sort of the way they do it.

M: Did you get pressured from the record company, Joni, to be less "self-indulgent"?

J: No. Basically, all they're interested in is their margin of profit. If I was a maverick and there's too much money in my experimentation that in order to recoup it they would lose money, they would take my power away soon enough. So as long as I can find a way to cut my corners, so they can still make their profit, we're straight. [laughs]

M: But when, let's say, Linda Ronstadt has so many hits, and Dolly Parton, do you think, "Why them, not me?" Do you want to flex your "hit muscle"?

J: I don't feel in competition with them. I feel we're doing quite different things. They are both produced for exactly that purpose — to make hits, whereas I'm painting.
Sometimes, you know, when you'll see a comment about "You remember Joni Mitchell from the '60s" or something like that. That hurts my feelings because I think, "God, it's not like I've been dormant all this time. I've been growing and exploring more than most people in the business." So, on that, I have a level of pride. When we have pride, you can get hurt on that level.

> Friends have told her not so proud
> Neighbours trying to sleep and yelling "not so loud"
> Lovers in anger "Block of Ice"
> Harder and harder just to be nice
> Given in the night to dark dreams
> From the dark things she feels
> She covers her eyes in the X-rated scenes
> Running from the reels
>
> Beauty and madness to be praised
> 'Cause it is not easy to be brave
> To walk around in so much need
> To carry the weight of all that greed
> Dressed in stolen clothes she stands

Cast iron and frail
With her impossibly gentle hands ·
And her blood-red fingernails

Out of the fire and still smouldering
She says "A woman must have everything"
Shades of Scarlett conquering
She says "A woman must have everything"
        ("Shades of Scarlett Conquering")

M: You mentioned the '60s, Joni. Some of the earlier songs had the charm of . . . people could sing them, people could whistle them. Now your songs seem to be too complex to sing or to whistle.

J: Well, for me to go on creating whistle songs, I would bore myself to death. I'm exploring something else now. I'm trying to find something fresh. I think America is a great country because it has such a rich ethnic heritage to be synthesized, and I would like to explore some of that contribution to American music.

    I experimented with more syllables in my sentences. I was criticized for that too, and I thought that was peculiar because it was different and interesting, and I thought, "Why don't they notice how interesting it is, you know? Like you want me to do what everybody else is doing, just so it's accessible."

    I have confidence in people. If I am interested in it, I am sure that there'll be some people that will be interested in it. Even if I feel unique, in that, I don't feel that unique.

    I'm certainly searching for beauty, but of an unusual nature. Okay. Take your average American beauty. There are a lot of beautiful blonds in *Vogue* magazine. They all look alike, don't they? Then there are kinds of beauties that are plain . . . All the great beauties were like that. Greta Garbo, Katharine Hepburn. Those women were not accessible as beauties. You know, when they came into the producer's office, everybody said, "Get that skinny, ugly, weird-looking chick out of here." Well, the same thing goes with songs.

M: Does it slide like water off a duck's back that your latest albums were not recognized as the expression of a maverick, or does it frustrate you to the point of wanting to quit yet again?

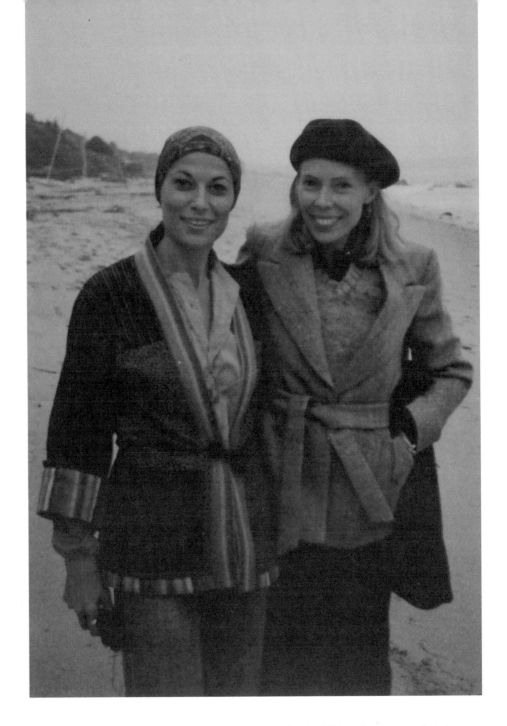

Joni and Malka, on the way to Neil Young's place soon after the '73 interview was concluded

Courtesy Malka Marom

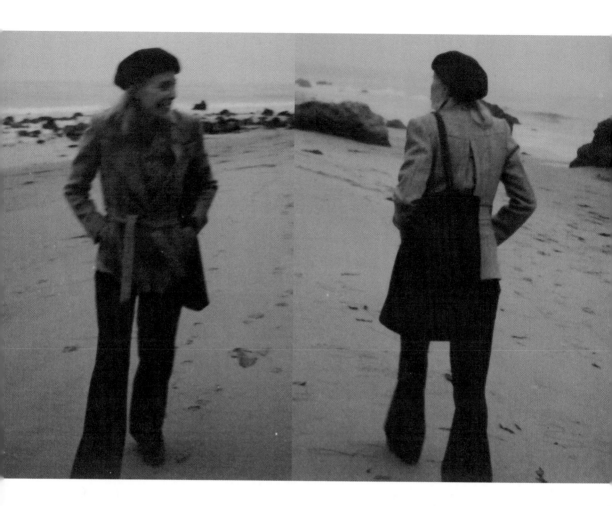

© Malka Marom

J: Well, when I'm dismissed as something that ended a decade ago, because I don't have the publicness of hits and slapping my picture into magazines. This is all available to me. It's all a matter of my own choice. The low profile I had hoped would give me some anonymity and invisibility, it hasn't. It's not the prize I want, deeply, but on a superficial moment when you're weak and vulnerable, you could feel underestimated. Basically, I know that the path that I have chosen is not going to make a big roar in that particular manner.

Also, I haven't been a good girl politically in some ways. I've been asked to MC at the Grammys and do those things, and I haven't showed up at any of them, which people find offensive. I don't like those kind of things. Not when the spotlight's on. I like to go and sit in the backroom. I like to be an observer. I don't like to be the centre of that kind of activity that much. So I would rather leave it to those people that like it, you know. There's plenty of people that like it. [laughs]

Those prizes are not too valuable to me. They don't seem to be a fair measure. Neither do Academy Awards. They're not given to the most imaginative, you know — the most imaginative kids in the school system were not the A students. So I'm kind of a freak. I was a freak in the school system and I'm kind of a freak now. But then I've always been a rebel.

> Well I looked at the granite markers
> Those tributes to finality — to eternity
> And then I looked at myself here
> Chicken scratching for my immortality
> In the church they light the candles
> And the wax rolls down like tears
> There is the hope and the hopelessness
> I've witnessed thirty years
> We're only particles of change I know, I know
> Orbiting around the sun
> But how can I have that point of view
> When I'm always bound and tied to someone
> White flags of winter chimneys
> Waving-truce against the moon
> In the mirrors of a modern bank
> From the window of a hotel room
>
> I'm travelling in some vehicle
> I'm sitting in some café
> A defector from the petty wars
> Until love sucks me back that way
>   ("Hejira")

M: Is it difficult to be a maverick or a freak, as you called it?

J: Yes. The time I get lonely is when I have friends from a few years back who are on a treadmill, who are at the state of opportunity to make a change, and can't find the creative energy or something to get them through. As a matter of fact, one of my friends, I almost shook him, I said, "The reason that I am prodding you like this is because I feel lonely. You're capable, you know." I don't want to be alone this way.

I want to be challenged, but I've a rough week about this, Malka, because I know I've made something unique, with the help of some unique players. When I say "a circle of magicians," part of the magic and the rareness is that they are looking for something fresh, and they are a minority. You wouldn't believe what a minority they are. Charles Mingus had a song called "If Charlie Parker Was a Gunslinger, There'd Be a Lot of Dead Copycats." And that's how I felt for the most part of this week.

This week, I became almost impossible. I became so excited with a sense of accomplishment of having made something fresh out of something that could have been hackneyed or completely in the past, you know, could have just been a regurgitation of an old idiom. But since we pulled it off somehow, it's made me very evangelical. I want everybody to do it, right? So I've been a little pushy.

For instance — I wonder how I can tell these stories without naming names. Okay, let's just say that there's a prominent band now enjoying current popularity that sounds like Bob Dylan. It sounds like the best band he ever had and it sounds like a slick Bob Dylan at the head of it. They came and played in town and everybody turned out to greet them. I think they have a number one hit or something. And among them to greet them was Bobby. Now I thought, this is very generous, but why isn't it annoying to him to see somebody stealing his licks like that. Why doesn't he say to them, "Get your own trip, be yourself." You know, "Why do you want to be me?"

M: Sounds like it isolates you, the maverick path you chose.

J: Oh, less and less, because in the last few years, maybe it's because I'm coming more and more into my real self. I have made some good friendships where I have found some people where there is a mutual understanding. You don't need very many of those people. They don't even have to live in the same town — just that they exist keeps you from feeling lonely.

I've had some very good relationships with men, you know.

M: Yet you didn't succumb to the magnet of marriage.

J: I couldn't. At a certain point, it was getting too planned, and I didn't know how to make it not planned without being a constant thorn in the side of the relationship.

I'm still not very good. My moods change a lot, which make for certain dynamics in a relationship that I've even been told are interesting but, at the same time, I always think, "Go on. Get yourself a nice girl. Get married." [laughs] This is how I think about them, you know. Maybe I'm a courtesan or something. Maybe in another era, I would be something else.

I still haven't figured it out, Malka. In the meantime, I have a man that I see steadily and . . . I have good relationships with men I've known before, so there's a continuance. I don't feel I wasted their time or they wasted mine. That's a good feeling.

M: Is it also a good feeling to be a woman in this business?

J: There was a time when I felt that the press and the men had put me safely into a nice little peer group of women and I felt it was too obvious for them to lump me into a gender group. The women were still mostly being shaped by a man. They had a producer who chose their material and directed them. They weren't in control of their own creative destiny, as I was. Neither are most men, you know; I've been very fortunate.

My growth has been slow, like a crescendo of growth, based on my dissatisfaction with the previous project, where I thought was weak, not what the critics thought. The critics dismissed a lot of what I thought was my growth and praised a lot of what I thought common about my work. I disagreed with most of them. So I had to rely a lot on my own opinions, not to say that I wasn't constantly asking them for advice and mulling it around, not dismissing it.

I still love to do that, ask people, "What do you think? Do you like this? Did you like it better that way? Do you like the dress I'm wearing? Should I wear my hair this way?" [laughs] I'm naturally insecure in that way. I have a natural feminine insecurity, but I also have a lot of nerve. Ultimately, what stuck to my ribs was my own decision.

I feel the way I was raised by my men friends in my teens, they always challenged me to keep up with them, then teased me when I did or when I almost did. I don't feel a woman in a man's world so much now.

I feel not only that I do get the respect I wanted, but now I also get this difficulty that accompanies it, which is suddenly men compete with me. So because they compete with me, I know they recognize my achievement, but now I have to work that out to make them and myself comfortable.

All your life it's a continuance . . . You get what you want but then you get something else with it, and you have to work on making that work.

M: You see it many times in the movies, when a guy is a very famous fighter, a stranger would come to him and pick a fight with him. Because, man, if he could beat this fighter, he's really the man.

J: Right. He gets a vicarious rep.

M: Does something similar to this happen to you?

J: Challenges. I've had a street musician playing guitar in the street, telling me that I didn't pay any dues and his girlfriend was better than me and that she was going to dethrone me.

I said, "Well, that's ridiculous. There's another throne waiting for her. Why do you have to kick me out of that chair? Get yourself your own chair." It comes at you in these ways.

I find that my accomplishment as a woman is intimidating, both to other women and to men.

M: You mentioned men friends in your teens, challenging you to keep up with them. Who is challenging you these days? Who do you consider your peers these days?

J: Let's talk about a certain kind of like-mindedness. Right now Weather Report, to me, is making the most interesting musical advances. So I am part of an alliance with them. We're going to tour sometime this summer. While I feel a peer to them, I also feel a student to them in some ways. Not that I'm detracting from my own accomplishment, but I think of them as real musicians. I think of myself as a painter, although I do have a fountain that seems to be deep and well stocked. I don't think I'll run out of melodic ideas, but the ideas that they're into seem advanced to me, and yet I feel that they're my peers while we're working together.

So let's talk about teachers rather than peers, okay? Leonard Cohen was a teacher

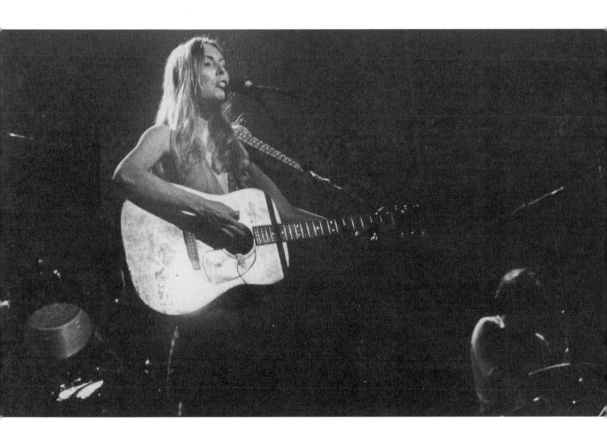

Joni on stage in 1974
© QMI Agency

of mine. Bob Dylan certainly inspired us all. Miles Davis taught me how to sing. More and more I'm beginning to show what he taught me — pure straight tones holding straight lines. The feeling when you sing and you open up your heart.

If you just try to remember to keep your heart open, it produces a warmer tone than if you really think you're hot shit, because the tone is going to get cold then.

That's the thing. You can be so flashy and incredible, there's a certain beauty that comes out of that too, but not out of arrogance . . . warmth is not gonna come out of it, you know.

I always kept Miles and his music, especially at a certain period, a lyrical period, in the area of music that I would play for myself but never thought of it as attainable. And now I'm playing with most of the players who made up that music.

M: What about the women — who do you consider your peers?

J: Among the women, I don't feel too inspired by them. Billie Holiday, yes. Edith Piaf was a great singer. And . . . an Egyptian singer. I bet you would know who she was. What's her name . . . She has an ability to express such deep powerful inner feminine strength and let out all her sorrow, you know, like in a gush. I don't think America . . . It would seem too much like losing to America. I mean the American style of singer is like a cheerleader, right? They're like cheerleaders because they're numero uno. The country hasn't really matured.

M: Is Oum Kalthoum the Egyptian singer you meant?

J: Yes! Oum Kalthoum. Great singer. Alright. [laughs]

> Critics of all expression
> Judges in black and white
> Saying it's wrong
> Saying it's right
> Compelled by prescribed standards
> Or some ideals we fight
> For wrong, wrong and right
> Threatened by all things
> Man of cruelty — mark of Cain
> Drawn to all things
> Man of delight — born again, born again
> Man of the laws, the ever-broken laws
> Governing wrong, wrong and right
> Governing wrong, wrong and right
> Wrong and right
> ("Shadows and Light")

M: Another common criticism, now even more than five years ago when we raised it first, is that because of the unique artistic lifestyle, and the opulent lifestyle, there is very little touch, if at all — real touch — with the general public. The general public struggles now with the life, let us say, of earning a living, searching for meaning and purpose, for success.

J: I'm still searching for meaning and purpose. You know, people have a funny idea that success, [that] luxury is the end of the road. That's not the end at all. As a matter of fact, many troubles begin there. They're just of a different nature.

I've had the experience of poverty, middle class, now extreme wealth and luxury, and that's difficult too.

I live in a beautiful place, like it would be a dream place. Many a day I walk through it and don't see anything. As a matter of fact, when I moved to New York . . . I tend to spend half the year there and half the year here [in L.A.], because I live like a princess here, I'm looked after. And there I have my kitchen laid out very sensibly. I know where everything is. I moved there so I would have a place where I would do my own shopping, where I would do my own housekeeping, where I would keep my own plants, to keep in contact with that, because there definitely is something you lose in the trade.

If I have to live with less, I can do it easily. I can live with much less. As a matter of fact, for my nature, it's too complicated to have so much because I can never find anything. [laughs] That's a silly little problem but you don't need that much. It's a big headache.

M: You have the choice to get rid of it.

J: Yes, but at this point, I feel like a monkey with . . . you know that thing where the monkey puts his hand in the jar and grabs peanuts and can't get the peanuts or his hand out? I'm in that stage.

I like the luxury of having a swimming pool. But if I could have a shack or a tent down there next to my swimming pool, I'd be very contented. [laughs]

> You read those books where luxury
> Comes as a guest to take a slave
> Books where artists in noble poverty
> Go like virgins to the grave
> Don't you get sensitive on me
> 'Cause I know you're just too proud

You couldn't step outside the Boho dance now
Even if good fortune allowed

Like a priest with a pornographic watch
Looking and longing on the sly
Sure it's stricken from your uniform
But you can't get it out of your eyes
("The Boho Dance")

J: I can live close to the earth primitively for short periods of time without luxury, then fly out to Paris and buy some fancy clothes and stay in a good hotel and drink good wine.

I think that, for me, to be able to afford to travel, to be able to afford not to have to tour, means that I can experience other aspects of life, even if it is going to Beverly Hills ballrooms with President Nixon presiding . . . I find it interesting when the Canadian battleships come into town to be invited to go out and explore that. There's some hoity-toity society things that I find interesting.

M: Since you mentioned Canada, did anything change for you regarding Canada since our first interview five years ago?

J: I think in a way that I feel beyond nationalism at this point. I'm proud of my background. Canada has a different character. It has a lot of character. Unfortunately, also, it has this huge inferiority complex. And if I'm around Canadians in a foreign country, I get very nationalistic.

But I've been given the opportunity to taste different cultures. Since I travel so much and I'm always crossing borders, I feel part of the culture wherever it is that I am.

M: Well, I've known you to cross quite a few borders over the years, and I've come to expect the unexpected from you, but Joni Mitchell and Charles Mingus — of all twosomes this one is really . . . way far-out. What brought this twosome about?

J: God, so many things. It feels as if I spent the last year in a circle of magicians. A lot of the way things fell into place, fell in the realm of magic, for lack of a better word. Just a series of amazing coincidences, unexplainable, too good to be true. And a lot of life hit me in the face, you know.

M: But Mingus and Joni Mitchell: who came up with this idea of combining you two — almost opposites?

J: The way it started out, as near as I can figure out, was Charles Mingus got word that he was ill, and when Charles, who was a very religious man in the deepest sense, in the sense of what I sometimes call "magic," discovered that he was dying, he wanted to reacquaint himself with God in a literary way. So he called up this friend of his and said, "Come over here, Daniele [Senatore]. I want to speak with you about God."

And Daniele thought, "He wants to speak to me about God, he's got the wrong person." So he went to a bookstore and he picked up a book of T.S. Eliot and he referred him to a section in the book called *Four Quartets*, which is a very comprehensive discourse on life and death and many matters. Charles read the book, couldn't understand all of it, and would discuss it with his wife, Sue Graham, who was literary in a different way. She ran a magazine in New York called *Changes*.

Anyway, Charles came up with an idea — the way he described it to me was there would be one kind of music, which would be very classical, overlaid with another kind of music, which would be a duet between the bass and the guitar.

He wanted me to play the guitar. And overlay it with a very educated Oxfordian kind of voice speaking T.S. Eliot, in a very literary manner, and interspersed with me translating it into common English, into the vernacular, and singing it. His analogy was that in the modern church someone would read from an ancient text, then side by side there would be a man shouting it out in common English or in street language. That was to be my role — the interpreter of the text.

So I read *Four Quartets*, found that I couldn't do it. I called Charles back and I said, "I can't do it, and the only way I could describe it, it's like as if I were to take three notes from your favourite bass solo and say, 'This is Charles Mingus's music.' I just can't condense T.S. Eliot down that way. You got the wrong person." So that was it.

About a month went by, and Mingus called me back and said that he'd written six melodies for me. So I went to see him.

I came to the door of his apartment. He was sitting in a wheelchair, a large man with a thick neck. All I saw was this hulking figure from behind in this wheelchair.

When I came around in front of him . . . Whoa! Man! His face was glowing. This beautiful face, full of the devil and beautiful light, with sarcasm around the mouth. A man who was capable of expressing many emotions.

He played me the melodies and, to tell you the truth, the music seemed to belong to another generation. In a way, that music belonged to the '50s. It didn't seem fresh to me. It seemed like I had been through it, which is odd, since I was never a jazz singer. But the force of his personality, the very specialness of our relationship, made me think, "Well, I'm gonna try this."

Charles gave me a tape with six melodies, which he called Joni 1, 2, 3, 4, 5, 6 and we went through a lot of his old material, looking for two more songs, figuring it would take eight songs to make an album.

M: What was the ailment that he suffered from?

J: He had Lou Gehrig's disease. I forget the medical name for it, but it's like a deterioration of the nervous system. First he was paralyzed, then his speech began to deteriorate, and finally his ability to swallow. That was in January. He died shortly after that. He just wasted away.

But he had a great capacity for fun and, all the way to the end, had something to enjoy. He loved to go for rides in the van. He was so uncomfortable. The only place he could sleep well was when they would load him into the van and drive around Cuernavaca to Mexico City.

M: He lived in Mexico?

J: He lived in New York, but when the disease really began to grab hold and the AMA [American Medical Association] could offer no solution, they turned their hopes to a faith healer in Mexico City, named Pachita. I went with them one night to this healer. It was lines of people, very mysterious, saturated in magic and Catholicism. Very mysterious. I stayed with Mingus and his wife for about ten days. It was a beautiful, radiant visit.

After my visit I went to New York to continue working on the music, and I was completely blocked. Music would not come out of me. But the painting began to, and every day, for fourteen days, I did a painting. They were not in my style. They were oddly reminiscent of Georgia O'Keeffe's, except that they all had people as their subject matter, and Charles was one of the reoccurring figures. Most of the album cover art was born while I was waiting for this musical block to lift off.

These melodies that Charles gave me, they were almost operatic to me. It was like learning an aria. They had so much range. They had more range than I'd ever sung in. And being musically illiterate, it was a lot to memorize. Some parts of it just wouldn't stick. It was like beyond memory. I couldn't comprehend it at first.

Something that I had dismissed as sounding familiar suddenly was — whoa! It was much more difficult than I thought, and challenging.

M: And yet you decided to take it on. Why?

J: Experientially, even though we come from different backgrounds and he expressed some emotions more overtly than I did, I felt very kindred to him. But I was surrounded by people . . . they thought it was an odd coupling. Mingus and Mitchell, like you said, it just sounded too weird, even though it was alliteration. [laughs]

Charles had been stereotyped into a violent person. This is what the public and most people, they would say, "Oh, he's such an angry . . . he's such a hostile man. He's a racist," they'd say to me. And I had been stereotyped, you know, into a tragic figure, because I dealt a lot with sorrow in my records, a lot of my humour would be missed in my music, a lot of my satire seemed to just go unnoticed. They wouldn't see that there was some saving grace to all this business. So we seemed odd to onlookers. I mean, nobody really thought that the project would come to anything.

A lot of times I thought that I couldn't do it — that I was really the wrong person for the job. And if I could have thought of the right person to turn it over to, I would have. But overall, I felt that it was meant to be, in that for the last four years I've been sticking my big toe into the lake of jazz, metaphorically, and Charles pushed me right in. It was a great education, a great opportunity to study with a great teacher. Very challenging.

There was this one note I have to sing. [sings] "When Lester took him a wife . . ." I mean, it's so low. I've used it in background but I've never sung in that register on a lead vocal. It's so deep, it's almost a joke.

Now it was difficult enough to memorize the melodies but then to set words to them, you know, the songs that I write would be more in my own conversational pattern against a rock and roll background. This was something else. It took a long time.

The first song was a bit of a Rumplestiltskin puzzle because I said to Charles, "What do you feel this piece of music is about?"

He said, "Well, this is about the things I'm going to miss, and the things I wish I'd done."

Sue, his wife, was so tender to him, she came rushing in and she said, "Oh, Charles. You know you've done everything."

I looked at him, and he looked at me and I thought, "No man has ever done everything. He must have a million pieces of music left in his head unfulfilled. Plus, the adventure is slipping away."

It wasn't too hard to project and put myself in his shoes. If I was going, I would miss the possibility of further romantic encounters. I would certainly miss the music. So I figured it would be music and women for him.

He laid a copy of his book on me, which was a very psychoanalytical and carnal autobiography. Beautiful. He's a fine writer. He's got a poetic soul, as well as a musical soul. In this book, there's a meeting with a woman who is to become his wife and she asked him what he would do if he had to do it all over again. And he says that he would come back bigger and better than ever. That he would . . . the next time he wouldn't even consider love. He would just be really hard about the whole matter. He would just be in it for the bucks. He would just be ruthless. Next time he wouldn't even have a heart. And at the bottom it says, "And if she believed that, she never would have become his wife." Right. It was his sense of humour.

I incorporated that into what otherwise would be a very sad song because it deals with realizing now that his life is coming to an end. And being stuck in this wheelchair in a skyscraper in Manhattan. The song is called "Chair in the Sky."

The rain slammed hard as bars
It caught me — by surprise
Mutts of the planet
And shook me down for alibis.
I'm waiting
For the keeper to release me
Debating my sentence
Biding my time
In memories
Of old friends of mine . . .
In daydreams of Birdland
I see my soul on fire

Burning up the bandstand
Next time
I'll be bigger!
I'll be better than ever!
I'll be happily attached
To my cold hard cash!
But now Manhattan holds me
To a chair in the sky
With the bird in my ears
And boats in my eyes
Going by.

There's things I wish I'd done
Some friends I'm gonna miss
Beautiful lovers
I never got the chance to kiss . . .
Daydreamin' drugs the pain of living
Processions of missing
Lovers and friends
Fade in and fade out again
In daydreams of rebirth
I see myself in style
Raking in what I'm worth

Next time
I'll be bigger!
I'll be better than ever!
I'll be resurrected royal!
I'll be rich as standard oil!
But now — Manhattan holds me
To a chair in the sky
With the bird in my ears
And boats in my eyes
Going by.

("Chair in the Sky")

M: Do you know why Charles Mingus chose you for this project? Did you ask him?

J: No. A friend of his turned him on to my records, and he was critical of some things because Charles was critical of music. He was opinionated about music. But he did come to the conclusion that I had a lot of nerve, and I think he probably liked nerve more than just about anything.

I think also that he wanted to ensure himself being remembered. And one of the things, oddly enough, that made him the most famous was the fact that Donovan mentioned "Mingus mellow" in an early song ["Sunny Goodge Street"]. And just that reference to Mingus, back in the early '60s, gave him a lot more notoriety than his own music because Donovan had a bigger audience, ironically.

So I think it was partially his ambitions speaking, certainly some musical respect. We had . . . we had some things in common.

M: Nerve, determination — fighting the odds to get the legs back from polio and trying to fight Lou Gehrig's disease. This I understand, but Las Vegas? Not your favourite place, if I remember right. Yet here, "The Dry Cleaner from Des Moines" . . .

J: [laughs] Yeah, I was in Las Vegas with my boyfriend, who was playing in a band there, and I thought, "How can you write songs in Las Vegas?" Well, this one born was a funny song about a dry cleaner from Des Moines, Iowa, who couldn't lose, who just everything he touched turned to gold.

Later I found a thing where Charles says, "I've been lucky. Everything I touched turned to gold." And I found out that he was a master of these one-armed bandits. He was a high winner on the slot machine.

I'm down to a roll of dimes
I'm stalking the slot that's hot
I keep hearing bells all around me
Jingling the lucky jackpots
They keep you tantalized
They keep you reaching for your wallet
Here in fools' paradise!

I talked to a cat from Des Moines
He said he ran a cleaning plant
That cat was clanking with coin
Well, he must have had a genie in a lamp
'Cause everytime — I dropped a dime —
   I blew it
He kept ringing bells
Nothing to it!

He got three oranges
Three lemons
Three cherries
Three plums
I'm losing my taste for fruit!
Watching the dry cleaner do it
Like Midas in a polyester suit
It's all luck!

It's just luck!
You get a little lucky and you make a little
   money!

I followed him down the strip
He picked out a booth at Circus Circus
Where the cowgirls fill the room
With their big balloons
The Cleaner was pitching with purpose!
He had Dinos and Pooh Bears
And lions — pink and blue there
He couldn't lose there!

Des Moines was stacking the chips
Raking off the tables
Ringing the bandits' bells
This is a story that's a drag to tell
(In some ways)
Since I lost every dime
I laid on the line
But the cleaner from Des Moines
Could put a coin
In the door of a John
And get twenty for one
It's just luck!
            ("The Dry Cleaner from Des
            Moines")

J: Mingus loved this song. Again, it was coincidence, but it suited him.

Charles Mingus was a man who had an enormous emotional spectrum. His book is called *Beneath the Underdog* and the way it opens up, it says, "I am three," and he proceeds to describe what those three are. One of them, the strong one, the observer, the detached one, the one that people call the God or the master in yourself, that is non-judgmental. He spent a long, long time in that personality, as most creative people do. The other one was a very open, almost naïvely open, childlike open, innocent personality. That's an unsung aspect of his nature, because that one would get screwed a lot. That one would trust blindly. The third one is the one that he's most famous for, because it was a most unusual one in a society where so much anger and hostility is repressed. You don't witness it unleashed. So Charles went ahead and unleashed it on people. [laughs] If he got annoyed with his bass player or somebody playing on the bandstand, he wouldn't tell them after the gig. He'd break down the music, go over, and say, "You're playing the wrong chord. This is the right chord."

He was known for punching people out. A friend of mine, John Guerin, said Mingus was a man who could clear a room with his fists or his eyes.

He had a very expansive emotional spectrum and this is why his music was so great and so difficult to play, because so many players couldn't give him enough attack on certain chords. They wouldn't be able to express that *Vroom!* They wouldn't be able to punch their guitar, punch their piano or scream in their horn enough.

After he died, I wrote a song for him. It's my music, but it's a condensation of the first four pages of his book, where he described the triptych nature of his personality, and the song is humorously entitled, "God Must Be a Boogie Man." Surely, if God made us, he must have a sense of humour. [laughs]

He is three
One's in the middle unmoved
Waiting
To show what he sees
To the other two
To the one attacking — so afraid
And the one that keeps trying to love and
    trust
And getting himself betrayed
In the plan — oh
The divine plan
God must be a boogie man!

One's so sweet
So overly loving and gentle
He lets people in
To his innermost sacred temple
Blind faith to care
Blind rage to kill
Why'd he let them talk him down
To cheap work and cheap thrills
In the plan — oh
The insulting plan
God must be a boogie man!

Which would it be
Mingus one, two or three
Which one do you think he'd want the world to see
Well, world opinion's not a lot of help
When a man's only trying to find out
How to feel about himself!
In the plan — oh
The cock-eyed plan
God must be a boogie man!
                ("God Must Be a Boogie Man")

J: The next one that I worked on was an old song called, "Goodbye Pork Pie Hat." This was a tribute to a fellow named Lester Young.

M: I'm sorry, Joni, who is or was Lester Young?

J: Lester Young was a saxophone player. He was a great horn player. He wore a porkpie hat, which is the vernacular for Porky Pig. Little hat with a small brim like Porky Pig wore. It was a popular hat in Harlem. Still see a lot of guys wearing these little short brimmed hats, but it was Lester Young that never took his off. So he became associated with this hat, and then people called him Porkpie. Charles assailed me with hundreds of stories about him. But somehow I didn't feel like I could just be a historian and take Charles's point of view. I had to experience something about it firsthand. And it was extremely frustrating, because it wouldn't come.

One night, Don [Alias], my boyfriend and I, we were riding back on the subway, and suddenly . . . Don, my boyfriend, is a black man, and we're not hassled, at least [not] in New York and Los Angeles. In Las Vegas we ran into a redneck that wanted to shoot us . . .

Now, Lester Young, on the other hand, was married to a white woman and he played a concert someplace in the South and they loved him at the concert, but then as soon as he got back to his hotel with his wife, they ran him out of town, violently. That was an important part, I felt.

Anyway, suddenly, Don and I, I can't remember why, but we decided to get off two stops earlier from our destination, and we came out on 50th Street. Smoke was coming up from the sidewalks and there was jazz in the night. You know, car hits a bump, it sounds like a rhythm track. And there's two small kids dancing and there's this crowd gathered around. So I'm thinking, "Whoa! Something's going on up here."

So we head towards it. When we get there, there's two little black kids doing this robot-like dance, and there's a whole group of black men standing around, mostly pimps 'cause it's close to the hooker district, you know, the place where all the strip joints [are] . . . Now we look up and on the marquee it says, "Pork Pie Hat Bar."

Here's a place where Charles' song, which is famous, "Goodbye Pork Pie Hat," has spawned a bar, and the bar has spawned an audience for two black kids dancing. So in a way, I thought these two little kids, one is Charles and one is Lester, they're the generation coming back up. You know, their music . . . They're the continuance of this whole thing. So I wrote that part into the song.

I wanted to get the past, which was Lester, and I wanted to get Charlie in the song too. So I got us all in there. And as a result, to me, it's a very successful song that has something immediate to say rather than just being a historical point of view.

When Charlie speaks of Lester
You know someone great has gone
The sweetest swinging music man
Had a Porkie Pig hat on
A bright star
In a dark age
When the bandstands had a thousand
　　ways
Of refusing a black man admission
Black musician
In those days they put him in an
　　underdog position
Cellars and chittlins'

When Lester took him a wife
Arm and arm went black and white
And some saw red
And drove them from their hotel bed
　　　Love is never easy

It's short of the hope we have for
　　happiness
Bright and sweet
Love is never easy street!
Now we are black and white
Embracing out in the lunatic New York
　　night
It's very unlikely we'll be driven out of
　　town
Or be hung in a tree
That's unlikely!

Tonight these crowds
Are happy and loud
Children are up dancing in the streets
In the sticky middle of the night
Summer serenade
Of taxi horns and fun arcades
Where right or wrong

Under neon
Every feeling goes on!
For you and me
The sidewalk is a history book
And a circus
Dangerous clowns
Balancing dreadful and wonderful
    perceptions
They have been handed
Day by day
Generations on down

We came up from the subway
On the music midnight makes

To Charlie's bass and Lester's saxophone
In taxi horns and brakes
Now Charlie's down in Mexico
With the healers
So the sidewalk leads us with music

To two little dancers
Dancing outside a black bar
There's a sign up on the awning
It says "Pork Pie Hat Bar"
And there's black babies dancing . . .
Tonight!
    ("Goodbye Pork Pie Hat")

J: "The Wolf That Lives in Lindsey" was a song that was written before I came onto this project with Charles.

Topically, it's an oddball on the album. I just left the song knowing that Charles agreed with the point of view. Musically I have to feel that it has a place. There's a lot more strength in my guitar playing. It's not just pretty pickin'. It scares some full-grown men. [laughs]

We recorded it, Don Alias on congas and myself, we recorded it as a duet. It has a lot of power, a lot of spontaneous communication, and when we were finished, I said to Don, "We need to get sounds of wolf choirs and water chimes." So we set up to put Emil Richards on with water chimes. That was on a Wednesday night. On Friday night I had to go to Berkeley. I was to play at a festival. When I got to the festival, I was extremely uncomfortable because they needed a headliner to draw in enough people to make enough money for this cause. At the same time that they needed me, people resent you when they need you, right? [laughs]

They expected me to come in like a prima donna, you know. I didn't want to be a prima donna, and I did want some space. Anyway, I made it complicated. It's my problem. I knew I was gonna play terrible and sing great. I was singing all the time, so I was really lubricated as a singer, but I hadn't played the guitar in about a year. So I knew it was gonna be clam land, you know.

I played the show. I sang great. Played terrible, as predicted. We went out to supper afterwards, and I was so tense. It seemed to me like all the tension at the table was emanating from me, and I kept saying to myself, "Oh, don't be silly. What do you think you are? The centre of the world?" But the fact of the matter was that I was so down, my frequency was spreading all around this table. So I excused myself, slipped away, and went back to the hotel.

At that point, I just shed it. I just said, "Forget it." And this beautiful thing started to happen among people. It ended up with a series of singing escapades, singing in the lobby with strangers, singing in the bar, even the bartenders were singing, and it culminated in going up to a party and I was leaning out the window. We were making a lot of noise. Security came up and told us to be quiet. The only thing I can see as a correlation was that we were howling out the window, because this fellow stepped up to me and said, "I have a tape of some wolves."

I said, "Really? I'm looking for a tape of some wolves. Would you send it to me?" He said, "I have it on me."

The piece was started off with a lead wolf . . . Awooo — space. Awoo — space. Then this choir of wolves begins to come in. It has internal chordal movement to it but it contains every note in the world. It would be like pressing down all the black keys and all the white keys. And it was exactly the same form as my music. It couldn't have been written better. As a matter of fact, people say to me, "Is that you singing?"

You have to remember that the wolf tape was added afterwards. They're following the voice.

It's so weird, Malka. So there was another . . . what do you call that . . . that's magic, isn't it? Freaky. [laughs]

Of the darkness in men's minds	His grandpa loved an empire
What can you say	His sister loved a thief
That wasn't marked by history	And Lindsey loved the ways of darkness
Or the TV news today	Beyond belief
He gets away with murder	Girls in chilly blouses
The blizzards come and go	The blizzards come and go
The stab and glare and buckshot	The stab and glare and buckshot
Of the heavy heavy snow	
It comes and goes	
It comes and goes	

Of the heavy heavy snow
It comes and goes
It comes and goes

The cops don't seem to care
For derelicts and ladies of the night
They're weeds for yanking out of sight
If you're smart or rich or lucky
Maybe you'll beat the laws of man
But the inner laws of spirit
And the outer laws of nature
No man can
No — no man can

There lives a wolf in Lindsey
That raids and runs
Through the hills of Hollywood
And the downtown slums
He gets away with murder
The blizzards come and go
The stab and glare and buckshot
Of the heavy heavy snow
It comes and goes
It comes and goes
("The Wolf That Lives in Lindsey")

J: Luckily, I have this circle of musicians. This is [what] I refer to as the circle of magicians. Wayne Shorter, incredibly profound creative person. Jaco Pastorius is one of the great music teachers of all times, aside from just being an awesome musician, and a great catalyst. He's kicked us all into gear. He's directly responsible for any growth that's perceptible in me.

Henry Lewy: Because Jaco, with his musical genius and his completely original way of playing the bass, which is not like a bass — he plays the bass, as if he were playing an orchestra — he thinks conceptually as an arranger, and it affected Joni's playing. She also started doing things on the guitar and on the voice that she had never done before. *Hejira* and *Don Juan's Reckless Daughter* were really a big collaboration between Joni and Jaco. It was the beginning of what we hope will be a long-lasting relationship musically.

J: Alchemists. That's what I would say this group of musicians are. You know, this is like mundane magic. But it's just as exciting as watching two birds disappear up a guy's sleeve.

Even little common things, like I had cut "God Must Be a Boogie Man" three times. Great musicians. People say, "You scrapped that tape?" because it was fine musicianship. But it didn't have that thing that makes your mouth fall open and makes you laugh when you hear two notes the way they butt up against each other.

There's a tremendous amount of affection in the playing on this album. It's hard to explain the difference, but most of the music on the radio is not coming from that space. It's just a lot of notes and dynamics and a lot of rooster strutting. They're equally valid emotions. They're beautiful in their own way, but for this I wanted to create a certain kind of theatre, which comes from love . . .

Love . . . it's a funny word to use. It's like love means different things to different people. It's like God.

Indifference is kind of the antithesis of love. I mean, that's probably the worst. Not hate. Hate and love are not that different.

Most of the recordings that go on in the studios come from a high degree of indifference. Most disco. The guys that play on disco records go out and laugh and make bad jokes about it. And yet disco is the biggest seller. But you got to know that the intent, the players that play those notes hated that music. Worse, they were indifferent to it. When it becomes dated, it's really gonna sound weird. Then you'll be able to hear that there's nothing to it, most of it.

M: Don't hate me, but I like the Bee Gees' "Stayin' Alive."

J: Well, the Bee Gees, they have some spirit on their records, and that's different. There's exceptions. But in any field of music, there is only a small percentage of genuine emotion.

Most singers are bad actors. They love their melodies, their notes, they don't know what they're singing about. If they do know what they're singing about, they get melodramatic on it. False . . . oh oh oh . . . Like false eroticism, false tenderness, false anger, you know, a lot of false emotions in modern music.

America is like really into Velveeta, do you know what I mean? Everything to be homogenized. Their music should be homogenized, their beer is watered down, their beauties are all the same. The music is the same track.

I don't want to fall into that trap. I have a pride in my experimentiveness.

M: What is your goal, Joni, at this point in your career?

J: My goal . . . if I have to have a goal, it's to make modern American music.

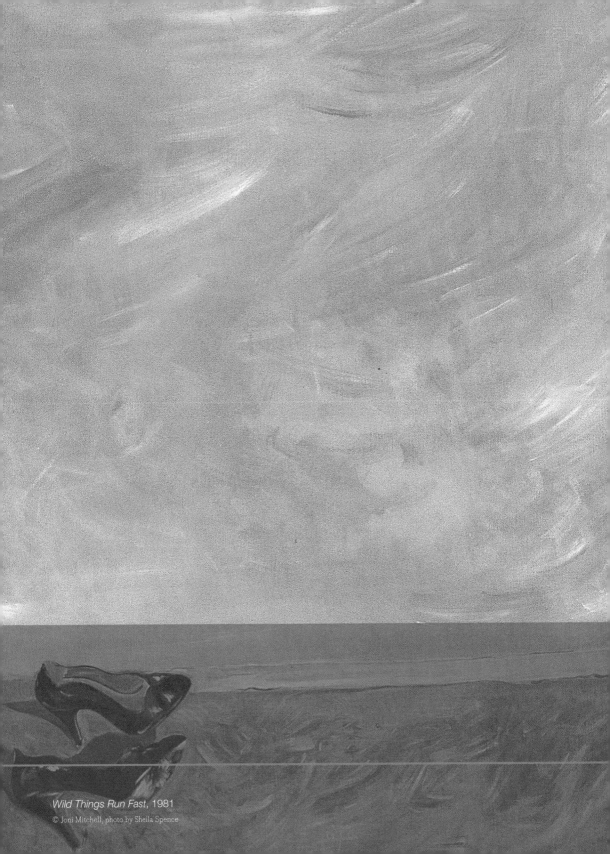

Wild Things Run Fast, 1981
© Joni Mitchell, photo by Sheila Spence

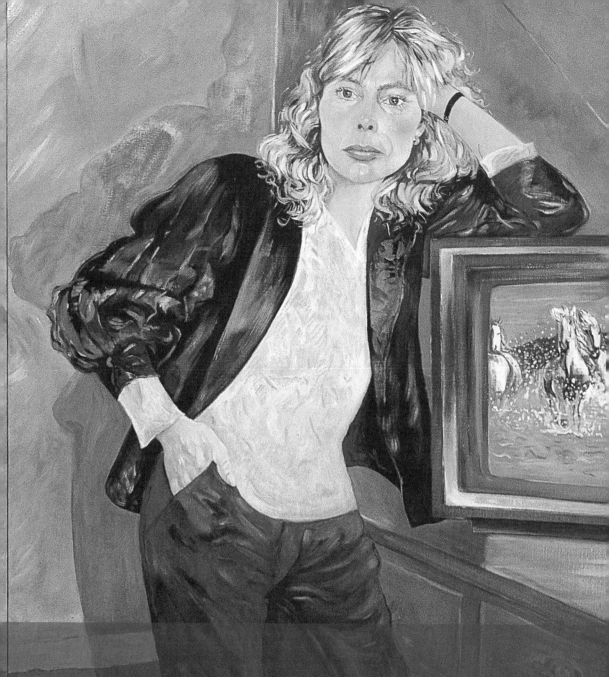

PART III

M: Thirty-three years have passed since we last recorded our conversation, and forty-five years since I first saw you sing at the Riverboat, nearly half a century ago, my God. Yet last night I saw you singing and dancing here at your home as if not a day passed since then, as they say, and I thought what a shame that I'm the only one to witness it. How wonderful it would be if you went on tour, like Leonard Cohen is these days. You saw his concert in Toronto, and you liked it.

J: Yeah, I thought it was the best I ever saw of him. I thought it was the best band he ever had, best orchestra, the best arrangements plus the repertoire — across the board, good collection of songs.

M: I thought he was amazing, especially if you consider how frail he feels in your arms when you hug him.

J: Yeah, he's very frail. Very delicate. Like my dad was at the end.

M: And yet on the stage. To see him bending and almost dancing. I thought he was really wonderful. He seemed to derive a lot of energy from the audience, from their love for him and his work. Are you tempted to go on the road?

J: No. I just was never addicted to applause or honorariums. The measure for me was the art itself.

Leonard's such a seducer he could probably believe that that many people could be in love with him. [laughs] I can't. I don't trust mass adoration. It doesn't feed me. I see it as a potential dragon. I'm not that addicted to applause that I want to manipulate the monkey to roar for me. I wouldn't get a thrill out of that, or try for a sense of victory. It wouldn't work for me. I'd rather that they forget to applaud. That they're so stunned, they're tranced in. That would be more exciting to me than the biggest applause of the night. Then I feel that I've accomplished something.

I'm really not a performing animal. I don't have that need. I prefer the creation of the song. I like the collaborations, the camaraderie of players, and small clubs.

I did small clubs when there was no hype around you back then, and when I packed a club of 300, 400 people, that was very exciting. I'd grin from ear to ear. I couldn't believe it that people were standing at the back . . . I loved it when it was small, little clubs. I never liked the big stage.

M: Because?

J: Because my music is just not for everybody.

M: And yet you sang at huge festivals, huge stages. The Isle of Wight [in 1970], for example.

J: Oh yeah. That was the worst audience ever on the planet for the artist. It was the "hate the artist" audience — 600,000 hate-the-artist people. It was very difficult. It was just horrible to play there.

I wanted to go on at night. I didn't want to see the audience, because audiences that big are there for the event, not for the artist, so you're looking at pandemonium frequently. You're not looking at rapt attention.

Also I'm the only one that has to go out there alone. Everybody else has got big amps and bands, and I can't make a big enough noise to mask the fact that they're all talking through every act at those things.

And it's precarious for me, because I'm small and vulnerable against an audience like that.

So I was booked to go on at night, but people were cancelling. And there came a cold spot in the middle of the afternoon, and my manager was off someplace necking with some girl. And I got railroaded . . . I became cooperative.

That's what I mean when I say I was very "feminine." There was a cooperative female acquiescing quality that I had at that time, and I allowed myself to be railroaded into the hardest spot in the concert.

The crowd was really rabid at that point, and a guy flipped out on acid, and people who had packed close began to stand up and move forward and they were gonna trample and be trampled. So I had to stand my ground and they did sit down and behave after that. It was a turning point in the festival.

M: What do you mean, "stand my ground"?

J: Well, you're in a fight or flight situation. Either you run — flight, you're full of adrenaline, you're in a middle of a nightmare — or you stand up to it. Standing up to 600,000 hostile people, it was a bit David and Goliath. [laughs]

M: How did you fight exactly? How does one stand up to 600,000 people?

J: Remember the Hopi snake dance in the desert? If I had not gone to see these men dance with live snakes, sidewinders, there would be no way that I could draw the strength to stand up to 600,000 people who were moving forward and probably gonna be trampled because they were packed so tight, and they were hostile.

If there's one rule to this game
Everybody can name real plain
It's, be cool!
If you're worried or uncertain
If your feelings are hurtin'
You're a fool if you can't keep cool
Charm 'em
Don't alarm 'em
Keep things light
Keep your worries out of sight
And play it cool
Play it cool
Fifty-fifty
Fire and ice

If your heart is on the floor
Cause you've just seen your lover
    comin' thru the door with a new fool —
Be cool
Don't you sweat it
Start right in right now
    trying to forget it
Be cool
Don't get riled
Smile — keep it light
Be your own best friend tonight
And play it cool
Play it cool
Fifty-fifty
Fire and ice

                ("Be Cool")

M: Since our last interview, hundreds and hundreds of artists have covered your songs, more than a thousand artists covered just "Both Sides Now." Although I sort of expected it when I first heard your songs, if anyone were to tell me then that "Both Sides Now" would play in elevators, or that "Woodstock," "River," and "Big Yellow Taxi" would play in department stores . . . Did you envision that they would become standards?

J: You can't predict . . . Well, like, Seal called me up one day and he said, "Come on over. I've written a standard." I said, "You can't write a standard." You write a song. And if it's good, and people like it, if you get three or four hundred covers of it, you've written a standard. You can't write it and predict that everyone will want to cover it. You know what I mean?

There was a funny article in the *L.A. Times*. The guy was ranting, "Why are all these people covering Joni Mitchell's 'River'? It's overexposed." That's what he said, and I thought, "This person has no concept of what a standard is. A standard is a good song enjoyed by many." A lot of singers wanted to sing it, and it kept the song alive.

You wouldn't predict that "River" would get that many covers. I wouldn't have. And be translated into many languages. There's a Hebrew version of it, you know.

M: Of many of your songs.

J: They don't have a river that you can skate away on in Israel. They were having trouble with that. So I said, "Just put a boat . . . 'I wish I had a boat I can sail away on.'" Bring it into your culture around it.

M: They have skating rinks now in Israel.

J: But they don't have frozen rivers.

M: No.

J: They won't unless the Ice Age comes back. [laughs]

> It's coming on Christmas
> They're cutting down trees
> They're putting up reindeer
> And singing songs of joy and peace
> Oh I wish I had a river
> I could skate away on
> But it don't snow here
> It stays pretty green
> I'm going to make a lot of money
> Then I'm going to quit this crazy scene
> Oh I wish I had a river
> I could skate away on
>   ("River")

M: Here in "River" you are stating, "I'm going to make a lot of money / Then I'm going to quit this crazy scene." Yet when you were offered a million dollars to appear one night in Vegas, you turned it down.

J: Elliot [Roberts] chewed on his wrist.

M: No wonder. A million dollars for one night! For one concert! Two or three hours max . . . In those days when a million dollars was a symbol of immense wealth.

J: Well, I kicked myself . . . I really wanted to do that. But to me, Vegas at that time was a symbol of the beginning of the rot, the decadence of America. It was just a seedy little place in the desert where you poured your money down a big deep hole . . . it was the kiss of death for serious music, really, in my opinion.

M: Still, not many people would reject that offer.

J: They are not gonna be that stupid. [laughs] That's stupid integrity, isn't it?

M: [laughs] When you wrote "Big Yellow Taxi," did you imagine that it would become such an important song?

J: I never think that any song is going to become an important song. I'm not ambitious for them.

M: Did you think it would be so deeply entrenched in our culture?

J: No. I just don't think that way. I'm writing from emotional disturbance, so I'm working through an irritant. I'm trying to exorcise the irritant articulately and draw it, if it's universal, to the attention of others, hoping that somebody out there will hear it and could do something.

M: Well, quite a lot or people all over the world heard it for many, many years, decades really by now.

J: David Suzuki said to me, "When did you write 'Big Yellow Taxi,' in the '80s?"

I said, "No, 1967."

He went, "1967?!"

I started to have a global consciousness around that time, before anyone else that I knew did. And I may as well have been Chicken Little for the way I was thinking.

That song was written in Hawaii. I used to listen to *Hawaii Calls* on Sunday nights. It was all Hawaiian music. I loved the sound of it. It was such a unique musical culture. There was so much joy in it and elegance and sway . . .

I landed in Hawaii at night, and I went into this hotel, this skyscraper in Oahu. I woke up in the morning, threw open the curtains, and there were beautiful green mountains and beautiful long-tailed white birds flying by, and then I looked down and it was cars as far as I could see. I was horrified. "They paved paradise / And put up a parking lot."

They paved paradise
And put up a parking lot
With a pink hotel, a boutique
And a swinging hot spot
Don't it always seem to go
That you don't know what you've got
Till it's gone
They paved paradise
And put up a parking lot

They took all the trees
And put them in a tree museum
And they charged all the people
A dollar and a half just to see 'em
Don't it always seem to go
That you don't know what you've got
Till it's gone
They paved paradise
And put up a parking lot

Hey farmer farmer
Put away that DDT now
Give me spots on my apples
But leave me the birds and the bees
Please!
Don't it always seem to go
That you don't know what you've got
Till it's gone
They paved paradise
And put up a parking lot

Late last night
I heard the screen door slam
And a big yellow taxi
Took away my old man
Don't it always seem to go
That you don't know what you've got
Till it's gone
They paved paradise
And put up a parking lot
("Big Yellow Taxi")

J: When "Big Yellow Taxi" was released, it was released as a single. The only place in the world that it was a regional hit was in Hawaii. Then over the years it was a hit in Nashville, by another artist. It became a regional hit by various artists in various places. And finally Counting Crows had an international hit with it [in 2002]. By that time, the whole world realized that we were paving paradise. By that time, there was a big audience that was cognizant of what the song was saying.

People approached me to use that song and other songs of mine when trees were coming down. They think they need my permission. I said, "You know, that's what the songs are for. Please be my guest." It just adds a little more than a good orator can do. It's kind of like your lawyer.

I would like to re-record it. To get the inflationary line up. I kept raising the price in performance, "Put all the trees in a tree museum, and charged all the people a dollar and a half just to see it." Those days are gone. $55 just to see it. $125. $3,000 just to see it. Finally I said, "An arm and a leg just to see it." [laughs]

M: I'm with David Suzuki on "Big Yellow Taxi." I mean it's really surprising that a young girl in her twenties, would have such insight . . . or is it really foresight?

J: I don't foresee impending disasters all around me. [laughs] It's not psychic. It's not anything paranormal. It's just being awake, being alert. I've got a fast eye.

M: How do you feel when people sing your songs, any song, or play it completely different, like with "normal" chords, and different arrangements?

J: I think it's great, I feel honoured. I like the idea of songs being sung. I like the idea that people who can't even sing are singing them. I love the arrangement of "Both Sides Now," with the big London Symphony Orchestra.

M: It's really beautiful.

J: That London Symphony Orchestra. All these Brits, so emotional on that . . .

That was a live performance in England, and there's a place where I get emotional and the orchestra swells up. Everybody's feeling it at the same time. You don't find that a lot on records, because of the way they're made now, that so many people are emotionally engaged simultaneously. The men were blowing their nose at the end of that take and women were wiping their eyes. And they all huddle into the playback booth, to hear it like little kids at the back of the room. It's very exciting.

M: You mean it was a live performance in a studio? You and the whole London Symphony Orchestra in one hall?

J: Yeah. It was the third take and that was it. There was no post-production on it.

And that performance then begat a movie called *Love Actually*. It was conceived when the movie director [Richard Curtis] put that cut of "Both Sides Now" on and much to his surprise, he was crying. It caught him off guard. And so he built a whole movie around it, *Love Actually*.

M: I would like to turn to what happened after you finished recording *Mingus* in '79 when our second interview took place. I wonder what you feel about the albums, the work, the poems, the stories, the music, that you composed and recorded since then. Let's start with *Wild Things Run Fast*.

J: It's just a rock 'n' roll ditty.

M: Really? That's how you feel about it?

J: You mean the whole album?

M: Yeah.

J: To me, that's the only rock 'n' roll album that I did, per se. I had a band that basically had its roots in rock 'n' roll. Before that, the bands had basically had their roots in jazz. And the songs are simplified; they're less wordy.

Coming out of *Hejira*, the writing was expanding to the point where it didn't even stay in a stanza. It was spilling over into kind of organic forms that you had to write out each verse because each line had a different length.

Somebody said that it was like I was improvising around a melody that only I knew. And, in a way, it was true because it was influenced by sax players who were riffing on a melody which isn't there, but it's a standard — you kind of know this is "Stardust," even though they're playing around it and they're not using the syllabication of the lyrics. They're playing thirty-second notes, if they want to, or sixteenth notes. I was trying to write like that with the liberty of a jazz horn player. This was a reeling in to a simpler kind of song structure than most, and it was a celebration.

One of the negative things about *Wild Things Run Fast* was that they counted the times the world "love" comes up on that.

Yes I do — I love you!
I swear by the stars above I do!
I swear on the streetlight on the corner
Shoving out the shadows!
One shadow cursing
Another shadow laughing
Underneath the streetlight
I don't know where they're coming from
I just see them passing
Underneath the streetlight . . .

Yes I do — I love you!
I swear on the buildings above I do!
I swear on a billion yellow
    and TV blue windows!
Gayboys with their pants so tight
Out in the neon light
Underneath the streetlight
Here comes a madman — madman
Kicking over garbage cans
Underneath the streetlight . . .

                                 ("Underneath the Streetlight")

J: "Yes I do, I love you." I forget what it is, fifty-four times or something like that. It was repugnant to that very cynical punk era, that it was such . . .

It just happened that I was in kind of a happy pocket there, and there was a lot of joy on it. And it was fun, really fun to play those upbeat songs with that band.

M: It was fun to hear it. Still, what do you think of it now?

J: I never listen to it. So I don't know what it sounds like now.

M: You don't listen to your songs?

J: No.

M: Do you happen to hear it on the radio when you are driving?

J: Sometimes when there's people over here, Val [Charles Valentine, Joni's friend] puts my music on when we're playing pool. At first I'm kind of embarrassed by it, but then every once in a while I hear something that I kind of like. But I'm always afraid that I'll go back and hear things, which I frequently do, that I want to change and I can't, so I don't really go back.

M: A similar thing happened to me about twenty years after I recorded my last album . . . I never listened to them because I was always afraid that, well, I heard flaws in them when I was recording them but they didn't have the budget for another take. So I never listened to them. Then, one day I was driving to Ottawa with friends and I hear this beautiful song. "Wow, who is that?" I asked. I didn't recognize my own voice. So it was not nostalgia.

J: Yeah, you gain some objectivity. Sometimes it's surprising that things hold up when you go back to them. Some of the old songs stand up. Even "Both Sides Now," which I hear in elevators and supermarkets, watered down on airplanes, I can sometimes find my way into because of what it's saying. I haven't outgrown it. But there are things that I had limited technology [for] that were very experimental that didn't quite work that I could fix now with Pro Tools . . . I gave Henry [Lewy] a gold-plated razor for a present one time because of the cuts we did manually.

Years later Henry suffered from bursitis. I didn't know this because I was sick. When I got well enough, I called him up and said, "Henry, I'm playing the piano better than I should. I haven't played it in three years, and all of a sudden I'm playing. You got to go into the studio and capture it."

"I can't. I'm sick," he said.

"I'm sick too. Let's go in," I said.

So we went in and he was so sick, he was like turning in the cobwebs. But I thought Henry's thing was slightly psychosomatic. I hate to say it. That's what they're saying about Morgellons, but I thought maybe I can trick him into getting well. So I put this incompetent second engineer in charge and he was making mistakes and Henry would say, "He's gonna ruin it," and I'd say, "Yes, he is." But Henry's hands would tremble on the console. And the second engineer butchered a lot of things. He made a lot of mistakes. So I took a real risk. "We've got to go to London and catch up with Jaco [Pastorius] and Wayne [Shorter]," I said.

And Henry, he's got his eyes closed and he's feeling sorry for himself. "London?" like that.

"Yeah, think of the good bread, Henry. We're gonna stop in New York."

"New York?"

"I'm crazy," I thought. I'm either going to kill him or I'm gonna challenge him into wellness.

So I dragged him and the second engineer. We went to see Dizzy Gillespie . . . and Henry stopped playing the "I'm dying." He's still limping. He still had the genuine injury of his leg. But spiritually he was not milking it so bad. By the time we got to England, he did it. He came back a lot. He lucked out. ·

M: I think that music and art have power to heal. I really believe it.

> Still I sent up my prayer
> Wondering where it had to go
> With heaven full of astronauts
> And the Lord on death row
> While the millions of his lost and lonely ones
> Call out and clamour to be found
> Caught in their struggle for higher positions
> And their search for love that sticks around
> ("The Same Situation")

M: You mentioned that you were ill when you called Henry, yet you travelled with him to New York and London. Was it the same ailment that kept you from performing "Both Sides Now" at the Vancouver Olympics [in 2010]?

J: I was invited to participate, but I couldn't — that was at the height of my illness, when I couldn't even wear clothing. I had to have alkalized soft cotton, and even then it felt like barbed wire. I couldn't leave my house for several years. Sometimes it got so I'd have to crawl across the floor. My legs would cramp up, just like polio spasms. It hit all of the places where I had polio. When it's severe, I can't walk. I had one attack where I had to crawl to the bathroom. And I had to turn around and back down the stairs. I started laughing . . . I'm so glad I don't have a man to be repulsed by this. I thought I must really look pretty funny. [laughs]

M: [laughs] Sorry, Joni, I don't mean to . . .

J: No, I love it. I think it's the right response. That's why I love it that you laugh when I'm telling you all the horrible things that are happening to me. It's so perfect. You're riding the middle way, the cusp . . . that's what genius is. You got a little angel on the other and Buddhism riding the middle way, you know, the balance between.

M: But it's not a relapse of polio, or a form of polio?

J: No. It's Morgellons. Morgellons is not like anything that ever existed before. But it has some overlap where it looks like, so it's subject to misdiagnosis. They go, "Oh, you had chicken pox, therefore, it's shingles. Give me my money."

"No, it isn't shingles."

"Oh, you're neurotic."

That's the battle. That's the stem of my anger. I don't want those people . . . I'd die in my house before I'll call 9-1-1. There's a lot to be angry at.

My music falls off cliffs if there are sudden changes. And there's dissonance or strange notes running through it. That's the way my life has been. Like today you're well, and then you get up in the morning and your legs are gone. And Morgellons is constantly morphing. There are times when it's directly attacking the nervous system, as if you're being bitten by fleas and lice, it feels like it's external, but in fact it's internal. It's in all the tissue — and it's not a hallucination. It was eating me alive, Malka, sucking the juices out.

M: Drained, that's how I felt when I had that head surgery, and when you're so drained, and in pain, you don't see the end of it, and you feel, "Oh, that's it, I'm fucked."

J: I couldn't indulge in that. It would get better, then it would get worse. It was a roller coaster. Finally, I gave up hope.

People have said to me in their naïvety, "Oh, Joni, you have to have hope." And I nearly bit their heads off. Hope? I've been through that hope/despair/hope/despair. It's a roller coaster ride. You have to transcend hope.

So when you transcend hope, what are you running on? Well, I had to give up hope and to proceed like an old warrior — like Buddhism, like path without goal. You can't have a goal. You do it because you do it.

There were a couple of years with this illness where I was very isolated. I kicked a lot of people out of my life. Suddenly I thought that there was a lot of deadwood in my life. I didn't have a sense of wasting my time with these people, but I thought I need to make different kinds of friends. I had found that kind of friendship with Jean [Grand-Maître, the choreographer of the ballet based on her songs]. I don't think they exist in this town, really, what I was looking for. I was imagining that I would come to a different kind of community, a community of artists.

M: Like the one that existed in L.A. when you first moved here?

J: Well, I see that me and my friends are becoming historical characters for the California scene; books are being written now. You begin to see that when the music scene moved from New York to here, really at the heart of it was Elliot [Roberts] and David [Crosby] and I. And the things that they did different came out of my stubbornness. Like, we got into artists' self-publishing.

M: You mean you were the first artist there that was self-published?

J: Yeah, because I just got out of a bad divorce, I wouldn't sign a contract with Elliot. I didn't sign contracts. I wouldn't let them have part of my publishing. And so all of them wanted what I had. My stubbornness made them move in a different direction than they had done in the past, and the whole scene moved that way.

M: Do you think that such a community of artists can exist today, or is it a utopian notion?

J: Yeah, it's a utopian notion. I guess being the only artist as I was growing up, I imagine a community of artists, where artistic discussions took place. I imagined that it was like that in Paris . . . Did you see Woody Allen's *Midnight in Paris*?

M: Yes.

J: It's brilliant. It's got a brilliant conclusion, like, enjoy the air that you're a part of.
   I always thought I'm a misfit in this. I would have been better off in Paris in the '20s. The way I dress would be more appropriate. I dress wrong for the scene. I

lead the conversation in ways that nobody wants to go. They're not interested in the same things. And it's so cutthroat competitive in an ugly way. But then when you read Van Gogh's letters, the same thing was happening there, and he was blaming it on Paris. He said, "If we all do like the Buddhists and we come and live in the yellow house with me — I've got lots of room — and we start our own school, we pool our resources, maybe some of that ugly competition that happens in the cities will go away, in this environment." So I say, "Same as it ever was."

And Woody's movie kind of brings that out very well in that you go back to the '20s and they wish they belonged to the grand epoch. They were always wishing that they belonged to the scene that their heroes did, the generation before, thinking they missed something. So you may as well enjoy the one you're in.

M: Were your parents alive when you became ill with Morgellons?

J: Oh yeah.

M: They knew about it?

J: No, I didn't have a name for it then. But I've been sick all my life.

M: Not like that, by the sounds of it. I mean, from what you've told me, Morgellons sort of invaded your being.

J: Right. They're body snatchers. The invasion of the body snatchers. [laughs] My body is like the earth. What we have done to the earth by overpopulating it, this disease has done to my body by overpopulating it. I want this out like I did polio.

M: Is Morgellons contagious, as polio?

J: No. My mother was so worried about catching the [polio] germ herself, she came to see me once, her haunted eyes over the mask. There was no comfort. I started to wait for her to get out of there.

M: So you were a whole year by yourself there?

J: Not a year . . . months. And then I was a year at home under her tutelage because I had to be home-schooled.

M: So you were already schooled in being alone since that age.

J: I know how to be alone, yeah.

M: That is so hard to imagine, Joni, you being alone.

J: Because I'm so social?

M: Not only because you're social, but also because you're so famous.

J: Oh, I could be dripping with sycophants if I wanted to, but that's not a very satisfying kind of company. I have a few of those still in my life that pass for company. And I can tolerate them. But they're give-to-gets.

M: They're what?

J: They're give-to-gets. They give you an apple — they want a Cadillac in return. [laughs] You have to watch out for that especially as you get older and ready to die. [laughs] They have to be really nice to you because you can die at any moment.

M: You mean, they think they can get your inheritance?

J: Well, maybe. That's what happened to Georgia O'Keeffe. She drew down a sycophant in her eighties. It gave her the strength not to die. He did manage to wangle a piece of her inheritance. The family contested it and they got some of it back. But she enjoyed him, and he didn't suck up to her. He wasn't a sucky sycophant.

We took a walk in the country one day, he and Georgia and I. And when we went back he picked her up and put her in a green plastic garbage can and went, "You're just an old bag of bones, Georgia." And she shrieked like a teenager with laughter. She was a tough old bird.

M: Was it while you were working on your album *Mingus*? Did she and/or her paintings influence your work?

J: Georgia? When I went there, the paintings she had there were the dregs. The best ones were gone.

M: You mean they were sold?

J: The ones that they showed me there — I asked if there was any work that I can see — he was afraid I'd buy because that was what he was lying in wait to inherit. He was wangling his way into her will. She had me stay and sign on her will. And he was doing the Brer Rabbit thing.

You know that story: the Brer Rabbit, "Don't throw me in the briar patch, don't throw me in the briar patch." They throw him in the briar patch. He goes, "I was born in the briar patch." So he was protesting a lot, "Don't put me in the will, don't put me in the will," so she went behind his back and drew up a will and had me co-sign on it, and he put on a mock fight: "I told you not to put me in the will." I was there for all of that drama. There was another will that came after the one that I signed, because she did go senile later. I think she was senile enough to believe that he was gonna marry her.

That's why I really watch out for any romance at my age. A friendship, yeah. I'll go for a friendship, but no romance. Because men like younger women, they're not gonna hook up with an older gal. And I know how young men were when I was ill. They wouldn't even throw a blanket on my bed if I fell down dying.

> Anyone will tell you
> Just how hard it is to make and keep a friend
> Maybe they'll short sell you
> Or maybe it's you
> Judas in the end
> When you just can no longer pretend
> That you're getting what you need
> Or you're giving out anything for them to grow and feed on
> > ("Jericho")

J: I did have one companion in my illness that behaved appropriately. He's dead now, Dickie Jobson. He fed me in the morning, fed me in the evening. He sat quietly in my company. Never said, "How are you feeling," or something stupid like that. He knew I was in relentless pain. He told me amusing things when he did break the silence. He gave me things to put my mind around. He had wonderful responses. I loved Dickie. He was the only person in my entire life that was a good companion when I was ill.

M: Were you curious to read the *I Ching* about your illness?

J: Well, I went back and looked at my luck. "Stuck at home with anger problems, get to know yourself, and take up a musical instrument." That's my luck! Unbelievable.

M: So did you follow it through — did you take up a musical instrument?

J: No, I have no drive. I couldn't follow things to conclusion.
    I used to be tenacious. I'd get on an idea and I'd stick with it until whatever it was, was completed. I would work and work — you couldn't wrench me away from it.
    But now I start, I'll get a stanza. I've got notebooks full of premises . . . the first verse and the point of departure . . .

M: I'm starting to forget where I placed the notebooks. [laughs] And sometimes, when a very good line comes to me during a walk and I don't have anything to jot it down, by the time I finally get something to jot it down, I lose the line. That's when I remember you telling me many years ago that you never lose it. It all goes to the . . .

J: Muse food. Let them go.

M: I remember it was always a source of comfort to me, always. Although it frustrated me to lose it.

J: I lose everything now. I just can't hold on to . . . can't remember what I just said. Everything is fluid now. That isn't necessarily old age because genetically my people lived quite long. But there's a lot of lethargy with my illness. I'm fatigued. And the medicines that I was taking give you what I call a Herx reaction, which is kind of brain fog.

M: Do you wish you had the drive back? Are you longing for it?

J: No, I'm not longing for anything. My creative energy went into survival and also into the furnishing the interior of [the B.C.] house with an art studio and a meditation studio. I have the desire to reflect suddenly. To be more amused where I am now irritated. I want to be able to transmute that response to amusement. I don't know whether I could accomplish it because of the illness.

I've become more irritable because of the disease, less tolerant. I don't think that's a good thing. I may jump on people a little quicker than I would before. Maybe I didn't jump on them quick enough before. [laughs] I need the balance, but I feel at this point that I've swum far enough.

I worry about the irritability. I don't want to turn into an old grump, but as one doctor said, "Sick people don't have good personalities." Thank you. That was the first friendly thing I've heard on this whole journey.

M: When were you catapulted on to this "whole journey"?

J: By 2007 I just began to decline radically. And I've been fighting it because I feel like I still have something left to do. But I don't really know what. I think I still have utility. That's the only reason I'm still alive. I feel like I've not totally fulfilled destiny, but according to my destiny pattern, I'm supposed to have spiritually attained.

Well, I've had a major leg up, spiritually speaking, but, in the meantime, because of all this bad behaviour around me, I'm angry, which is the low end of insanity in Buddhist terms. So, in a certain way, I'm at the bottom of the pit, spiritually speaking.

What does a voice at the bottom of the pit have to say? Well, Job says it very well. I've already done that. I've already been the voice at the bottom of the pit because this is my second time down, right?

M: I remember years ago you said, "We're just writing the same songs, not as good as we used to write when we were young."

J: Did I say "we"?

M: Yes, because you meant Bob Dylan and yourself.

J: That's interesting because my songs did change. When was that?

M: I don't remember. It was twenty or twenty-five years ago, I think.

J: I did take a growth spurt as a writer on *Hejira*, I think . . . Around *Hejira* and *Don Juan's Reckless Daughter*, to a degree, I think I went to another level as a writer.

That's what I'm hoping to do as a painter. I was good then, but in terms of originality, like in really pioneering a new territory, as a painter I haven't really done that yet, and I'm not sure that it's possible because I think painting is more mined out than music.

I mean, that there were musical laws left to break at the end of the twentieth century amazes me; that I did things that were outside the law amazed me. I knew that what I was doing sounded fresh. I didn't know what the law was because I was self-taught, but certainly the law keeps those things from being common.

One thing that I used actually had been forbidden. I only used it in one song. It's called the "devil's interval." The church had forbidden it because you're gonna get a doubt feeling in your body, that's what those chords evoke. They don't want any doubt in the church so they outlawed it. It's a weird interval, this devil's interval. You wouldn't want to use it a lot. It's not even attractive, really, but it falls under the words in a piece called "Sunny Sunday."

The story is about a girl in a bad relationship who every once in a while takes a gun to the front porch and shoots at the street light outside. She always misses. But she's set in her mind, the day she hits that goddamn light is the day she's gonna have the strength to leave this guy. But she always misses, so that's where I put the devil's interval: [sings] "That one little victory, that's all she needs" — right in there "one little victory." So theatrically it's perfect, it's got the doubt transition underneath which kind of creates irony. You see what I mean?

> She waits for the night to fall.
> Then she points her pistol through the door,
> And she aims at the streetlight
> While the freeway hisses.
> Dogs bark as the gun falls to the floor.
> The streetlight's still burning;
> She always misses.
> But the day she hits,

That's the day she'll leave.
That one little victory, that's all she needs!
She pulls the shade;
It's just another sunny Monday.
She waits for the night to fall.
("Sunny Sunday")

J: The church forbade the devil's interval for many years. So you never hear anybody ever do it in music, but in terms of the play, you couldn't have a better illustration, emotional illustration to accompany the text there.

That's one of the laws that's a known law. The other is the suspense of sus chords that I've told you about before. Using them a lot is like keeping you in the state of no resolution.

Well . . . look at my life — chronic illness, the bomb hanging over us. There were external iconic situations and personal chronic situations of tension. And stalker after stalker after stalker in my yard.

M: Yes, I remember the stalkers. I brought up the *I Ching* before, because I remember it was when you taught me to read the *I Ching*. I don't remember what year it was, but I remember that because of stalkers a security system round your house was connected to the police and I triggered the alarm a few times — scared the shit out of me. And I remember thinking how brave you are, to live alone — alone at night, with stalkers murdering artists in this town.

J: Many stalkers. Many, many, many. Some of them very dangerous. Necrophiliac fantasies and one guy was going to cut his left testicle off because he might better know the nature of women. A lot of Manson-type butcherous stalkers. They didn't get me. [laughs] Like Leonard says, "They'll never get us, Joni."

So far so good. But my nocturnalism comes from years of being stalked here.

M: You mean your insomnia started because you were stalked?

J: Right. I'm the night watchman. A lot of my insomnia comes from — I can't sleep until it's light outside. I am scared of the dark, but I'm so used to being scared of the dark that I don't even notice it. You know what I mean?

I'm not sitting in a fearful state, but it has affected my sleep patterns.

They should call this Job's disease because in the Book of Job, my song Job ["The Sire of Sorrows (Job's Sad Song)"], he says, "Let me speak, let me spit out my bitterness — / Born of grief and nights without sleep in festering flesh."

Up in B.C., I have Hans to help me, so there is a neighbour who's like an uncle. Also he has populated a lot of the coast, so if anybody messes with me, you can call on this family.

There's wolves and coyotes up there, but I don't feel scared up there.

M: When you do get to sleep, do you dream in black and white, colour, sound, in music?

J: All of the above, and smell even sometimes. It's like living fully.

M: Does it inspire your songs or your paintings?

J: "Paprika Plains" was inspired.

I want to attempt to paint my dreams, especially the ones where Chögyam [Trungpa] came to me, which were very mystical. I have tried to paint it once and I don't think I succeeded. I need to try again.

M: Let me return to the *I Ching* for a moment: did you use the *I Ching* as a tool in your work?

J: Oh yeah, I did one song that I wrote which is a very unusual song. When Donald [Alias] and I met, I carried a little portable *I Ching*, not as good as the Wilhelm [translation], but good enough. We threw on the first night that we met, we each threw a change, and I wrote down the highlights of the contents of the two things, it was really accurate. I wrote a song based on those two things called "Stay in Touch."

"People will be envious
But our roles aren't clear
So we must not rush
Still
We are burning brightly
Clinging like fire to fuel
I'm grinning like a fool

Stay in touch
During times like these
The wise are influential
They can bear the imperfections
They can keep the harmony
No doubt about it
No doubt that's essential
No doubt."

So part of the change was: wood over fire. That's always been a tricky one for me — "burning brightly / Clinging like fire to fuel / I'm grinning like a fool / Stay in touch." That's based on two things that we threw from the *I Ching*. Commingled. And it really made a profound little song about the beginning of a romance. But that's the only thing that directly [references the *I Ching*], other than — "I was driving across the burning desert / And I spotted six jet planes / Leaving six white vapor trails / It was a hexagram of the heavens."

That's the six straight lines of the creator — the first change in the *I Ching*. That's another mention of the *I Ching*.

M: It didn't occur to me until now that your song "Amelia" was based on the *I Ching*.

J: It would be a good tool for understanding people.

I was driving across the burning desert
When I spotted six jet planes
Leaving six white vapour trails across the bleak terrain
It was the hexagram of the heavens
It was the strings of my guitar
Amelia, it was just a false alarm

The drone of flying engines
Is a song so wild and blue
It scrambles time and seasons if it gets through to you
Then your life becomes a travelogue
Of picture-post-card-charms
Amelia, it was just a false alarm

People will tell you where they've gone
They'll tell you where to go
But till you get there yourself you never really know
Where some have found their paradise
Others just come to harm
Amelia, it was just a false alarm
      ("Amelia")

M: For a heavy lady, you can be hilarious, even in very serious songs, and since you . . .

J: I can't stand myself if I get too serious.

M: This is certainly not too serious: "Love takes so much courage / Love takes so much shit."

J: [laughs] That's a good one, isn't it? That's worth a guffaw. [laughs] "Love takes so much shit."

M: It's the line that comes before it.

J: "Love takes so much courage / Love takes so much shit."

M: Exactly. You couldn't in your right mind put those two together. [laughs]

J: It's astute. You have to be out of your mind to be astute?

M: That is why it is so funny, because it's astute. While I still have enough light to read a few lines — "Don't need to look so good / Don't need to talk so wise."

J: That's not me. That's my hero — Kipling. I only changed a little bit of his writing to bring it up to date, and I changed the ending. People think I did it as a feminist, but I did it because I disagreed with his idea at the end.
    Read me the last verse and I'll tell you what it was.

M: "If you can fill the journey / Of a minute / With sixty seconds worth of wonder and delight."

J: I changed that. What did he have? It had to do with endurance . . .
"If you can fill the journey of a minute
With sixty seconds worth of . . . distance run —
then the earth is yours and everything that's in it.
And what is more, you'll be a man, my son."
That's Kipling's. And I thought: that's not how you inherit the earth. That's a soldier's way to tell a boy. That isn't what I want my son to get out of it. I wanted to get the idea changed because: how do you inherit the earth?

The earth is yours, if you can fill the journey of a minute with sixty seconds worth of "wonder and delight." Then the earth is yours and everything that's in it.

"Wonder and delight" is renewal of innocence. You can always get your innocence back if you can have sixty seconds worth of wonder and delight. If you can delight in a bird song or the light on the water.

"Wonder and delight" is hardly ever used in modern plays. It's overlooked and underused.

M: "For a true artist, each work should be a new beginning where she tries or he tries again for something that is beyond attainment." I'm paraphrasing Hemingway.

J: Exactly. I'm in total agreement with that. You're always shooting for something, keeping a carrot in front of your nose for growth. Some people, though, they hear the groove, it's saleable and they stay there. People go, "*Court and Spark* was commercial; why didn't you stay there? You had a winning formula." This has been a criticism of me.

Well, I didn't think there was a great deviation between *Court and Spark* and *Hissing of Summer Lawns*. I thought the changes from album to album were very subtle. Everybody saw them as dramatic departures. The only thing that I did on *Hissing of Summer Lawns* is I cut the jazzers some slack, so they went further into jazz in their performance and that was the kiss of death. It worked on people's prejudice, "that jazzy stuff that she does."

Hissing got trashed. But meanwhile out there was Prince. That was his first Joni record, and it was his Joni record of all time. I became the hero for that. So while getting publicly trashed by the press, and a loser to the businessmen and to the public, to the young artists coming up — whoa! They could still see that there was something going on there.

Then I just got even more experimental with *Hejira* — trashed again.

More experimental with *Don Juan's Daughter* — trashed again.

But by that time Charles Mingus was totally intrigued with me and sent for me to work on his last project, which was an honour and also — now you're being pulled into meat-and-potatoes jazz. But meat-and-potatoes jazz, as good as it was, is still retro. It's done.

So I thought now I'm going straight into the jazz world, collaborating with a jazz master, but I've got to come in as an innovator, without disturbing him. Even Jaco [Pastorius] backed me up. Jaco said, "What are you doing this tired old shit for? Your work is more progressive than that." I kind of knew it, but it's not for me to say. I was surprised that Jaco also knew it and with that leg up, I had the courage to take it.

And so I gave the call and I pulled that band together and I gave them some very unorthodox instruction, which they followed but they didn't grasp. They didn't get it till about ten years later. One by one they went, "Did you hear that shit we played?"

M: Your instructions must have been quite unorthodox, if those terrific musicians didn't grasp them till years later. What were they?

J: Well, what I told them was "There is no leader here. I want to break up the traditional relationship between the drums and the bass locking up. We are all following the words."

When you tell this to jazzers — they're not word people. They're note people. But I told them you got to follow the words and the words are wordy, but you got to get in between the words. You can't scribble over them. You can't dominate them. You got to support them, and in the breaks where there are no words — *Bam!* There's a kind of a free for all. Everybody is playing off of everybody else.

M: What attracted you to jazz initially?

J: I had an icon. I loved Miles. I had some Miles records. I had the hottest new sound in jazz. And I loved Jon Hendricks' lyrics, and Annie Ross and [Dave] Lambert. Miles in particular, because I loved the sound of the Harmon-muted trumpet.

M: And that was when you were how old?

J: Fourteen, fifteen, sixteen.

M: So young!

J: Before I became a musician.

M: Where did you find those records?

J: Painting . . . I did a UNICEF Christmas card. They paid me in Miles Davis. I did a mural on somebody's wall. They paid me in jazz records.

M: Did they know that you liked jazz? Or was it just a coincidence?

J: I was a beatnik to them . . . I was doing satire on the beats. People thought I was serious but . . .

M: "Reality can permit itself to be unbelievable, inexplicable, out of proportion. The created work [. . .] cannot permit itself all that." This is from the writer Aharon Appelfeld.

J: No. You have to be selective. That's what I like about the song form, as opposed to writing my book. The song gives me a corset. When you take the corset off, I'm overwhelmed. The structure of the melody gives me an architecture and it forces me to be economical. Give me a blank page, I could drown myself in details and twist and turns and digressions. The song enables me to reach clarity.

M: Because there is a certain discipline to it?

J: Especially in a song, because the way I write songs, I'm trying to tell . . . Like when they ask me to do songs for a movie, they always reject them because I tell the whole movie in the song. [laughs] I end up kind of reiterating it.
    [With] *Midnight Cowboy*, they asked me to do it and they rejected it for that reason, that I told the whole movie in this song, right? Put it at the end over the

trailer, everybody knows the plot by then. My music is always rejected by movies. It's never been accepted. [laughs]

I was in an all night movie
When I heard the usher say
Here comes the midnight cowboy
Got his gun hired out for pay

You were walking kind of faded
From the Netherlands Hotel
With your hat tipped off to ladies
Really looking well

Aw Joe, why don't you go back home?
Really hate to see you falling down
Get out of town

Well you came to New York City
With a calendar full of gold
Now they locked it up in the bedroom
And they kicked you out in the cold

Now you can't afford a little blanket
You can get one from a friend
You can trick one off the corner
You can even keep the change to spend

Hey Joe, why don't you go back home?
Really hate to see you come falling down
Get out of town

There's a soldier in the depot
He's a fighting nightingale
Wearing western boots and buckskin on
Reading fortunes from the penny scale

Now today he's got a quarter
For the photograph machine
But tomorrow he'll be lonely lonely
That's the way it's always been

Poor Joe, why don't you go back home?
Really hate to see you falling down
Get out of town

I was in an all night movie
When I heard the usher say
Here comes the midnight cowboy again
Got his gun hired out for pay

You were walking kind of faded
From the Netherlands Hotel
Hat tipped off to ladies
Tipped off to gentlemen as well

Well Joe, why don't you go back home?
Find yourself a girl and settle down
Get out of town
Get out of town

Find yourself a girl and settle down
Hey Joe, looking more lost than found
Get out of town
("Midnight Cowboy")

M: I'd like to move on to a couple of lines from . . . God, I can barely see even with these glasses.

J: Your glasses are beautiful. The blue and the black in the middle. I've been looking at them all the way through. As the light just changed, they're really nice now. I've never noticed the black. The blue I noticed. Beautiful glasses.

M: Thanks. Here, like a child, I jotted stars near the verses from your "Come In from the Cold."

J: Oh, that's the song that I intentionally plagiarized a line because I found that Leonard and Bob lifted lines from literature. I caught them with their hand in the cookie jar and I was feeling kind of self-righteous. And so in order to eliminate my self-righteousness, I stole from Camus. See if you can spot . . .

M: "Back in 1957 / We had to dance a foot apart"

J: "And they hawk-eyed us / From the sidelines / Holding their rulers without a heart."
    They really would come with a ruler, and if you got too close they'd stick it between you, so there was no genital contact in waltzes.

M: I've never seen this.

J: Yeah. We had to dance a foot apart. So this is from life. Go on. I want to show you where I stole from Camus.

M: "And so with just a touch of our fingers / I could make our circuitry explode."

J: "We could make" — does it say that?

M: No, it says, "I could make."

J: Misprint. Change that to "We could make our circuitry explode."

M: "All we ever wanted
   Was just to come in from the cold
   Come in
   Come in from the cold
   We were so young,
   Oh come in
   Come in from the cold

   We really thought we had a purpose
   We were so anxious to achieve
   We had hope
   The world held promise
   For a slave
   To liberty
   Freely I slaved away for something better
   And I was bought and sold"

J: "And all I ever wanted / Was to come in from the cold." Keep going because I want to show you the plagiarism . . .

M: "I feel your legs under the table
   Leaning into mine
   I feel renewed
   I feel disabled
   By those bonfires in my spine
   I don't know who the arsonist was" [laughs]

J: [laughs] Yeah, which one of us. Who is doing this? "Which incendiary soul"

M: "But all I ever wanted"

J: "Was to come in from the cold"

M: "Come in
   Come in from the cold

You were so warm
Oh come in
Come in from the cold

I am not some stone commission
Like a statue in a park
I am flesh and blood and vision
I am howling in the dark
Long blue shadows of the jackals
Are falling on a payphone
By the road
Oh all they ever wanted
Was to come in from the cold"

J: I think this is the Camus one.

M: Look at how I marked it.

J: You marked it? Because this is stolen, I can't even remember this part.

M: "Is this just vulgar electricity"

J: That's mine.

M: "Is this the edifying fire"

J: Okay, that's Camus, "edifying fire." That's his phrase.

M: "It was so pure / Does your smile's covert complicity"

J: See this is Camus's vocabulary, not mine. I would never use words like Camus: "covert complicity" and "edifying fire." Because it impedes Irish English as opposed to Cromwell's English. I would never use Cromwell's English. Irish tells a tale with small words. You don't have to look it up in the dictionary, unless it's *hejira*, which is a borrowed Arabic word. If you use Cromwell's English, it gets so heady, cerebral. You have to say, "What do these words mean?" And you don't get the picture. You want to have a direct communication, then see the picture.

M: Look, at how underlined this stanza . . .

J: That's what I did in my reader. I underlined lines that I liked.

M: "When I thought life had some meaning" — past tense
"Then I thought I had some choice
I was running blind
And I made some value judgments
In a self-important voice
I was out of line"
In brackets, it says here . . .

J: The Greek chorus in the song is what's in brackets. It throws off the rhyme scheme of the main text, but not when it's in the background, where it's just a counter melody.

M: "But then absurdity came overnight"

J: That's where I like you to laugh. This is optimistic. This is Buddhist.

M: "I long to lose control"

J: "Into no mind" — which is Buddhism. "I long to attain."

M: "All I ever wanted / Was just to come in from the cold."

J: Yeah, it's a pretty good description of that pocket of pain.

M: What pocket of pain inspired "Magdalene Laundries"?

J: "Magdalene Laundries" . . . Hans up in Canada said to me, "Joni, you're basically a cheerful person, but you write these melancholy songs. I think it's because you write late at night. You should write in the daylight." So [in daylight] I sat out on the rock and I got the music for "Magdalene Laundries," which, if you play it, it's very like the landscape there.

Then I went to the supermarket and in the checkout line there was a newspaper. I never buy the newspaper, but there was a woman ahead of me with a big order, so I was reading this thing about the Magdalene laundries. It was front page news that some land had been sold in Dublin for development by the Catholic Church and in grading it to build on it, they unearthed all of these unmarked graves. Magdalene of the Tears, Magdalene of the Torment . . .

And it told a little bit about the Magdalene laundries. It was really compelling to me, so using my experience with nuns in hospitals, and my experience [of] how I was treated as an unwed mother . . . you can easily project from your own personal share of prejudice. Although I was never incarcerated in a place where I could never get out. I could understand their situation to a degree. And so I wrote it as if I was an inmate there and I wrote it with considerable authenticity, and it enabled the last of the Magdalene laundries to be closed. So there's another song that went into the culture and did some good.

Most girls come here pregnant
Some by their own fathers.
Bridget got that belly
By her parish priest.
We're trying to get things white as snow,
All of us woe-begotten-daughters,
In the steaming stains
Of the Magdalene laundries.

Prostitutes and destitutes
And temptresses like me —
Fallen women —
Sentenced into dreamless drudgery . . .
Why do they call this heartless place
Our Lady of Charity?
Oh charity!

These bloodless brides of Jesus
If they had just once glimpsed their groom
Then they'd know and they'd drop the stones
Concealed behind their rosaries
They wilt the grass they walk upon
They leech the light out of a room
They'd like to drive us down the drain
At the Magdalene laundries

Peg O'Connell died today.
She was a cheeky girl,
A flirt
They just stuffed her in a hole!
Surely to God you'd think at least some bells should ring!
One day I'm going to die here too,
And they'll plant me in the dirt
Like some lame bulb
That never blooms come any spring,
Come any spring,
No, not any spring . . .
　　　　　　("The Magdalene Laundries")

J: The Irish were very upset about it. The press was all over me when I performed it: "What business was it of mine? Was I Irish? Was I Catholic?" One girl confronted me in Saskatoon [at] a place called Lydia's. It was on the patio and she was very testy with me. She went [mimicking an Irish accent], "That song of yours, 'The Magdalene Laundries.' Are you Irish then?"

I said, "Well, my mother was."

And she said, "Are they Catholic?"

I said, "No, Protestant."

"Well, what business is it of yours? I mean, it was bad enough with Sinead and the Pope but at least she was one of ours." She said, "Do you know I'm living here in Canada and I'm living in sin with a Protestant? I haven't told me mother yet. Actually, the truth of the matter is, I married him. So I'm going to use the song to break the ice," she said. "Anyway, it was well put." She put me up on the carpet for a while and then she went, "But anyway, it was well poot."

M: I noticed, Joni, when we talk, your past and present tense get interwoven. Do you feel that the past and the present are interwoven in your life?

J: I never thought about it.

If past and present are woven together, your recent actions are setting into action things that are happening now. It is a long and mysterious chain of events. Everything that you do counts. Like, if I had not gone to see the Hopi dancers dancing with live snakes, sidewinders, there would be no way that I could draw the strength to stand up to 600,000 people at the Isle of Wight.

M: I find that past and present are united even with the future.

J: The subconscious knows no past, present, and future. Like, when I tried to quit smoking, I went to a hypnotist and he tried to hypnotize me and he said to me, "You're gonna laugh now" and I laughed, but I laughed because I wasn't hypnotized.

He said, "You're not hypnotized."

I said, "I know. Why is that?"

He said, "Well, what I think it is, is that the gap to your subconscious is wide open."

I said, "Well, why is that?"

He said, "Well, little kids have that but generally, they're told by seven to quit daydreaming. And they work on it, and eventually it seals."

So I suppose if that's true, I have easy access to the subconscious.

M: And therefore easy access to the muse? Do you think there's a relation to . . .

J: I am driven by my own muse. That's why I would never let a producer on me, who was gearing me towards commerce and telling me, "That's wrong" or "You can't do that."

That's the only moment I had trouble with Henry [Lewy], where my ideas of distortion made him look like a bad engineer and his ego stepped in. Twice, in thirteen

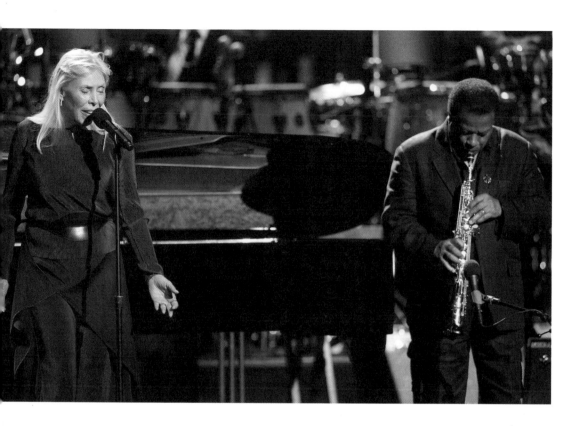

Joni and Wayne Shorter perform during a 2007 all-star tribute concert for Herbie Hancock
AP Photo/Rene Macura

years. Other than that, there was no ego involved, like [with] Wayne [Shorter]. The way Wayne works is the difference between a genius and a talent.

The talent will come in, a great player. He'll listen to my music, he'll write out the chord changes, he'll notice how weird they are and he'll go, "Oh, this is deceptively simple." Then he'll figure out a part. He'll play it. The first time, it'll be a little rough. The second time, it'll be better. The third time, he's not gonna deviate. You'll get up to take four, and I'll ask him for take five, thinking maybe he'll put a variation on it, but he won't. He's got his part, he's done it, and he's giving you a dirty look like, "Don't you have it already?"

A talent is pretty good to work with.

A genius like Wayne is always exploring, so he's gonna be more inconsistent. He's gonna be all over the place. Because he's going into new territory. The great things nearly always come on the edge of an error. What comes after the error is spectacular. So if you are hung up on the error, you missed the magic.

If you're hung up on concept, then when a lucky accident happens, you're still stuck in the tunnel vision of "No, that's not what I wanted." So you're approaching it intellectually and not fluid enough or open enough to see "This is better than what I had in mind" and go with it. I think it takes a degree of alertness and fluidity.

Jaco [Pastorius] also, as out of control as he was, he was doing the things that I was trying to get bass players to do, but they wouldn't. One of the bass players who wouldn't, told me, "There's this really weird bass player in Florida. You'd probably like him."

I said, "Would he do this?"

"Yeah, he's weird."

So I sent for him. And, sure enough, he — Jaco — and I were craving the bass to do the same things. I wanted the bass to be less supportive and more of a show-off. Jaco was the biggest show-off on the bass that you ever saw. And he would play notes on the bottom end that were technically outside the chord, which then makes it impossible to write because the bass note is supposed to indicate what key you're in. And you have to set up the staff again and rewrite it. So I'd say, "What's the problem? We're not doing it on the paper anyway. We're going straight to tape." But most bass players wouldn't.

I was so grateful for Jaco, who had a progressive vision of a new way to vent the bottom in of music.

There are some jazzers who think that I'm trying to do jazz and getting it wrong, but I don't want to make jazz. It's been done. I want to make something new. I'm trying to be a new tributary. By getting directly at my muse and expressing the harmonies that depict my emotions accurately in their complexity, I'm trying to make something that's new, that's outside the laws of jazz.

M: An artist doesn't need a producer, you said, "a record producer is a babysitter." And yet you did have a record producer.

J: On?

M: With Larry Klein, no?

J: Because he was my husband. I had married a bass player and he had turned into a producer. I guess he felt we spent too much time alone otherwise.

My manager, Elliot, said, "Why is it that every man you go with has to produce you?" Well, they do. It doesn't mean they take me over. It means we waste a lot of time with me fighting for my rights, you know, it was a lot of "Joni, you're so controlling."

When [an inexperienced producer] was hired to do the box set, they paid him a lot of money and gave him power over me. And he was deluded enough to think he knew more about my art than I did. [He] was hired to pick my repertoire. He was not qualified. And once given that power, he wouldn't let go. And he started telling me stuff. So I told him, "Okay, on the first album, I want you to just give me a recording with no opinion on it. I want to hear what's on the tape . . . I never heard what's on the tape," because that album was all screwed up, Crosby fucked it up. I mixed all my albums [after *Song to a Seagull*].

So what did they do?

"Oh, we're listening to 'Sisotowbell Lane.'"

I said, "'Sisotowbell Lane' is one of the ones that we're leaving alone. We're not mixing that. Why have you spent three weeks . . ."

"Well," he said, "but Joan, these songs, they all sound different."

I said, "Look, 'Marcie' is a narrative. You're singing in concert style to the back of the hall. It's more of a belter style of holding long notes. 'Sisotowbell Lane,' you're singing it like you're sitting five inches from the person around a campfire. It's a different style of singing. The vocal quality is . . ."

He's going, "Don't worry about things that you don't know about."

"You're gonna try and make them all sound the same? You can't! And if you do that, what a travesty it would be. You just don't understand. You should not have been put at the helm. Give me back the reins."

It's for that, that you get called a control freak. Some stupid asshole gains control, doesn't know what he's doing, and you go, "Give it back to me, you moron" as nicely as you can. [laughs] You do three or four rounds diplomatic and then you go, "You're a fucking know-nothing." And then you get rude, right?

Finally, he finds a few men in Minnesota and they say to her, "You could have caught more flies with honey than with vinegar." And you say, "This was not a situation for honey. You don't have time."

M: You don't have time because studio time is very expensive, and you wanted to cut costs — so that you could stay under the radar of the record executives? [laughs]

J: With Klein I had to go, "Well, this is very nice" and "Oh, that's beautiful." I had to spend an hour with the clock ticking stroking ego . . . "But here we had a problem," you just say, "I can't play to this. The bass player is playing back of the drummer."

"Oh, the bass player always plays back of the drummer."

"Well, not a drummer from Shreveport, Louisiana. He's playing as far back on the beat as you want to be. If he plays behind him, just because that's the way it's always done, it's gonna drag the time, and it's slow and I can't sing to it."

"Well, that's your problem."

I said, "No, get the bass player back in here. Have him sing on top of it."

"Well, that's not the way it's done."

"Well, that's the way it's got to be done."

I couldn't get it across.

It's the same with [that producer]. These people, they think you're after something invisible.

Well, although I'm probably getting a little more emotional than we want, over there I can stay calm.

M: Control, ego, at work with men, women . . .

J: Yes, it's an interesting topic.

In all fairness, Klein led me in that direction with the sound of that board, which was a different, more contemporary sound. He and I did some very good collaborations. But *Dog Eat Dog* was a nightmare. I had to fight for every note that I put on that record. People think Klein took me over, but he didn't. We just changed the palate, and I played nearly everything on there, everything was under my guidance.

M: *Dog Eat Dog* was a nightmare to create, you say, yet it's a very good album. It's really special.

J: Yeah, because it was my political awakening.

I can't decide
I don't know
Which way to go?
The options multiply
The choices grow
Which way to go?
What should I buy?
What should I be?
Which way to go?
(Doctor, Lawyer, Indian Chief)
So much comes at you
Too much for me
Which way to go?

Elusive dreams and vague desires
Fanned to fiery needs by golden boys
In ad empires
Fiction
Truth
Fiction
Truth
Fiction
Truth
Fiction
Fiction of the boob tube
Fiction of the papers
Fiction of the image
    and the image makers
Fiction of the magazines
Fiction of the movies
Fiction of the "Buy me," "Watch me,"
    "Listen to me"

I can't decide
I'm so confused

Which way to go?
I'm being useful here
I'm being used
Which way to go?
Some line gets drawn
What line is this?
Which way to go?
Could be a threshold or a precipice
Which way to go?

Elusive dreams and vague desires
Fanned to fiery needs by sexy boys
In flaming TV fires
Fiction
Truth
Fiction
Truth
Fiction
Truth
Fiction
Fiction of obedience
Fiction of rebellion
Fiction of the goody-goody
    and the hellion
Fiction of destroyers
Fiction of preservers
Fiction of peacemakers
    and shit disturbers

Fiction of the moralist
Fiction of the nihilist
Fiction of the innovator
    and the stylist
Fiction of the killjoy
Fiction of the charmer

Fiction of the clay feet
    and the shining armour
Fiction of the declaimers
Fiction of the rebukers
Fiction of the pro and the no nukers
Fiction of the gizmo
Fiction of the data
Fiction of the this is this
    and that is that — Ahh!

I can't decide
I don't know
Which way to go?
The more you learn
The less you know
Which way to go?
Some follow blind
And never know
Which way to go?
To lead you need some place to go
Which way to go?

Elusive dreams and vague desires
Fanned to fiery needs by deadly deeds
In falling empires
Fiction
Truth
Fiction
Truth
Fiction
Truth
Fiction
Fiction of the diplomat
Fiction of the critic
Fiction of the Pollyanna
    and the cynic
Fiction of the coward
Fiction of the hero
Fiction of the monuments
    reduced to zero
    ("Fiction")

M: Was it the nightmare in the making of *Dog Eat Dog* that triggered this verse from "Taming the Tiger": "I'm a runaway from the record biz / From the hoods in the hood"?

J: No. The men, the executives, were like sexual tourists in my business. They were grabbing their crotch and saying to secretaries, "Swing on this, bitch." One guy pulled it out and said, "Watch me, watch me" and came all over his secretary's desk.

    And I thought, "With men of this kind of character running the music business, how can there be any room for grace or elegance?" They have no morality, no ethics. It's just a dirty dog race.

    I was surrounded by pigs at the time. Pigs.

M: When you wrote "Sex Kills," was it triggered by those record executives, or by AIDS?

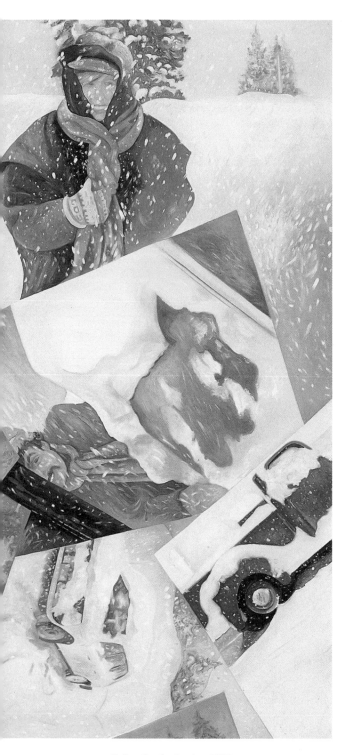

J: It has something to do with both. Yeah, sex sells and sex kills. It has that to do with AIDS. You have to go through it verse by verse. I'll see if I can remember. It has to do with justice.

> "I pulled up behind the
>   Cadillac;
> I was waiting for the light;
> And I took a look at the licence
>   plate —
> And it said 'JUST ICE'
> Is justice.
> Governed by greed and lust
> Just a strong doing what they
>   can
> And the weak suffering what
>   they must."

I was over in Brentwood and there was a white stretch limo in front of me. We pulled up to a light and I looked at the licence plate and it said, "JUST ICE."

Then I went to this little café and there was one person there. He said my name. I walked over to his table. He introduced himself, he was a lawyer.

I said, "A lawyer. I just saw a licence plate that said 'Just Ice.' You think there's any justice in America?"

He said, "Joni, you need to read Plato's *Republic*."

Before the Avalanche, 1982
© Joni Mitchell, photo by Sheila Spence

I said, "I do?"

And he said, "I guess lawyers aren't very popular."

Out of my mouth came "Not since Robespierre slaughtered half of France," because Robespierre was a lawyer and he went crazy. He couldn't kill enough.

It was one of those things when I went, "Oh, write that down." But I did remember it. I got Plato's *Republic*, I read it, and saw that Socrates' utopia was completely unjust to artists. You couldn't be a poet and a painter and a musician. It was illegal. Illegal! I don't know what the punishment was.

Anyway, the good line in Plato's *Republic*, to me, was the man in the street's line. They asked a man in the street what is justice, and he said, "Just the strong doing what they can and the weak suffering what they must." That's the bright line in the whole bloody book.

M: Moving on to "Stay in Touch":
"During times like this
The wise are influential
They can bear the imperfections
They can keep the honey"

J: "They can keep the harmony / No doubt about it / No doubt."
Yeah, "harmony." "Honey" is a misprint.

I make more sense than that. I don't get poetic for poetic's sake. See, that's "muddying the waters." You can keep the honey. What does that mean? Oh, I don't know. It sounds nice.

M: "Every song
Just a one-night stand.
Formula music.
Girlie guile!
Genuine junkfood
For juveniles!
. . .
I'm so sick of this game."

In this, from "Taming the Tiger," it seems you went further than *Dog Eat Dog*, no?

J: Yeah, I'm out of the music business, and those are pretty clear reasons. That's what my take at that time was, which hasn't changed much, but I'm not that mad at it now.

That's the exorcism, the frustration of having to work in an arena that is getting so perverse, that the standards are dropping, the sediment is rising to the top. That the business is run by sexual tourists, as I told you before. Lunch with lap dancers. How can I do my work in that climate? They can't possibly see the value of my work in that climate. I'm not in a whorehouse. [laughs] Nobody's gonna rent me for the night, do you know what I mean?

M: [laughs] Here is another one from "Taming the Tiger." I love that song. "It's hip / It's hot / Life's too short / The whole thing has gotten / Boring!" [laughs]

J: I guess anger does have its role in art, doesn't it? I guess it does.

M: And a healing element, no matter how angry you are.

J: That's what I find with Nietzsche. But you can't appreciate Nietzsche until you're in the bottom of the pit. And not everybody in the bottom of the pit is willing to face that much truth. So they're gonna stay at the bottom of the pit.

M: While we're at the bottom of the pit, I loved these lines from your "The Sire of Sorrow (Job's Sad Song)":
"Once I was blessed; I was awaited like the rain,
Like eyes for the blind, like feet for the lame.
Kings heard my words, and they sought out my company.
But now the janitors of Shadowland flick their brooms at me.
Oh you tireless watcher! What have I done to you?
That you make everything I dread and everything I fear come true?"
You obviously read the Bible.

J: Yeah, many times.

M: In what translation?

J: In many translations. Mostly the Gideons I read many times from cover to cover in hotel rooms in my youth. Then the one that you gave me.

When I set Job to music, I used several different Bibles because these translations have pretty much the same content but a little different language so that I could, as much as possible, get my rhymes without having to paraphrase.

M: I'm sorry to stay in this mood — "Nothing is sacred / The ceremony"

J: "Sinks."

Now this is Yeats. "Innocence is drowned / In anarchy / The best lack conviction."

I had to make it rhyme with "Give me some time to think." That's my line. I had to rewrite him a little bit. When I take something that someone else wrote, I sometimes have to add a little bit, but I'm very delicate to add it within their own style. I have to make it sing.

The funny thing is, the Yeats estate is run by the granddaughter and a lawyer — women. They sued Van Morrison for setting the Yeats poem to music. They were very, very sticky. Only classical music. And here in my version, to sing it, I had to take it out of the prose and restructure it to his first stanza, and I didn't quite have enough material. So I had to add lines to extend it to make it go into that shape. And when I found out how strict the granddaughter and the lawyer were I thought, "Oh my God." But it turns out, blessedly, they were fans. They just said, "Put 'adapted from' and you're fine." They let me do it.

M: "Being open to the miraculous," you called the coincidences that seem to unfold over the decades for you. Like, you pull into a gas station and you find the last verse to "Barangrill," or you go for a drive and on a licence plate in front of your car it says: Just Ice, but you see it as Justice. What led you to see the evangelist as a rock singer in "Tax Free"?

J: The evangelists at that time came on TV about 2:30 in the morning. It was Oral Roberts — and also Reagan was holding hands with Billy Graham. And there were billboards on Sunset Boulevard at that time, pink with black letters: "Rock and roll is the devil, signed Jerry Falwell and the Moral Majority."

Preacher preaching love like vengeance
Preaching love like hate
Calling for large donations
Promising estates
Rolling lawns and angel bands
Behind the pearly gates
You know, he will have his in this life
But yours'll have to wait
He's immaculately tax free
      "Multiple hundreds of thousands of . . ."
Tax free
      "Hundreds and millions of dollars"
            Tax free
      "A hundred billion dollars!
      And who is paying the price?
            Who who
      Your children are"
Pissed off
Jacked up
Scream into the mike
Spit into the loving cup
Strut like a rooster
March like a man
God's hired hands and the devil bands
Packing the same grandstands
Different clothes
      "Pot in their pockets!"
Different hair
      "Sexually active!"
Raise a screaming guitar
      or a bible in the air
Theatre of anguish
Theatre of glory
God's hired hands and the devil bands
Oh come let us adore — ME!

Lord, there's danger in this land
You get witch-hunts and wars
When church and state hold hands
Fuck it!
Tonight I'm going dancing
With the drag queens and the punks
Big beat deliver me
      from this sanctimonious skunk
We're no flaming angels
And he's not heaven sent
How can he speak for the Prince of Peace
When he's hawk-right-militant
And he's immaculately tax free
      "Our nation has lost its guts!"
Save me
      "Our nation has lost its strength"
Tax free
      "Our nation has whimpered and cried"
Save me
      "And petted the Castros"
Tax free
      "The Khomeinis' and the Kaddafis'"
Save me
      "For so long"
Tax free
      "That we don't know how to act like a
      man"
Save me
      "I think that we should turn the
      United States Marines loose on
      that little island south of Florida and
      stop that problem!"
      "I am preachin' love,
      I am!"
            ("Tax Free")

J: Immediately after I wrote this song, I was blacklisted by the Evangelicals. I was forbidden literature. But I got letters of congratulations from this one big place I thought was crackpot, the Crystal Cathedral. That minister wrote me a letter of congratulations saying, "We need more artists like you." And I went, "What? I can't believe that I'm getting a letter of congratulations from this guy."

Later, the Episcopalian Church also wrote me a letter of congratulations. They've got a very progressive bishop who comes out of marine biology who's in trouble with the mother church, so much so that they were trying to reinstate the heresy act. I heard her on the radio being asked, "How can you reconcile Genesis with your scientific background?" She said, "Easy. Genesis is allegorical." And I went, "Hallelujah! A thinking Christian!"

In the meantime, Chögyam Trungpa tells everybody in this church:

"You like this music?

"No, it's money music."

"You like this music?"

"No, it's money music. Who do you like?"

He said, "Joni Mitchell."

"Is that money music?

He said, "No." [laughs]

So I had this one lonely Buddhist, and all the rest of the churches with a couple of exceptions are down on me.

M: You mentioned Chögyam before . . .

J: Chögyam Trungpa had a powerful influence on my life in a very short space of time.

M: In what way?

J: Chögyam zapped me out of "my complications," and he took the "I" thing away. The I thing: "I want . . ." But when the I thing is gone, there's nothing to want — except that I still smoked cigarettes. My smoking was so reflexive, it was beyond want. [laughs]

But seriously the I thing: the ego; what is the birth of the ego?

Original sin. I think theology missed the point on that story. All of them. They use it as a device to keep women down. Eve screwed up. It was really interpreted in ways repressive to the female. Whereas I believe that the intelligent way to interpret it is that Eve was a metaphor for the planet, and we are expelled from Eden. What guards it on the outside? Cherubs and the flaming sword. What keeps us from Eden is the very concept of good and evil — dualistic mind.

Now this is when I got into Buddhism; Buddhism is very kindred in its thinking although it doesn't deal with these stories. Dualistic mind keeps us, in Buddhist terms, insane. Buddhism is the only theology that I know of that is actually attempting to get back to the state of mind before the fall. Maybe Hinduism, also.

Here, when Adam and Eve got their fig leaves up and God says, "Why are you doing that?"

"Because we are naked."

"How do you know you're naked?"

It's the awakening of, it's the birth of ego.

Now the trouble is with abolishing ego, which you need to be enlightened, is ego discerns. You don't have any discernment — "Oh, this doesn't taste right." You're like a dumb dog. You'll eat shit because you can't say — "Oh, I'm eating shit."

> I met a friend of spirit
> He drank and womanized
> And I sat before his sanity
> I was holding back from crying
> He saw my complications
> And he mirrored me back simplified
> And we laughed how our perfection
> Would always be denied
> "Heart and humour and humility,"
> He said, "Will lighten up your heavy load"
> I left him then for the refuge of the roads
>   ("Refuge of the Roads")

M: Were you introduced to Buddhism by Leonard Cohen?

J: No, I was introduced to Buddhism at art school when that infatuation with the East was floating around. I wasn't drawn to the mystical East at that particular time. They all seemed kind of like mystical gobbledygook to me.

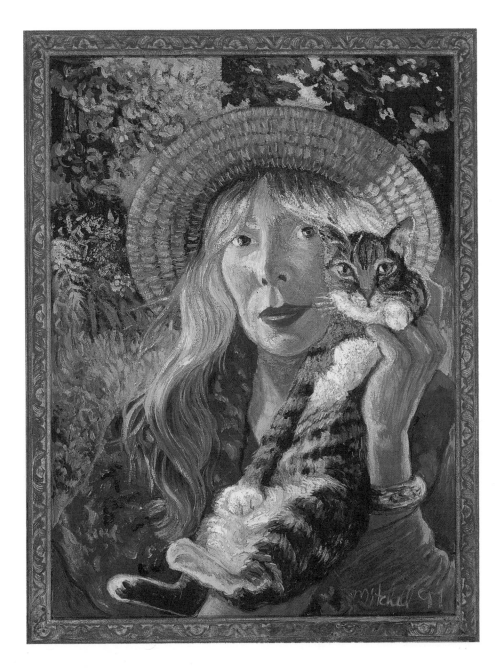

Taming the Tiger, 1997

© Joni Mitchell, photo by Sheila Spence

Later, I remember riding down Sunset with Leonard on the way to a restaurant that was some kind of Indian religion or fellowship, with white women in saris. We passed a building, a little shack that had a hand-painted sign that said "Scientology," and I said to Leonard, "What's Scientology?" and he said it was some crackpot religion. He later joined Scientology in New York, then found it kind of scary and got out. He eventually took up with a monk at Mount Baldy, a Japanese Zen roshi.

There came another time that we went, Leonard and I, to see the great Karmapa, who was the head of Chögyam Trungpa's lineage. He was visiting L.A. and he was in the home of a Hollywood movie star, with a podium, kind of, built up for him. Leonard had gone on behalf of his roshi. I had gone along with him.

Well, there was a receiving line, and as we approached Karmapa in this line, there were a couple of American monks on either side and I saw the monk recognize me and whisper something in his ear. Then when my turn came in, he invited me, "Oh, come and see us at the palace." And I thought, "Oh, the world's an Italian restaurant." Like, everyone sucks up to a celebrity.

I did some drawings of Leonard's teacher, Roshi, for a cookie drive; they were printed in a Zen magazine called *Zero*. So I had a little bit of contact with Roshi. He was a jolly little guy. He liked to drink and he liked to smoke and he liked to giggle, all things that I'm fond of — not so much the drinking, but smoking and giggling are up my alley. So I did spend a little bit of time in his company and Leonard's. This was in the early '70s when I was staying with David Geffen.

I'm gonna tell you a couple of stories.

One New Year's Eve, I was supposed to meet Leonard and Suzanne at the club On the Rocks, and I was at a New Year's party at Ringo Starr's. When I was leaving to get to On the Rocks for midnight, it was about eleven thirty, into the room came Mae West and two wrestlers — kind of like a Gorgeous George, a bleached blond bodybuilder on each arm. [She was] wearing a pink negligee with marabou feathers, and in her eighties still looking recognizably Mae West. She swaggered in and I couldn't leave. I sat down and talked with her and I remember the dialogue between us was pretty funny.

Anyway, midnight hit. There was all of the hurrah of that. And I went over to On the Rocks. In the meantime, Leonard had left. So I called with my apologies and we planned to get together the following night. And I remember we were sitting on the floor and suddenly Leonard said to Roshi, "Roshi, how do you get rid of . . ." envy or jealousy, I can't remember.

Roshi was distracted and just kind of giggled and ignored him. So I said, "Easy,"
because I have anger problems, but I don't have envy problems. "Easy," I said, and
my cigarettes were sitting on the table. So I picked them up and I said, "You just give
it up, like smoking." I dropped the pack of cigarettes on the table, like I gave it up and
then I made this bawdy English joke about desperately needing another cigarette.
Leonard just looked at me like I was from Mars.

It was never quite the same between us after that, and I don't know if it was that,
that I answered a question which was meant for Roshi.

Or . . . there was another thing.

Roshi served me a cup of tea, and I received the tea on the palm of my left hand, I
kind of guarded it, pulled it.

And Leonard said, "How did you know how to do that?"

"Do what?"

"Well, you took it in the correct manner."

"That's the way my father does it." It's just kind of practical. Nothing's gonna spill
if you do it that way and you draw it back towards you. There's a grace to the movement. My father, I could remember him receiving a cup of tea in company like that,
cautiously.

Following that event, Roshi came up to me and I hugged him, because I enjoyed
him. He was giggling and I was giggling. We were finding kind of the same things
funny that night. I hugged him. He was a little tiny man, in his seventies at that point.

Next day I get a call from Leonard and he says, "Roshi wants to move in with you."

I said, "Great. I've got a spare room. He's welcome to stay here." Because I know
he's gonna be up at Mount Baldy most of the time. He was married at that time to
a young Japanese girl who was a math, kind of, wizard. I didn't know much about
Buddhism and monks at that time. "He's welcome to stay here."

So they came over and, at the time, I was dating a very handsome actor, and so he
was here also. I was entertaining them in the living room, but I treated Roshi like an
elder monk, with more respect than the younger men.

Suddenly, Roshi jumped up and he said, "C'mon, Cohen, Roshi lonely. Let's go."

I realized, oh my God, I didn't know that he had some kind of romantic designs on
me, which I never would have guessed. And I was kind of horrified, coming from a
Christian backwoods, like, "Oh, you monk, you're not supposed to be human."

M: Something like that happened to me also, with Roshi, I mean. Also in the '70s, while I was on a shoot in Montreal, I get an invitation from Leonard to come to his house for dinner. So I walk in and I see this amazing-looking elder, almost like a halo around him, sitting cross-legged on a chair by the table. And I said to Leonard, "Who is this luminous elder?"

"That's my teacher. I call him Roshi," Leonard said.

So I turn to Roshi and start talking to him. Like, "Pleased to meet you, how fortunate you are to have Leonard for a student . . ."

Leonard interrupted with that grin of his that I love, "Roshi doesn't understand a word of English."

"Wow, is he ever radiant, Leonard, what a glow about him . . ."

"Yeah, but you know, he can't get it up. Would you get it up for him?" Leonard said, joking or teaching some illuminating Buddhist lesson? I couldn't tell.

It certainly illuminated to me that under my sort of bohemian, debonair, woman-of-the-world spirit is the daughter of my father: a religious observant Jew, who, though a bit shocked and very embarrassed, reverted to the Jewish traditional way of learning: answering a question with a question. "Why would you follow a teacher who can't get it up?"

"For the balance," Leonard replied, barely able to keep a straight face. "I have one teacher who can't get it up and one teacher who can't get it down."

J: Oh! That's why Leonard said, "One of my teachers can't get it up. One can't get it down." Irving Layton . . .

M: Strange how your Christian upbringing and my Jewish roots grab hold even after we think that we moved on . . .

Moving on to another stanza that I underlined. "Are you just checking out your mojo / Or am I just fighting off growing old."

J: Right. Middle-age crisis.

M: How old were you when you wrote this?

J: In my forties.

M: And you were "fighting off growing old" in your forties?

J: No. My marriage had just gone bad. Klein was bringing to the house the girls who were coming up behind me, who were emulating me. He was going out to dinner with them, and not letting me come along, and saying, "Don't come in here because you're disruptive. You intimidate them . . ."

It was true. Because they looked up to me, it would bog things down.

So in my own house, I can't go into my studio. There are girls in there that are getting good reviews while I'm getting bad reviews. He's going out to dinner with them. In the meantime, I have a miscarriage. He leaves me in the middle of a miscarriage. So I thought, I'm losing my instinct. I'm going feral. I was a suffering animal with no one in my corner, and being shunted: "Stay in your end of the cage, while I bring in your competition into the house and you can't come in here . . ." So I started painting what I call my gilded cage. I started painting murals on the doors to that room there.

People would go, "Oh, you're a victim." No, I'm not a victim. I have had to witness very bad conduct from the man that I have chosen, and my men friends . . . whether it's a sickness of our generation or the artistic men that I know, but irresponsible, selfish behaviour.

M: On a lighter note, Joni: "Man from Mars, / This time you went too far."

J: Read it again?

M: If you hear it in my accent, it's even funnier.
"Since I lost you . . .
I can't get through the day
Without at least one big boo hoo
The pain won't go away
What am I going to do?
Man from Mars
This time you went too far"
[laughs]

J: [laughs] Well, Nietzsche's like that. Nietzsche cracks me up like that because there is that same kind of audacity. Because he is a man without a country, like me.

M: You consider yourself a person without a country?

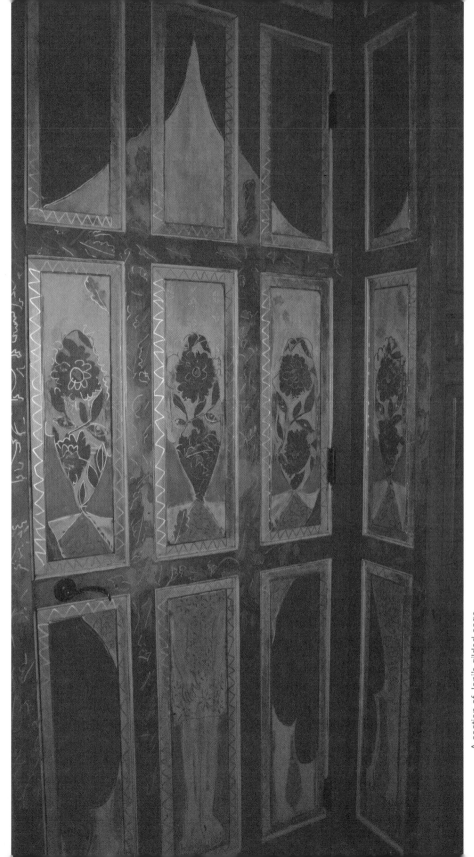

A section of Joni's gilded cage

J: Yeah. Way outside the box.

M: You don't consider yourself a Canadian, or an American?

J: I consider myself like a salmon. Does a salmon consider himself a South American or an American? I feel that these are artificially imposed categories. I feel an affinity to the crocuses coming out of the ground. I get a rush from meadowlarks' song. I'm not a Canadian in that I don't really know Ontario or Manitoba. I've had little experiences here and there, in Alberta and Saskatchewan where I've been many seasons, and especially British Columbia, where I spend so much more time there than anywhere. That little plot of land I have up there is home. But none of this is nationality. This is regionality. Saskatchewan, when it comes right down to putting up a statue of me, does not consider me a Saskatchewanian because I wasn't born there. Alberta, because I was born there, although I wasn't raised there, does consider . . . It gets really stupid.

> I'm going to take you to
> My special place.
> It's a place no amount of hurt and anger
> Can deface.
> I put things back together there
> It all falls right in place —
> In my special space
> My special place.
>   ("My Secret Place")

Canada . . . Canada gave me a Juno [award] finally after all of these years. For best producer. [laughs] For best producer, after my whole career, at the end of my career.

What I do best has never really been recognized in the award centre. It's ridiculous. Most of the award shows, you're forced into a position where you're supposed to be so humble when you're awarded, [while] the people are making such arrogant mistakes up there. Like, for instance, the Billboard award, which was also supposed to correct a mistake. It was called the Century Award. When I went to receive it, David Crosby was up there and he's going [mimicking his voice], "I'll tell you what a good songwriter Joni Mitchell is, man. When we came back from Woodstock, talking about it, and two days later she had a song written from what we said."

And I went, "I didn't get that from what you said." Already he's tailgating on it. Crosby had nothing to do with the writing of "Woodstock."

So can you understand? You don't feel humble. You feel pissed off. And it's inappropriate when you're being honoured to feel pissed off. [laughs] I've never really received an award for what I do best.

M: I cannot believe this, really: what about that music award in Sweden, the Polar Music Prize, that's like the Nobel Prize. You were the first woman artist to receive it — after Paul McCartney, Dizzy Gillespie, Quincy Jones, Elton John, Mstislav Rostopovich.

J: But the Album of the Year award, the day after I get finally get the Album of the Year award [in 2007], in the newspapers it says, "Serious songwriters, then and now" and I'm in the "then" column. So the whole system of awards to me is completely absurd . . . Same as it ever was. I'm a woman. It's a man's world. They don't want to give me prizes. It's like Mary Cassatt. Do you know who she was?

M: No, I'm sorry, I don't.

J: She was a painter. She was the one that invented Impressionism. She's painting in her studio and into the studio comes Manet. Manet comes in and looks at her work, trivializes it, and says, "Why are you doing all that 'dot dot dash' stuff?" Next thing you know, he's doing "dot dot dash" stuff. So is Seurat. The whole movement is born. And who gets the credit? Manet. They call him the father of Impressionism. They all copied this "dot dot dash," and formed a club called the Impressionists. And they called themselves "members of the academy." And Mary Cassatt was called an "associate of the members of the academy."

So history is "history" — it's not "herstory."

I'm a minnow in the industry but I'm greatly influential.

Like, the day that Whitney [Houston] died, Clive Davis was there, and I met his sons. A friend of mine who was in the backroom told me later that Clive's sons came back and said, "We just met Joni Mitchell. Who's Joni Mitchell?" And Clive Davis said, "Well, she's not as big a star . . . she's not as big as Whitney, but she's more important."

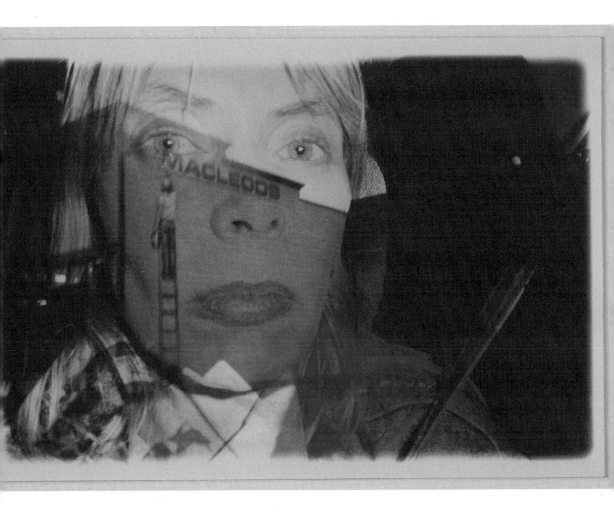

Photo Series, 1986
© Joni Mitchell, photo by Sheila Spence

I never was a big seller. Maybe *Blue* sold several million over time. Over time, some of my records went platinum. But they don't come out of the chute that way.

I didn't have very many radio hits. I had the hits in that "Circle Game" went to summer camp. A lot of them went into curriculum. "Big Yellow Taxi" became grade three in New Jersey curriculum. School kids in New York State of all races and colours sang that in lieu of "Old MacDonald." I'm proud of that [more] than if it went to number one on the charts. A lot of my music went into the culture sideways.

So I've been very influential. I've had a lot of fresh ideas. I was the first to do this, and the first to do that. I will never get the credit for it and I don't really care. The influence has been there, the ideas have introduced people to the possibilities of direction.

Let me digress. In 2000, they did a documentary rounding up the music of the twentieth century. I didn't even know about it. I turned on the TV, and I went, "What's this?" It was a British production. They showed a clip of me in this pink dress from this concert I did in England, just seconds of it, and then the narrator leaned against the wall, the way doctors do, and he goes, "I never liked Joni Mitchell. She's too twee." And then they moved on. That was the end of my segment. There was a put-down of my singing [from] some years ago and basically it was because I wasn't like a belter. Belters are very impressive. Whitney Houston, to me, was spellbinding when she came on.

M: I feel a tremendous sense of loss when a brilliant talent like Whitney Houston self-destructs.

J: Yeah. She was a gorgeous girl. She was a stellar singer, that I can go, "Wow!" And Mariah Carey too. Those belters are very impressive but they'll never replace the more intimate singers. For me, Billie Holiday still remains my favourite.

There were these girls, they came to see me in D.C. They were black girls and they had gone to all the young black singers and none of them liked Billie Holiday. They said she was a victim. Well, that's Diana Ross's fault. She depicted Billie Holiday in that way in the movie. I don't believe that Diana Ross's persona is anything like Billie Holiday's persona and the way she played it — very dramatic — but I don't believe that that's how Billie was. Just the thump bent of her voice, the strings of character that I hear, are nothing like Diana Ross's. But Diana played her own soul in that circumstance and it's very different.

M: You feel a kinship with Billie Holiday.

J: Right.

M: Why is that? Just a gut feeling?

J: It's a spiritual . . . I like her world-weariness, and something transcendental in her soul that rose above. There's never self-pity or ego in her voice. It's just a triumph for the soul over adversity. When these girls came and they were fans, one said, "She's a victim," I went, "A victim? Not in her art."

She fell into some bad company and some bad people got power over her. In spite of all of that, there was a part of her they couldn't spoil, that remained pristine in spite of bad company.

M: What do you think of those singing competitions? Do you ever watch them on television?

J: No. I watched one karaoke competition because I only get one channel in Canada, and there was one little girl, she was a punk, dyed-black hair and tattoos, and she was a great little singer. She was individual. She had her own thing. And she had some subtlety and some nuance. And she was beaten out by a good-looking blond Texas belter. And the judges panel, that's what they like. They like volume. As a matter of fact, I watched two of those episodes where they were encouraging her, the blond Texas belter to be more of a Texas belter. It's not . . . it's contemporary taste. It's just not mine.

There was this wonderful singer out of Scotland [Emeli Sandé]. I think she's black, not so much by her speaking voice but by her singing voice. She's a great new talent, the first one I've heard in twenty-something years. I wrote her name down but . . . anyway, she's a singer-songwriter. She was studying to be a doctor and then her music kind of took her over.

And she said, "When I was young, I used to sing like Mariah Carey." So she's got all those belter chops. But then she said, "I decided I wanted to be a real artist. I discovered Joni Mitchell and Nina Simone."

And the guy said, "Nina Simone and Joni Mitchell don't have anything in common."

And she said, "Well, yes they do."

I forget her exact use of words but basically what she was saying is it's a more personal, intimate way of singing.

Now the thing is, Nina and I have a lot in common.

When I met Nina, she came running through the shopping centre calling my name, "Joni Mitchell, Joni Mitchell!" And she came up to me and grabbed me. She's a big woman, swung me off the ground, kissing me, going, "'Ethiopia,' girl! 'Ethiopia.'" Swinging me around in circles, this big barrel of woman.

And when you think about it, we both sing intimately and we both have a passion for meaningful songs and we both play the piano. We have a lot in common. So why can't they see it? Because she's black and I'm white?

M: It's not only that you're white, Joni, you are blond.

J: [laughs]

M: I couldn't resist. [laughs]

J: When I'm having fun, I could be pretty blond.

M: When you start dancing, oh man, love that blond side. Well, it's not blond. It's black, as a matter of fact, the way you dance.

J: Yeah, I've had black people come up . . . I don't work my moves in front of a mirror or anything, and I'm inhibited because every time I went to dance, my mother would slap me down as a kid. Like, "Don't draw attention to yourself, don't show off." Anyway, B. Williams paid me a dubious call. I went out to dinner with him and some people and he went, "I liked the way you moved on stage. Nobody moved like you."

M: That is true, by the way.

J: "I would have fucked you," he says. All the nerve. And in past tense, to boot. It was doubly insulting. [laughs]

M: How good to laugh . . . You know what keeps surprising me during all the years, the decades I've known you and your work, is the affinity — yours with the black dance, music, singers, musicians, culture — and theirs with your work. Critically they appreciate your work more than most everyone of any other colour. Not long ago I saw this quote: "You don't realize what effect Joni Mitchell had on black musicians."

J: Oh, I do. I am aware and I'm honoured.

When I got my doctorate at McGill, it was amusing, one insult after another, until it got to the last speaker, a black guy from New York. He was a bass player and a writer for, I think, the *Village Voice* and he did a rap poem. "She's So Black" — that's what it was. "She's so black — da da da. She's so black . . . it took you fifty years to give her this award."

M: Well, according to the transcript of that event on the 'net, it was Greg Tate of the *Village Voice* who said you are "so black that black folk hear her as an inventor and not a vulture. So black that she's finally getting an honorary degree in her motherland after, what, four decades?"

J: They hate it when people do blackface. I thought, "Why didn't they object? Because it was not a clichéd black?" White people did not get that album.

M: You mean your album *Don Juan's Reckless Daughter*?

J: Yeah, I remember Janet Margolin said, "What is she trying to tell us? That black people have more fun?" But I got great reviews for that album in *Ebony* and all the black magazines. The black culture just ate it up. The brother reviewed it like a black artist. And when black culture puts me on *Vibe* magazine, did this piece, and it said, "All you kids with your tight abs and your one hit, you're not gonna last. Look at these people — Miles Davis, Joni Mitchell, and Carlos Santana. They're lifers." No white magazine would put me on that list.

M: Black/white divisions, even in music . . .

J: Once, at a party, Henry [Lewy] was there and also this band, a black band. They asked me if I would like to sit in. And I said, "Do you know 'Will You Still Love Me Tomorrow'?"

It was in the '80s. They had a guitar player, who became my friend, Rick; a piano player; a bass player; and a black girl vocalist. So I start to sing and I get to the first verse and I can't remember the second verse. We're coming up on it and Rick is watching me and he intuits that I'm gonna miss it and he covers — gives me the words so I finish the second verse. And I can hear the piano player behind me, I can feel he's like a horse that wants to gallop. So I get off the stage and I said to this piano player, "You've got it." He gets a whole verse to play, to gallop. Then I got back up on stage and we did the last verse and then I stepped down. And there was a record producer there [who] said to me, "How did you do that?"

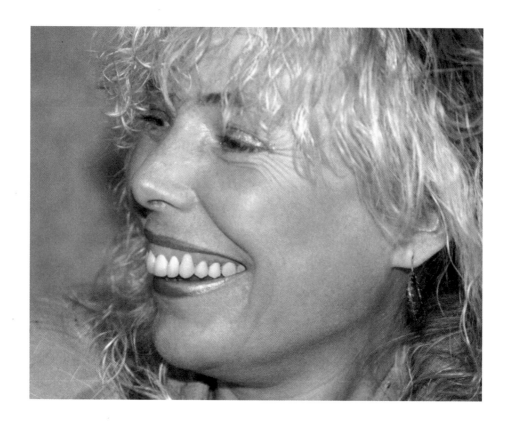

Joni, 1983
QMI Agency

I said, "Do what?"

"You came up with an arrangement on the spot."

I said, "Well, the piano player was interested to take off, so I gave him some room."

And that producer looked at me, the concept would never have entered this guy's head — of freedom.

Janet Jackson did a really rare and beautiful thing. Janet Jackson was being interviewed for her album. They were driving around in her car, and she's going, "Never mind my album, listen to this." And she's playing a track from *Chalk Mark in a Rain Storm*. She kept playing it. She's being interviewed for her own album and she's going, "This is on a whole other level." Like, "Check this one out." Can you imagine?

It's so foreign to me from all of the petty folkies, "You can't play that song because that's my song and this territory." All that small-mindedness.

What Janet Jackson was saying to that interviewer was "Our father told us, 'Find out who's the best and then beat 'em.' But this is on a whole other level." That's what she's saying.

The generosity and the excitement of finding something that she felt was on another level, I know. That's how I feel about Duke Ellington. At this point, there isn't that much left standing. It's unfortunate, because I have friends who still make music. I can listen to their things, even though really, in my heart of hearts, it's derivative. But they're very proud, "Oh, this is kinda like the Byrds." But why would you want to . . . ? But people do. They want to work in the tradition and that's what they want to achieve: kind of like the Byrds. And I can't adjust myself. I don't have to be mean, I can even enjoy it in a club, but really, for my own art, I just wouldn't go there. I don't want to do something kinda like anything.

Well, I have this birthday on the Day of the Discovery. So I have this abnormal need to plant the flag where no one else has been. It's the innovators I bow down to. Especially Duke Ellington or Charlie Parker, they were at the beginning of an explosion of a new idea. Others stole right and left from Duke and made the genre out of him but there was some stuff that was too far-out and too individuated that they couldn't . . . His harmony was weird and personal and it depicted a spirituality more sophisticated than his imitators.

M: At one point, Joni, remember when you were approached to write your autobiography, you told me that you want to start it with the line, "I was the only black man at the party."

J: Yes, to me, that was one of the more interesting scenes in my life. It started when I went one afternoon, down Hollywood Boulevard, looking for a costume to go to this Halloween party with friends of mine. I was wearing pink high heels and a jersey summer dress. It was an Indian summer.

I'm walking along in these stilettos and a black speed walker went by in a jogging suit, blue with white racings. It was the '70s. He was wearing a 'fro. And he had a New York walk, which they call the "diddy bop," where the shoulder comes forward and the fingers curl back and one leg is shorter than the other. It was a New York kind of street walk.

So he was diddy bopping by me, and as he went by he said to me, "Mmm, mmm, mmm, looking good, sister, looking good."

I broke out into a big grin and started mimicking, but in pink high stilettos, I was trying to get that walk down behind him. And he turned around to have another look and he caught me diddy bopping in pink high heels. He laughed and he kept speed walking away and he waved to me.

It was this beautiful exchange, as we glided by one another, and I went, "I'm gonna go as him."

So I turned into a wig shop, bought a 'fro, bought mutton chops, bought a moustache, bought some weird sunglasses, bought a Hollywood hat with rooster feathers in it. Not *Super Fly*, not a broad brim, but a little one. Went into a drug paraphernalia store, got a gold Superman medallion for around my neck and an obscene coke spoon to wear around my neck. Bought all of this stuff. And elevator shoes, cordovan leather, like Prince wears, you know, with a stacked heel, to give me some more height. Oh, and Egyptian brown, it was the Max [Factor] pancake colour that was contrived for the great black beauty Lena Horne.

Then I went over to Peter and Betsy Asher's, and it was burning a hole . . . I had to try all this stuff on. So I said to Peter, "Do you have a shirt and maybe a brown jacket, something you don't mind if I get makeup on it? And a pair of khaki pants or something, as long as you don't mind if I get paint on it, throw them in here." Because Peter is about my size.

He threw them into the bathroom and I put the makeup on quite quickly. And, as I put it on, I couldn't believe it — because as it went on, initially it looked like pancake, but as it dried it looked chalky for a minute and then it seemed like my body oils came up through it and it didn't look like paint at all. It had a sheen. It wasn't oily.

Then I went, "Oh my God. Even the way my fingers were at that time, the shape of them and everything. The palms were pink so they had pink pigment in them. It was unbelievable.

It changed the planes of my face and then you put these weird sunglasses and the blue eyes went away. And I had one gold earring on. When I came out, all of us, we couldn't believe it.

Oh, for the final costume, I used my rock award around my neck.

The next thing you knew, it started a fad. The black community was wearing these gold medallions. It was my rock award that was on a ribbon, that's all. But they became very fashionable and they went into the bling thing. They had sort of translated themselves into diamonds.

M: But long after that the kinship continues . . .

J: I like the ghetto thing. And much to my surprise, some gang leaders are fans and that's an interesting phenomenon. For instance, one of my friends had to go into the coloured zones and detag walls. That's very dangerous work.

M: I'm sorry. De- what?

J: Detag walls. Gangs' tags. They put their insignias on walls. You wipe them off, they'll kill you. It's good that my friend got this 300-pound black guy with him, because when you're detagging gang stuff, you need a big mighty gang lord at your side, who was also . . . serving time. That's what they were doing. Anyway, he mentioned something about going to dinner with me that night and

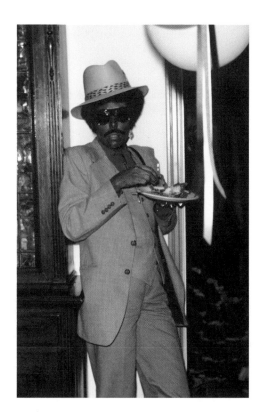

Joni in disguise at Peter and Betsy Asher's party
© Henry Diltz

this guy [said] he's such a fan of the music, which is interesting where music travels, that it travels into war zones, because that's what that is. It entered foreign countries because that's what that is. It's a foreign country at war.

I'm always amazed when it goes into those places. You think, "Okay, well, it takes a lot of sensitivity to like that stuff, and a lot of emotionality." And there is a guy who's second in command in a war zone who liked it. So it kind of gives me hope in a way.

M: You don't realize . . . I'm starting to sound like the African-American guy who says, "You don't realize what an influence Joni Mitchell had on black music."

J: I do, because I know Stevie [Wonder] for instance he considered his and mine philosophical music which I found very flattering. He and I were up for a lot of awards at the *Court and Spark* time, and those two projects were really fresh in the context of the business at that time. [His nominated album was *Fulfillness' First Finale*.] But neither one of us won very much, actually. I had five nominations and I won best arrangement or something, a behind-the-curtain award. Anyway, I thought that was gonna be a year for real music. He really was the most interesting . . .

There was one book called *Music of Living Legends*. It was a textbook and he and I were the only people included as twentieth-century composers at that time, from the pop field. He was like into Mozart and I was kinda like into, I think, Beethoven. Freddie calls me Beethoven in drag.

M: Who calls you this?

J: Fred Walecki, the guy who sold me a lot of my instruments. He comes from a classical cellist background family.

M: Does it bother you that you're becoming anonymous in some places? Like when you hear someone say, "Who is Joni Mitchell?"

J: I never really wanted to be famous because you would not be able to wander around. I always wandered around by myself.
I [once] went to a Korean doctor and he went, "Where's your bodyguard?"
"What bodyguard?"
"Where's your bodyguard?"
"I don't have a bodyguard. I don't want a bodyguard." I already made myself too exotic to fit in most places. It's bad enough as it is. I lay myself more vulnerable than most celebrities.
The press . . . I'm afraid of journalism. Even you, and you're my favourite writer of all, and I know you'll give me as fair a break as possible, but . . .

M: "I'm afraid of my own truth," you said at one of our interviews.

J: Yeah, because . . . people aren't gonna understand. They're not gonna understand . . . The standards are so low, Malka. There used to be a hard taskmaster to bring you up to a standard, but the standards are so abysmally low [now] and if you talk in terms of those standards, you're just a horrible human being. And the journalists, they try to lead me into a place where . . . I can't really speak my mind without stepping on people. I can't really talk honestly about this without people hating me. I feel stupid. It's like I've been hated enough.

M: Well, the press, the media are competing for the sensational and controversial, they have to sell and outsell saleable material.

J: I was their dream-come-true because I was so outspoken.

In the beginning . . . I was a pro six months after I picked up the ukulele — six months and I was a pro! That's the North American continent. Like how could I be a pro? Because I was young, I guess, and sort of cute. When you're that green and you're making money at it, America loves beginners . . .

And in the beginning, in the honeymoon, when I was a new artist, they always say nice things but after that, the longer I'm at it, the higher I raise the bar, the higher, the higher. You're too different, therefore you're dangerous, kill it. That's predictable, that's happened to every innovator.

But it gets you sometimes, like when the press and, in particular, the *New York Times*, Steven . . . I forget his last name, wrote, "She thinks she is a poet." I thought, "Well, I know I am a poet." If Jim Morrison, who chants old movie titles — "Riders on the Storm" — is a poet, I'm a poet. If Dylan is a poet, I'm a poet. If Leonard is a poet, I'm a poet.

A woman who was an expert on who was a poet and who was not put out a book called *Forty of the World's Best Poems* [*Break, Blow, Burn: Camille Paglia Reads Forty-Three of the World's Best Poems*], which is quite pretentious really. Not in the English language, but in the world! And she included my "Woodstock" in it. Then she called me for an interview for *Interview* magazine. So she comes in, and I've got her book. It's sitting in the living room in a pile. And at the beginning of it, she said to me, "You could have been a poet, you know."

Right? Well, you just put one of my poems in *Forty of the World's Best Poems* book and now you say . . . So I said, kind of, a little on the edgy side, "What prevented me?" I said.

And she said, "A book."

I said, "Well, I have a book." And I wanted it to be a book of select verse. I wanted to select what I think is a song from some poem, condense it down, but Random House said no. They were gonna call it "rock lyrics" because poems don't sell.

So there, I'm a rock lyricist and not a poet. In the pigeonholing of it all, I'm out-side. You know what I mean? It's not like any other rock lyrics. It's poetry.

I then decided, "Okay, this has gotten ridiculous, this exclusion has become absurd." So, before I sing this song, I'm going to send it to the *New Yorker* and have it printed. I sent them "Bad Dreams Are Good," and they were almost not gonna print it because I was academically incorrect. I said, "Well, are you gonna take out Bob Dylan's 'ain't' and put in 'isn't'? This is my poem. Take it or leave it." So they did print it and they put "poet–rock lyricist."

M: At least they didn't say "folk singer lyricist."

J: Right, but this crazy pigeonholing.

And the woman at Random House, when I was saying I wanted to do a book of poetry, like —

"A strange boy is weaving

A course of grace and havoc

On a yellow skateboard

Through midday sidewalk traffic

Just when I think he's foolish and childish

And I want him to be manly

I catch my fool and my child

Needing love and understanding."

That's got some meat on it and some poetry in it. You can't tell me that's not poetry. Those are the kind of things I wanted to isolate from "Help me I'm falling in love again," which is a song lyric.

She told me, "You're not a poet."

I said, "What am I?"

She said, "I don't know, but you're not a poet." Like that.

I said, "Well, did it ever occur to you that I'm a new kind of poet?"

The stuff that I'm reading doesn't have any humanity in it. Yeah, it doesn't seem to have anything to do with the living, do you know what I mean?

I think that the poets are housed in academic situations and don't seem to have any life. They're writing the most bloodless, egotistical stuff. They must just go through the faculty room to their typewriter or their computer now.

A strange boy is weaving
A course of grace and havoc
On a yellow skateboard
Through midday sidewalk traffic
Just when I think he's foolish and childish
And I want him to be manly
I catch my fool and my child
Needing love and understanding
What a strange, strange boy
He still lives with his family
Even the war and the navy
Couldn't bring him to maturity

He keeps referring back to school days
And clinging to his child
Fidgeting and bullied
His crazy wisdom holding onto something
    wild
He asked me to be patient
Well I failed
"Grow up!" I cried
And as the smoke was clearing, he said
"Give me one good reason why!"

What a strange, strange boy
He sees the cars as sets of waves
Sequences of mass and space
He sees the damage in my face

We got high on travel
And we got drunk on alcohol
And on love the strongest poison and
    medicine of all
See how that feeling comes and goes
Like the pull of moon on tides
Now I am surf rising
Now parched ribs of sand at his side
What a strange, strange boy
I gave him clothes and jewelry
I gave him my warm body
I gave him power over me

A thousand glass eyes were staring
In a cellar full of antique dolls
I found an old piano
And sweet chords rose up in waxed New
    England halls
While the boarders were snoring
Under crisp white sheets of curfew
We were newly lovers then
We were fire in the stiff-blue-haired-
    house-rules
                ("A Strange Boy")

M: You never wanted to be famous you said earlier, Joni, well, have I got a surprise for you . . . [laughs]

A few weeks before I flew here, I'm taking my shoes off before a class at this yoga/Pilates studio that I've attended for quite a while, when one of the instructors comes to me and says, "Malka, I didn't know you're famous." I said, "What makes you think that I'm famous?" "I saw a documentary on Netflix about Joni Mitchell, and you appear in it."

So just imagine, Joni, I'm just saying a couple of sentences about you in that documentary, and that instructor thinks I'm famous. Imagine you, a full hour on Netflix validated you to a Mega Super Famous Celebrity. [laughs]

J: Yeah. [laughs] That's why I was so grateful to Ted Turner, so are all the old actors and actresses who are still living, they're not scrapped; this whole world keeps them alive. And I remember thinking, "Gee, I wish we had something like that to keep the music alive," because it got so radically pigeonholed and I had so few hits that they just circle them ad nauseum — and it's not my best work. My whole catalogue is dying, and these little ditties are the things . . .

For a while Beethoven had a similar problem.

A friend who invented the metronome, I don't remember his name. He's an Italian inventor. For the sake of conversation, let's call him Metronomi.

So Metronomi comes to Beethoven and he says, "I make these wonderful music boxes and rich people are like children, they like to spend their money on toys. And these are wonderful toys. But they're made out of brass. If you could write something with a lot of brass in the arrangement, which would translate into this [toy], and write something with a bit of the French national anthem and a bit of the English national anthem, because people like to hear something they can identify with. We'll put this music on these discs and we'll sell them and you'll become famous and we'll make a lot of money."

And Beethoven went, "No," because Beethoven wouldn't pander. "No! I'm not gonna contrive something to what they like."

"Come on," Metronomi says. Anyway, he convinces Beethoven to do this.

So Beethoven writes this piece of music and, sure enough, he becomes famous in Paris and England and they want him to come there and tour and play. So he goes over there, and what do they want him to play? This godawful ditty that he hates. That's all they want to hear. They don't want to hear any of the good stuff.

That's the danger of it. If fame and fortune is not your motivation . . .

> No tongue in the bell
> And the fishwives yell
> But they might as well be mute

So you get to keep the pictures
That don't seem like much
Cold white keys under your fingers
Now you're thinking
"That's no substitute
It just don't do it
Like the song of a warm, warm body
Loving your touch"
In the court they carve your legend
With an apple in its jaw
And the women that you wanted
They get their laughs
Long silk stockings
On the bedposts of refinement
You're too raw
They think you're too raw
It's the judgement of the moon and stars
Your solitary path
Draw yourself a bath
Think what you'd like to have
For supper
Or take a walk
A park
A bridge
A tree
A river

Revoked but not yet cancelled
The gift goes on
In silence
In a bell jar
Still a song . . .

You've got to shake your fists at lightning
   now
You've got to roar like forest fire
You've got to spread your light like blazes
All across the sky
They're going to aim the hoses on you
Show them you won't expire
Not till you burn up every passion
Not even when you die
Come on now
You've got to try
If you're feeling contempt
Well then you tell it
If you're tired of the silent night
Jesus, well then you yell it
Condemned to wires and hammers
Strike every chord that you feel
That broken trees
And elephant ivories
Conceal

        ("Judgement of the Moon
        and Stars [Ludwig's Tune]")

M: You mentioned the muse in relation to Picasso, earlier at the restaurant, just before we were interrupted. What were you going to say?

J: I get criticized when I go relating to Picasso, but Picasso said to his secretary, "I need a new period. You get me a new house. And I'll get myself a new woman." And they did.

The men in my life did create a new pocket and a new direction and muses, like John Guerin. *The Hissing of Summer Lawns* was a point of departure, because I'm hanging out more in jazz clubs with him, because that's his world.

They all . . . even association with Carey who was more like a friend in Greece, who liked a certain kind of San Francisco rock 'n' roll. Some of the stuff on *Blue*, even though I only had a dulcimer there up in British Columbia, it went from less delicate to more bold, because I wrote that song for his birthday.

M: For Carey's birthday?

J: Yes, for Carey . . . I won't say his last name, because I don't think he wants to. "Carey, get out your cane."

> Come on, Carey, get out your cane
> I'll put on some silver
> Oh you're a mean old Daddy, but I like you
>
> Maybe I'll go to Amsterdam
> Maybe I'll go to Rome
> And rent me a grand piano and put some flowers 'round my room
>
> But let's not talk about fare-thee-wells now
> The night is a starry dome
> And they're playin' that scratchy rock and roll
> Beneath the Matala Moon
>
> Come on, Carey, get out your cane
> I'll put on some silver
> You're a mean old Daddy, but I like you
>
> The wind is in from Africa
> Last night I couldn't sleep
> Oh you know it sure is hard to leave here
> But it's really not my home

Maybe it's been too long a time
Since I was scramblin' down in the street
Now they got me used to that clean white linen
And that fancy French cologne

Oh Carey, get out your cane
I'll put on my finest silver
We'll go to the Mermaid Café
Have fun tonight
I said, Oh, you're a mean old Daddy but you're out of sight
                    ("Carey")

J: The muse for a man is a woman; for a woman, it's a man. Occasionally, I've written about women, like "Shades of Scarlett Conquering." But I used the first person, not like . . . Like a lot of Leonard's stuff is sung in the first person. But it's his "I." My "I" was a better device for a woman than "you."

"Bad Dreams" has a "you" and it's critical. It wasn't written about [Larry] Klein, but he got very upset about it.

And I suddenly realized for a woman to go, "You're this and you're that" critically, it's a patriarchal stance. Dylan can do it and get away with it, but I can't. So it's better for me to say "I," and people have the choice to see themselves in it, make that "I" their "I." Or it's my "I" and they can arm's-length themselves. But the "you" is a "lookee here."

So as much as I didn't like being called a confessional poet, I returned to the "I" device — "I am Lakota."

Can't you see that these "I"s are theatrical? That they're not all personal? But, no, they just assume everything I write is personal. I was never in the Magdalene laundries. But I understand the roles I sing, believe me.

"I wasn't a married girl
I just turned twenty-seven
When they sent me to the laundries
For the way men looked at me."

They sent this poor girl, fictional but typical, into this prison of slavery to be a drudge for the rest of her life simply because when she walks around the street, the men give her attention.

I was not in those institutions but I can write with genuine empathy. I can feel for the girls that get caught up in those situations, and that song has a ring of authenticity.

So does "I am Lakota," enough so even though I'm not Lakota, they sent for me to march with them on a broken treaty. At the time that this came out — "Courts that circumvent — choke Lakota / Nothing left to lose" — we're dealing with a current book and treaty and they were about to march on the Black Hills and they sent for me to march as a dignitary, which I did.

Now, I really did them a disservice because I think that they wanted me to draw attention. But because I don't do that, I didn't tell the press that I was going, so it was very secret. I marched with them, but I didn't realize what my mission was until afterwards. I went, "Oh, I gypped them. I should have called the press on this to draw attention." But I'm not a press-driven person.

I am Lakota	I am Lakota
Brave	Faithful
Sun pity me	Rocks pity me
I am Lakota	I am Lakota
Broken	Meek
Moon pity me	Standing water
I am Lakota	Lakota
Grave	Oh pity me.
Shadows stretching	
Lakota	I am Lakota!
Oh pity me	Lakota!
I am Lakota	Standing on sacred land.
Weak	We never sold these Black Hills
Grass pity me	To the missile-heads —
	To the power plants.
	We want the land!
	("Lakota")

M: Do you think that your affinity with the Native people stems from the geographical closeness, that you lived so close to the Native people when you were a child?

J: Yes, they came into town in their beaded leathers. It's in "Paprika Plains."

"In their beaded leathers they came to McGee's general store
And then smashed, smashing their alcohol bottles down on Railway Avenue."

I saw them as a child with their culture intact. They wore satin skirts and beaded smoked-leather moccasins and beaded jackets.

There was one incident, as a child in Maidstone, a Native woman went down the back alley [of the family home]. There was no dry cleaners in the town, so [my mother] had her coat lining out. It had a silver-grey satin lining. And she'd use gasoline on it to dry clean it and it was airing. So [the Native woman] went down the back alley, and my mother told me to go out and grab the coat off the line. The Indian would steal it for the satin.

It was a 300 population hamlet, two blocks of downtown. Sometimes during rationing, a call came: "McGee's has a brick of Neapolitan ice cream. There's one left." So my mother sent me down to get it.

When I got there — they had a box step, tiered all the way around, but wooden — there were a group of Indians and these tired, skinny horses with a buckboard parked out in front. And they were sitting, about ten of them on the steps, and I had to go by them, all in their beaded leathers, and very mahogany-coloured skin.

And I stopped and I wouldn't go in. I came back. My mother always said it was because I was scared. But I remember that it wasn't that I was scared. I was fascinated that a group of adults could sit like that quietly. And I loved their clothes. I was fascinated by the self-decoration, the solemnity, and the quiet. Whenever people congregate it's "blah blah blah blah" — I'd never seen adults sit quietly like that before.

When I was three feet tall
And wide eyed open to it all
With their tasseled teams they came
To McGee's General Store
All in their beaded leathers
I would tie on coloured feathers
And I'd beat the drum like war
I would beat the drum like war
I'd beat the drum
I'd beat the drum like war

But when the church got through
They traded their beads for bottles
Smashed on Railway Avenue
And they cut off their braids
And lost some link with nature
I'm floating into dreams
I'm floating off
I'm floating into my dreams

I dream paprika plains
Vast and bleak and God forsaken
Paprika plains
And a turquoise river snaking
("Paprika Plains")

When we recorded "Paprika Plains," I did an hour of improvisation, whittled it down to ten minutes in January, and then wrote a song around it, opened it up in August, and inserted the improvisation into it. Same piano and everything, but it had been tuned a lot of times, and I said, "You're gonna have to leave a gap there to tune up, because you're now out of tune with the piano."

"Oh, the princess and the pea." Again, it was Joni's sensitivity.

Mostly it's longer pauses between things, like a four count instead of a two count, so I need to lengthen it. Add a little more silence in before you hit this next note. But cutting air into the tape was the hardest thing. These days, with Pro Tools, you can move it in increments, and listen back, and move it in increments. But back then with tape, physically, you've got pieces of tape dangling off the console.

"You couldn't hear when you put the strings on it," they told me. The strings sawed across the splice. And the professor from Berklee Music couldn't hear it. The engineer, Henry [Lewy], couldn't hear it.

But when I met Mingus, first thing he said to me was "The strings on 'Paprika Plains' are out of tune!"

And I went "Yeah! Can you hear that?"

And he looked surprised.

I told him that nobody could hear it. "I'm glad! Thank you!"

I think he was kind of disappointed. He was trying to take the mickey out of me, like "your pitch isn't that good" or something.

M: Something similar happened to me back in those razor blade tape-editing days. I was editing my interview with Pablo Casals, weaving the interview with his recordings of Bach, and brought it to time, only to find that the producer wanted me to cut it shorter by a minute and a half. "But don't cut the minute and a half from Casals, cut it from Bach," that producer told me. "You can't cut a minute and half from Bach," I told her. "Cut it, cut it, no one will notice the cut," she said. But ten minutes or so after it was aired, I get a phone call from Glenn Gould, "How did you do the cut in Bach? It's a great cut . . ."

J: Sensitivity, it is a social pariah of sorts, but it's very rich and rewarding. You can hear things that other people can't hear, like dogs hear high signals.

M: For a girl who didn't read, you've got heaps of books, even in the pantry, and in your dining room, or what would be considered the dining room, it's filled with books stacked on every surface.

J: A lot of them I haven't read yet. Some of them are presents, some of them I've read partially.

M: Do you like to be surrounded by books?

J: No, it's not decorative. It's just that they ended up here because either . . .

M: You don't have any more space for them?

J: This is a nice place to read. But the ones that I'm reading now are stacked by my bedside. I've got five books going kind of at once. I get to a certain point . . . until I realize that it's kind of propaganda. And then I start another one.

Van Gogh and Emily Carr are writers that I love. They, both being painters, have a succinct way of describing things in snapshots, kind of. It's a painter's way of communicating, I think. It's the way of a visual person communicating. Even in a song.

Like "The Jungle Line," which I saw completely as a film, in black and white '60s-style cinéma-vérité. Against this black and white film, Rousseauian-style animation starts to come up. *Douanier* [Henri] Rousseau, the painter, enters down the stairway into a jazz cellar in New York where a jazz band is playing. As he sits there, from time to time with the wave of his hand, Rousseauian-coloured foliage appears. Like, he hangs a moon above a five-piece band. He puts a flower behind a waitress's ear with a wave of his hand. That poem is a black history poem and it gets quite surrealistic in places. You're trying to describe a film that was never made in that song. I can clearly see what the film of that should be.

Rousseau walks on trumpet paths
Safaris to the heart of all that jazz
Through I bars and girders — through wires and pipes
The mathematic circuits of the modern nights
Through huts through Harlem through jails and gospel pews
Through the class on Park and the trash on Vine
Through Europe and the deep deep heart of Dixie blue
Through savage progress cuts the jungle line

In a low-cut blouse she brings the beer
Rousseau paints a jungle flower behind her ear
Those cannibals — of shuck and jive
They'll eat a working girl like her alive
With his hard-edged eye and his steady hand
He paints the cellar full of ferns and orchid vines
And he hangs a moon above a five-piece band
He hangs it up above the jungle line

The jungle line, the jungle line
Screaming in a ritual of sound and time
Floating, drifting on the air-conditioned wind
And drooling for a taste of something smuggled in
Pretty women funnelled through valves and smoke
Coy and bitchy wild and fine
And charging elephants and chanting slaving boats
Charging, chanting down the jungle line

There's a poppy wreath on a soldier's tomb
There's a poppy snake in a dressing room
Poppy poison — poppy tourniquet
It slithers away on brass — like mouthpiece spit
And metal skin and ivory birds
Go steaming up to Rousseau's vines
They go steaming up to Brooklyn Bridge
Steaming, steaming, steaming up the jungle line
                    ("The Jungle Line")

M: You mentioned that Emily Carr is an artist you love. How and when did your admiration for her start?

J: When I read her books. I'd seen her paintings — we both painted the British Columbia forest, we loved the B.C. forest, we loved animals, we got sick . . . She never really said what she had, but she got sick all around the world, like me. She got sick in London, she got sick in Paris, she got sick in San Francisco. The only city that didn't make her sick was New York City, which is interesting.

And she would always return with this desire to capture the spirit of the B.C. forest. She admired the way the Indians were able to personify the spirits in totem language. She'd say in frustration when it wasn't working, "I can paint the trees, but I can't paint the spirit of the trees." I think she did. I think she did more than she thought she did. But I don't know what she was after, what she thought she didn't get.

It's her writing that I like. Her sense of adventure, and her descriptive ability as a writer, excites me even more than her paintings. Very economical, pre-Hemingway, Victorian times — the economy of her language and her ability to cut straight through. What she can say by omission, what she can intimate by leaving things out . . . There's just certain things about her, I think she's a great writer. I admire her greatly.

M: Can we turn to another that you admire greatly? Van Gogh. What is in Van Gogh that attracted you, that compelled you to paint him?

J: It's the only painter that I stood in front of his paintings and got a lump in my throat. That caught me off guard. Like "Both Sides Now" did to the man who was inspired to do the movie *Love Actually*. Toller Cranston did that to me in his Olympic skate. It's inexplicable how a gesture can do it or how a painting can do it. It's not a sad painting. There's nothing to make you cry. Why does it make you cry?

I wasn't such a Van Gogh fan until I went to the Van Gogh museum when I played a concert in Amsterdam in '73, and there it was laid out chronologically, and so you see Van Gogh struggling, chronologically. You see he doesn't have a sense of proportion. He's not greatly gifted. He's struggling and struggling and then you watch it come in.

M: Years later you painted yourself as Van Gogh.

J: Yeah, well, that was because after years and years of showing signs of growth, the press was diminishing it. The public voice was not recognizing the growth in my work. It was very frustrating and it also affected the record company, who swallowed it, and a certain amount of the buying public. So there was this negative, ignorant influence, and I thought, "What do I have to do? Cut my ear off?"

So I basically cut my ear off in effigy and I put it on [the *Turbulent Indigo*] album cover. It was black humour, but there was a certain amount of truth in it. And they got it. I got a sympathy win. They gave me Album of the Year that year, and I won a Grammy for that album cover. People kind of got the message in a way. It was one of my communications that connected.

Chögyam has a chapter that explains the hate-the-star thing. There's a love/hate thing going on there that the public has with celebrities. Like the litigation battles I had in the '80s.

M: You mean, the court cases with your former housekeeper?

J: Yeah, lawyers fell away because she was such a pain in the ass. She went through lawyer after lawyer, but she finally got a guy with parasitic sharks in his office who held on tenaciously and that put me through the emotional ringer.

But in the criminal court, the judge who tried the criminal case that she brought against me, said, "I looked at this case from both sides now, and I really don't see a case at all." [laughs]

M: That's great! [laughs]

J: But she took it to civil court, and the civil law, it's a con game. My lawyers were fleecing me. They dragged it out for five years and they repressed things that would have helped, and I couldn't figure out why. It was an education in corruption. It's interesting that I'm wealthy enough to see so much corruption.

You see a certain kind of corruption when you're poor . . . In that way, I think I've seen it from both sides. [laughs] I've had a full and rich life in that I've seen so much from so many different vantage points, from destitution to prosperity.

M: In your latest recording of "Both Sides Now," the one with the full London orchestra, you sing in the low register, not a hint of your soprano . . .

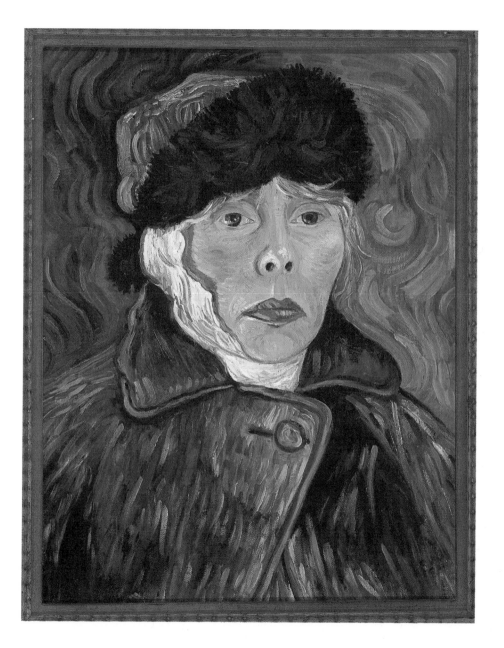

Turbulent Indigo, 1995

J: I'm not really a soprano, I'm really an alto. I started singing high because I started off mimicking folk singers and the girls were all sopranos, Baez . . . and I'm a mimic of sorts.

M: You had a tremendous range.

J: Falsetto. Soprano was false. But it was effortless. But my mother, thirty years into my career, said that she was an alto and so was my grandmother and I thought, "Fine time to tell me." My soprano began to decay on Rolling Thunder [Revue].

M: I listened to your recording before I flew here, and what I noticed this time is the breath. Whatever you did in the high notes, you did it using your breath. And you know the breath is in some ways more powerful than the note itself.

J: The breathing in between?

M: You are holding the tone and then it sort of turns into . . . hhaaa [breathes out].

J: Oh, let it disintegrate, it just peters out.

M: It has a vibrato, even in the breath. Even in a whisper. Keep in mind, I was listening with earphones.

J: Well, that's like painting, see? Like feathery lines . . . Nowadays, the style, a great singer has to belt. She has to grandstand.

M: Do you listen to music of recording artists of today?

J: Duke Ellington.

M: I mean new artists.

J: No.

M: You're not curious?

J: What I've heard doesn't interest me. I haven't heard anything exciting.

M: What about somebody like Lady Gaga?

J: I don't know. It's pageantry. It just doesn't . . .

M: And hip hop music?

J: If I see one more crotch grab . . . It's become a cliché. I like hip hop. It's the Charleston. I like the groove. I always loved black dance, but what has happened in hip hop is it's aggressive. If you go back to Duke Ellington, and Johnny Hodges, it's bordello music, so seductive, but it's like, "Oooh, they're playing to the ladies." Well, they're not playing to them anymore. It's more like men dancing for men, showing off their physical prowess. It's not great art anymore, because it's not yin-yang. It's too yang or too yin.

M: I wonder if it is not because I'm of the older generation that I see today's performers, like Beyoncé — a beautiful singer, so talented — and she's singing while dancing all over the stage, and up and down risers, and as if that's not enough to tantalize the audience, she's wearing next to nothing. I cannot imagine myself performing like that.

J: Me either. I mean there's burlesque . . .

M: It's so hard to do.

J: Well, it's hard, it's physical.

M: I cannot imagine you doing this.

J: I could though, but . . . I don't like the spirit of it. It's decadent. It's tragic really. That should be the rotten underbelly of a culture . . . The sediment has risen to the top. That's the way I look at it. It's not a graceful culture. I guess I have an appetite for grace, which is not in vogue.

The music is like bubblegum cards. When you have that many pieces of music, you're never gonna get to know them.

M: To me, it mostly sounds like the same song.

J: There's no imagination. Even in the '50s, all the songs that made it onto the airwaves sounded different. The Everly Brothers sounded different from Elvis. Everybody went for their own unique sound. But now everybody wants to sound like something else. There just is no concept of . . . individual is dead, that's all. Culturations just don't want individuals. They want worker ants and that's what they got.

M: It bothers me that I cannot catch the lyrics they sing.

J: The lyrics don't matter. They're just kind of chants. They're very repetitive. The '50s stuff, where we started from, was kind of like that too. I used to get Dell song-books. It didn't matter to me that they didn't mean anything. "Tutti Frutti." I would buy them anyway and learn the words so when it came on, I'd sing along. It didn't matter. No word was too dumb. It's fine when you're young like that.

> You wanna make Van Goghs,
> Raise 'em up like sheep.
> Make 'em out of Eskimos
> And women if you please.
> Make 'em nice and normal;
> Make 'em nice and neat;
> You see him with his shotgun there?
> Bloodied in the wheat?
> Oh what do you know about
> Living in Turbulent Indigo?
> ("Turbulent Indigo")

M: But as we grew up, I think our generation put a high value on the words, that's why the concert tour of you and Dylan, "just" the two of you, was a huge event. But then I was surprised to find out that Dylan didn't speak with you throughout the whole concert tour.

J: He didn't speak with anybody. Look out if he does speak with you. The time that he spoke kind of briefly to me [mimicking Dylan], "That song, that song that kills those chords. You gotta show me those chords. That song. That's a great song. If you sing that, you can go anywhere after that." [laughs] And then he just set out to break my guitar. He basically sabotaged me again and again and again and that was it.

M: Was it his strange silent treatment that inspired the song that you told me about, the one in which you called Dylan "Romeo" and me "Martha" . . .

J: Oh, "Talk to Me." "We could talk about Martha / We could talk about Jesus and Hitler and Howard Hughes / Or Charlie Chaplin's movies / Or Bergman's Nordic blues." It's like, "Are we not an artistic community? Can't we talk about art, painting, philosophy, history . . ." Do we have to talk about [mimicking Dylan], "Are you still with that drummer? Does he get you off?" Do you have to come close up with the camera on my lips and say [Dylan's voice], "Say something about sex, Joni."

So you know what I said? "I'm not gonna say anything sexy. I'm gonna say something revolting." And it came to my mind, "Men fake coming," because you never hear that said. The cameras went down and every guy in the room went blank. That was the end of that.

> Oh, I talk too loose
> Again I talk too open and free
> I pay a high price for my open talking
> Like you do for your silent mystery
>
> Come and talk to me
> Please talk to me
> Talk to me, talk to me
> Mr. Mystery
>
> We could talk about Martha
> We could talk about landscapes
> I'm not above gossip
> But I'll sit on a secret where honor is at stake
> Or we could talk about power
> About Jesus and Hitler and Howard Hughes
> Or Charlie Chaplin's movies

Or Bergman's Nordic blues
Please just talk to me
Any old theme you choose
Just come and talk to me
Mr. Mystery, talk to me

You could talk like a fool I'd listen
You could talk like a sage
Anyway the best of my mind
All goes down on the strings and the page
That mind picks up all these pictures
It still gets my feet up to dance
Even though it's covered with keyloids
From the "slings and arrows of outrageous romance"
I stole that from Willy the Shake!
You know — "Neither a borrower nor a lender be"
Romeo, Romeo talk to me

Is your silence that golden?
Are you comfortable in it?
Is it the key to your freedom
Or is it the bars on your prison?
Are you gagged by your ribbons?
Are you really exclusive or just miserly?
You spend every sentence as if it was marked currency
Come and spend some on me
Shut me up and talk to me
I'm always talking
Chicken squawking
Please talk to me
                ("Talk to Me")

M: Wow, that's "open talking," alright. Here you were quoting "Willy the Shake," and I'm quoting you . . . as have many others over the years. Do you ever quote your own songs?

J: I have a friend who comes over every week and I'd start into a sentence and he'd cut me off and come to a conclusion, before he hadn't even heard the rest of the sentence. Again and again and again. I had to quote him:

"Land of snap decisions
Land of short attention spans
Nothing is savoured
Long enough
To really understand
In every culture in decline
The watchful ones among the slaves
Know all that is genuine will be
Scorned and conned and cast away."

M: And that is from?

J: "Dog Eat Dog." I'd start a sentence. He jumps in. *Boo!* "Wait a minute," I said, "Hang on. Save your comment till the end."
Annie Leibovitz also. When I showed the video of my ballet to Annie . . .

M: Annie Leibovitz the photographer?

J: Yes, I did a photo session with Annie Leibovitz. I had just done my ballet and I wanted to leap around and get her to do action shots of me in movement, but she wanted to pose me and she stuck me in this position that was very uncomfortable, and I kept saying, "Annie, I hope this looks good because it feels terrible." I'm supposed to be lounging but I'm in pain. "Does it look like I'm in pain?"
At the end of it, I wanted to show her and this girl from *Vanity Fair* the video of the ballet.

M: Just to clarify, Joni, are you referring to the ballet, *The Fiddle and the Drum*, that's based on your songs?

J: We did a video of that ballet, which I'm proud of because it transcended stylistic problems that I've had to deal with. So I put it on and Annie goes, "Oh, long dissolves. I hate long dissolves." Right straight to it. "I know, I know, I couldn't do anything about it, look, reserve judgment. Just take the trip."

We get into the second song, she goes, "He hates women."

I said, "No, Annie, 'Sex Kills' is the name of this piece. Listen to the words and look at the dance. I'm gonna start it over from the top. Every time you talk, I'm gonna start it from the top again."

So the girl from *Vanity Fair* said, "Don't you hate it when the artist is in the room?"

I said, "Of course you do, because you can't say all your catty things. But save them till the end. Just take the trip."

Now we get into the third song. We started from the top, Annie, she took the trip, and at the end she goes, "I can see your music."

And I went, "Yes!" Because [Jean Grand-Maître] did such a good job on the choreography. I told him it's got to be literal. "Make them see the music."

"I've got to listen to your music again," Annie said. And I looked over at her and she had this expression on her face, which I've seen on a friend of mine's face who had a lot of phobias — fear of flying being one — and after I made her fly to The Last Waltz because I was the only woman there, just to have a woman with me, she had this kind of "I did it!" look on her face. So now I looked at Annie and she had that kind of look. It was like soft, internal, self-surprised, and kind of glowing.

"What are you thinking right now?" I said.

"I'm thinking that I try too hard," she said.

I said, "Yes, you do! I've been on sessions with you, quite a few. You're well established. You don't have to worry like that."

She said, "I'm gonna change . . . the next shoot, I'm gonna change the way . . ."

And, apparently, she did. I don't know whether it was for better or worse. [laughs]

M: Annie Leibowitz was right, you could really see your music in that ballet.

J: After the premiere of the ballet, we went downstairs and we came up in an auditorium with a few art students from the art school in the building. It was ten o'clock at night or something, but there was a good little crowd there, impromptu. And we were to talk about the ballet. The one thing I really remember about it was, there were quite a few Native painters in the room, men at the back, and this thirty-ish Indian woman near the front. And at the end of the talk that Jean and I gave, there was a questions and answers. And the Native woman stood up and she said [mimics in a deep voice], "I used to think your work was silly." The two girls at the back went, "Oh, shut up." She turned around and she said, "You shut up. I used to think your work was silly. But now I don't." And she sat down. I cracked up. I really wanted to know, "What did you think was silly and why don't you think it's silly now? It left me with some curiosity. What happened? What changed your mind? What was your aversion and what is your attraction now?" I never did ask the question but . . . I loved that speech: "I used to think your work was silly, but now I don't." [laughs]

M: I saw the ballet at the Four Seasons Centre for the Performing Arts in Toronto; my hands nearly bled from applauding the live performance, and strange, but I loved even more the video version of it.

J: You know, the assumption was you can't dance to Joni Mitchell's music. As a matter of fact, after the ballet, this one fellow wrote, "When I was young, I took some Joni Mitchell records to a party." And they went, "You can't dance to that." And the Alberta Ballet proved if you know how to dance, you sure as hell could dance to Joni Mitchell. So it was a great reprise for the music and all the dance that it contained, to do that ballet and to see Jean so sympathetically articulate my rhythms with dance.

M: When you saw the ballet, and you heard the reaction of the people to your old songs, did you feel like holding the guitar and starting to sing?

J: I've been trying to . . . Freddy is helping me set up my VG-8, but my computer dropped.

M: VG-8?

J: A VG-8 contained all my tunings, but I didn't play it for a long time because I've been very ill since 2007, and by sitting idle, the computer dumped everything that we programmed, so we've got to do it over and he's not well also. So the last three years we were inching our way to getting this thing up and going.

M: You were described in a book or a magazine I read as "the James Joyce of guitar tuning." It maintained that you originated thirty-five guitar tunings.

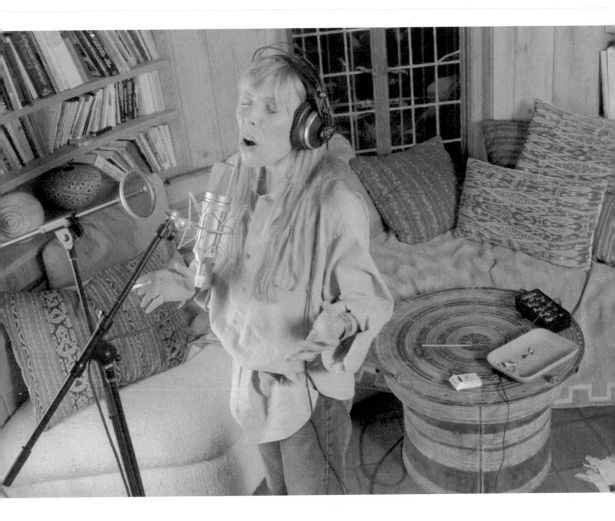

Joni in 1989 in her L.A. living room, where the marjority of the 2012 interview was recorded

© Neal Preston/Corbis

J: More . . . I don't even know how many.

M: Someone will probably find the number on the web.

J: On the web, there are these old clips of when I was still Joan Anderson, I hadn't married Chuck Mitchell yet, and the men on the show are staring at me like I'm from Mars. It's really a revelation because that's the beginning, and I didn't realize there was living evidence of the beginning, before even the Mitchell thing.

I'm doing folk songs for the most part. One I do, "Urge for Going," which was one of the very first songs I wrote and, I never thought of it till I saw this clip, but the language, it's more literate than most folk songs and there's words, they don't seem like abnormal words to me, but they do to a man in the camera shot next to me. A word will hit and he'll [roll his eyes] like that, and then there's a comment on one of these clips where the host of *Let's Sing Out* says, "She's looking directly into the camera." And I thought, "What is this?" It's like my dad going, "You're shaking hands with him like he's an equal." I find it very strange.

I awoke today and found the frost
perched on the town
It hovered in a frozen sky, then it
gobbled summer down
When the sun turns traitor cold and all
the trees are shivering in a naked row

I get the urge for going
But I never seem to go
I get the urge for going
When the meadow grass is turning brown
Summertime is falling down and winter
is closing in

I had me a man in summertime
He had summer-coloured skin
And not another girl in town
My darling's heart could win
But when the leaves fell on the ground
Bully winds came around, pushed them face down in the snow

He got the urge for going
And I had to let him go
He got the urge for going
When the meadow grass was turning brown
Summertime was falling down and winter was closing in

Now the warriors of winter they gave a cold triumphant shout
And all that stays is dying and all that lives is getting out
See the geese in chevron flight flapping and racing on before the snow

They've got the urge for going
And they've got the wings so they can go
They get the urge for going
When the meadow grass is turning brown
Summertime is falling down and winter
is closing in

I'll ply the fire with kindling now
I'll pull the blankets up to my chin
And I'll lock the vagrant winter out and bolt my wandering in
I'd like to call back summertime
Have her stay for just another
month or so

But she's got the urge for going
So I guess she'll have to go
She gets the urge for going
When the meadow grass is turning brown
All her empire's falling down
And winter's closing in
And I get the urge for going
When the meadow grass is turning brown
And summertime is falling down
            ("Urge for Going")

M: Are you excited now that you're packing to move up to your place in British Columbia?

J: Yeah. I should have a seventieth birthday party there, like we did my sixtieth. It's gonna be a nice house. And the basement, this archival basement that I put in, it's a fireproof room. I'm shipping everything up there. Then I'm gonna sort it, so that

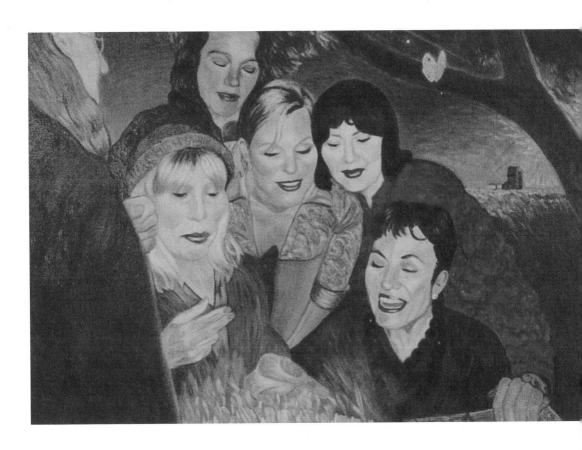

The Birthday Party
© Joni Mitchell

when I pass, at least it's not scattered all over the place and there's some kind of organization.

M: That should take a bit of time . . . I mean, hopefully, it would stretch to when we'll celebrate your eightieth, and judging by your genes, your ninetieth and the hundredth as well. [laughs]

J: You'll like the [way] my kitchen door slides back and it's completely open, like a Mexican house.

M: How wonderful that you don't have to close anything like we do in Muskoka, because you don't have mosquitos.

J: Yeah, we do. A lot of mosquitoes. And I have no screens on in the house.

M: No screens?

J: Nowhere. The architect made no allowance for screen or for . . . He doesn't care about me. He just cares about the Joni Mitchell house. [laughs]

M: [laughs] Is it all open or do you have walls to hang your paintings?

J: It's not a good house for paintings. The walls are stone hard, you can't put the nail where you want it. Did you move the big red poppy painting to your apartment?

M: Yes.

J: I love that painting. I like that better than any of Georgia O'Keeffe's flowers. It's beautiful. That vermillion, the red, that particular red. You told me a story about it a long time ago, but I forget what it was.

M: It was the first painting that my friend Helen Lucas painted in colour after years of black and white. I loved it at first sight, I wanted to buy it the moment I saw it, and when I moved to the house in the Village there was a perfect place for it over the fireplace . . .

J: Yeah, you couldn't find a painting in the world that would grace that place more.

M: Yes, I was dying to buy it but I was afraid that she wouldn't charge me for what it's worth, even for half its worth, because we were close friends. So I was still trying to figure out how to approach her on this when I was unpacking the heap of boxes that the movers lugged to the house, and in walks Helen carrying that painting. And she says, "I want to give it to you as a wedding present, but I don't know if you will like it."

She was reluctant to bring it because she thought I might not like it. And I was reluctant to buy it because I feared she will not charge us enough and she needed the money at that time.

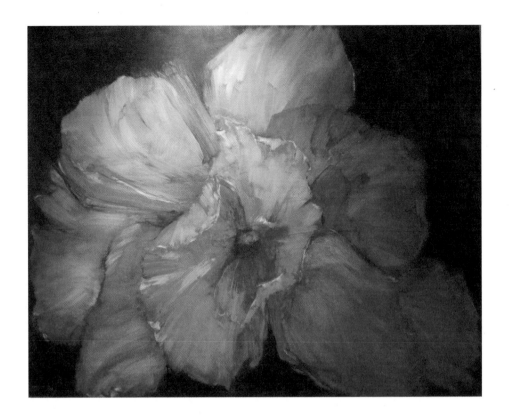

Helen Lucas's flower painting

© Helen Lucas, photo by Jen Knoch

J: The red, it's a transparent crimson. The brush she used, the transparency of the strokes on the petals . . . Completely confident she got it right the first time. She didn't fuss.

M: It looks like a vagina . . .

J: Well, flowers do. They look like sex. They all do. [laughs]
    It's nice talking about other things other than mine.

M: Getting back to your new house, is it near the ocean like your old cottage?

J: No, it's high up, there's quite a drop-off from the deck down, and there's rocks all the way out. I go to the edge of the rocks and dangle my legs off, that's okay, as long as it's in the house. But I can't walk on any of the ground. I feel like I'm gonna twist my ankle all the time.

M: You have to get good country hiking boots.

J: It's not the boots. It's the muscles. It's just that you're coming from walking on flat surfaces, to walking where everything's uneven, so you're rickety when you first get up there, and it takes a little bit of time. I used to run over those goddamn rocks like a deer, at night!

I remember I invited this guy up there one time for a romantic interlude and there was a place I wanted to take him. There was a high tide that night, and the inlets are full of logs, and the trail was full of ankle twisters. So I said, "Well, let's just walk across the logs."

You've got wet logs floating in the ocean. We're carrying sleeping bags and a lantern. He's completely green to the neighbourhood, so I took his lantern, his sleeping bag, I've got everything and I'm leading the way, and when we get to this place, he had no desire for me and I wondered why. [laughs]

There's a beauty to growing old.

M: And power, according to Isak Dinesen, the woman who wrote *Out of Africa*.

J: She's a very big Nietzsche fan also.

M: Isak Dinesen said that when women are old enough to be done with the business of being women, and can let loose their strength, they are maybe the most powerful creatures in the world.

J: I don't really want to go necessarily in that direction. I guess it's the Buddhist desire in me, I don't like to think of myself as a powerful woman. I watch people vicariously using my power. I would never use it. You know what I mean?

M: No, as a matter of fact, I don't.

J: You know, my housekeeper would go into a restaurant and say, "I'm Joni's confidante," and they'd send champagne to her table. And she'd get very uppity and she'd behave like stars do, vicariously. "The food is not right . . . I'm an associate of Joni Mitchell." She would do all of these things that I would never do, and they would put up with it and they'd indulge her in it, as if she was a star. I've seen people around me using my power vicariously that I would never use myself. "You live here like a star / Rent-free suite"

M: "Big blue pool"

J: "That you sing by"

M: "Trips to . . ."

J: ". . . to tropic shores / Clothes from fancy stores. / You want too much."

M: "You want too badly / You want everything for nothing."

J: That's a give-nothing-to-get. Give-to-get. There's just some people that feel entitled. Like, "I'll hang around her. She's rich and she'll just give me . . ." And the more you give them, the cheaper they think you are. Even though I always pay the bill.

M: I could see when we went out to dinner, the server went with the bill directly to you. I was amazed that he didn't even say, "Are you going to split the bill?"

J: I'm always amazed when somebody takes me out to dinner.

M: I marvel at your openness, Joni, while I feel that there's something sad about it, not you. You state it just as a matter of fact, open as ever.

J: Oh yeah. I still don't edit. I should maybe have more discriminating awareness as to what to spit out or what to not; I mean, I still don't have the sense to guard myself.

M: Well, in that case, could I ask you something trivial, silly, really, because you look great, not only for your age, but really beautiful. And since you have a song called "Face Lift," and you live in Hollywood . . . Were you, are you, tempted to do a facelift?

J: Oh, not at all. I see women with facelifts that are horrible and they're delusional. They really think they look nice. Me, I have to think: I look awful, and rise above it and forget what I look like. [laughs]

I was always on the cusp of beauty. Some thought I was, some thought I wasn't. In my teens I was more neurotic about it, but as I became a writer, I didn't wear any makeup. I didn't wear it even on TV. They thought it was because I was religious or something, but I never thought it would enhance me.

> We pushed the bed
> Up to the window
> To see the Christmas lights . . .
> On the east bank
> Across the steaming river
> Between the bridges
> Lit up
> Paris like.
> This river has run through both our lives
> Between these banks of our continuing delights!
> Bless us!
> Don't let us lose the drift . . .
> You know
> Happiness
> Is the best
> Face lift
>
>   ("Face Lift")

M: You told me recently that you have been talking to yourself. What are you telling yourself?

J: I'm thinking out loud. It's the same thing that I would have done before, only I would write it down, but now I can't write very much. I write every day a little bit, but I don't do anything with it. I don't have the thing that makes you finish.

M: You have the spark, but you cannot start the fire.

J: Right. I get ideas. I write a little bit down. I think more on that topic, just think, "Where else can I take this?" This is the spark of it. Where do I go from here?

M: When I talk to myself, I split myself into two people, and I tell one self, "Do this, don't do this, you are silly." Is that how you . . . ?

J: No, I'm reliving old injuries. I'm reliving them and I'm telling the person off that I didn't tell off. I'm trying to expel anger. And it hangs in the air and I go, "Was that very satisfactory, when you said that to them? No." And then I kind of do it again.

It's almost like a writing process.

Since these people have been injurious to me, their bad conduct has affected me, it's stuck in me, like a poison dart. How do I get these poison darts out? What would I like to say to these people? Well, it starts like a kind of an inarticulate rage, and it does no good at all. It begets war.

I'm not a vindictive person. The kind of vengeance I like is the thing that stops the war. You get your respect back. They realize they cannot step on you. But you do it in such a way that it doesn't fan the flame. I've done that a few times. It's very satisfactory for revenge. That's the only kind I like. Anything that fans the flame and creates further enmity is not very satisfactory to me. But now I'm experiencing my ugly side.

M: You're trying to exorcise it like that.

J: I guess that's what I'm trying to do. Because I've asked myself, "What are you trying to do?" Are you gonna be like one of those crazy people walking down the street, shaking a fist at the sky? If you keep this up much longer, it could become your behaviour. It can stick.

"Are you working through something or are you developing into something?" It's a good question. I think I'm working through something because it's quieting down. It's kind of like my primal scream.

M: I find that the anger is mostly directed at myself: "Why did I do this? Why didn't I do that?" And sometimes I forget, and I talk like this in public too.

J: Yeah, you could be training a bad habit. It's too much time alone that brings it on. And with it a new problem. Too many strangers are coming into my home. Too many people know I'm home and live alone and have nice things.

The world's a cold and hostile place. So I figure that if I could get my dogs to stop shitting . . . they'd snuggle up to me and we get to walk. I can talk to them instead of to the walls. [laughs]

> I wish I had more sense of humour
> Keeping the sadness at bay
> Throwing the lightness on these things
> Laughing it all away
> Laughing it all away
> Laughing it all away
>   ("People's Parties")

J: I want to show you the video of this homage that they paid to my songs at the Hollywood Bowl with this great jazz band when I was too ill to be there. Brian, Brian Blade, the musical director said, "Joni, if only it was you up there."

The difference would be . . . If I had my chops up, every night is going to be different. Every night I'm gonna lay on a different word and I'm gonna syncopate it different. Real jazz, improvisational. Brian would be watching me like a hawk to see where I'm going to go. He's gonna watch my shoulders and he's gonna see where I'm gonna go, right or left, or if I'm gonna hold something. He's gonna play a lick, I'm gonna hear it, it's gonna influence what I sing next. I'm gonna echo him, and with that calibre of musician now you're interacting.

M: Sounds like you're dying to sing, Joni, with that band. And that you were talking to yourself in order to limber up your singing voice, and your writing voice . . .

J: I'm not up to it yet. When I sing, I get nervous energy. My fingers go like this . . . The fingertips kind of jingle a rhythm. Have you ever seen that when I'm not playing an instrument?

M: Nana Mouskouri goes like this too when she sings. Quite a few singers have that.

J: Whitney Houston did. Joe Cocker. There weren't that many.

Anyway, in the second half of that homage, Brian reads from the *Hejira*. Not from the *Hejira*, but from liner notes, and I thought, "I wrote that?" I don't know how I wrote them. It's like I look back and there's parts on it that have been shed. Who was that person? Like the pink high heels in the garage. And the person who wrote these liner notes . . . I can't write like that anymore, anymore than I can draw like I did when I said to Leonard's friend Mort [Rosengarten], "I don't like the way I draw." And he said, "Draw me and don't look at the paper."

I was trying then to shed this fantasy head for a more realistic approach. But this kind of writing in the liner notes, I'm just kind of surprised because I can't relate anymore. I can't imagine writing anything like that now.

M: These liner notes and whole albums, you can download them [illegally] from the internet these days. Does it affect your retirement fund that people can download your music without paying?

J: Yeah. That's like stealing from a shoe store and fifty percent of your stock or eighty percent of your stock is being stolen on a daily basis.

M: Such a high percentage?

J: Absolutely. And at a certain point, if you're not bringing in enough, you're not a big enough fry and the [record company] dumps you. The more they dump you, the sleazier the people who answer for it.

On the other hand, look at Jean and my ballet. We didn't make a dime, it cost me money to do it. And yet it's playing in Brazil.

M: You mean a video of your ballet is playing there?

J: Yeah. The video cost me money to make. I didn't get paid at all. I never will. But it is travelling the world, so your art is reaching people. And I want to educate and make aware of certain things that will help the planet. For that, I don't really care if I get paid or that it cost me money to participate in it. Because I hope that the payment will stimulate cultural awareness.

M: Hopefully that would also be the payment for all your songs that people download for free.

I'd like to turn to Nietzsche now, you'll be glad to hear. [laughs] You mentioned Nietzsche before, a few times before.

J: There's a lot of Nietzsche in my songs. I think that what I have in common with him is you can keep your religions as long as you know that it's allegory. Let's not believe in Santa Claus into adulthood.

But the main thing I took from Nietzsche is a support . . . he's describing how Germany decayed. And I take that thought, and I show how America is decaying.

"I picked the morning paper off the floor
It was full of other people's little wars
Wouldn't they like their peace?
Don't we get bored
And we call for the three great stimulants
Of the exhausted ones
Artifice, brutality and innocence."

It's basically, since innocence is lost, it's innocence defiled. It becomes a new obsession. People want to fuck children because they're innocent and they want to make them dirty. They want that innocence but they want to fuck it because they're not innocent. So in decadence, there's an increase of pedophilia.

The next verse, "no tanks have ever rumbled through these streets," it's describing peace time.

Machiavelli knew this. He said, "Peace. People don't know what to do with it. It always degenerates into fornication and fashion." Isn't that a great quote? What is the point of peace if people are just gonna change their clothes and fuck a lot.

The whole song ["The Three Great Stimulants"] is a warning. We are repeating history. We are now on the brink as Rome was in its fall, Germany in its fall. And we're slipping further and further into pornography, into the cesspool of it all.

"No tanks have ever rumbled through these streets
And the drone of planes at night has never frightened me
I keep the hours and the company that I please
And we call for the three great stimulants
Of the exhausted ones."

The decadent ones, the ones that are going down. Artifice, brutality and innocence.

"And deep in the night
Our appetites find us
Amuse us and blind us."
In one verse I say, "bind us."
"Deep in the night
While madmen sit up building bombs
And building locks and bars
They're gonna slam free choice behind us."

M: You admire Nietzsche even though his name is almost synonymous with anti-Semite.

J: Erroneous rap for being anti-Semitic. He was not. He was dying of syphilis and he described that kind of a Jew in the gold market. And that's what got him the anti-Semitic rap.

M: It seems you have — let's call it a kinship, not only with Nietzsche, but with Yeats, Kipling, Picasso, and Van Gogh. I don't see women in here.

J: No. I think it's because my dad would come home and go, "Oh, gee, I just had such a nice night out with the boys." And my mother would go out and she'd come home and she'd go, "Those damn women." My mother didn't get along with her mother. She had a lot of brothers. My father had a lot of sisters and really trivialized women basically, but enjoyed men's company.

And in my own interactions growing up, I found the girls conspiratorial, arbitrary, envious, like their mothers who were driving my mother crazy in the neighbourhood. The boys lacked imagination, but there was a camaraderie with them.

M: But you do have women friends, lifelong women friends. So it's not as if you have an aversion to women.

J: I think women have an aversion to me. Even Betsy who is a lifelong friend observed that I'm more myself in the company of men.

And men always said, "You're one of the boys." So I said to Tony [Simon, a friend since childhood], "Why was I one of the boys? Was I not feminine?"

"Oh no, you're plenty feminine. It's just that we could be ourselves around you."

So I'm comfortable with men. I make them comfortable. I like their goofiness. And a lot of times I don't know the "lipstick" conversations. I didn't know how to talk to girls.

"Oh, Joni, do you have to talk about Nietzsche? Couldn't you talk about nail polish?" Betsy used to say. It's mainly that. That I'm a bit of a cad.

M: I think Dylan said, in one of the clippings I read, "Joni is like a man . . ."

J: Oh, that thing. Well, they asked him, "What do you think of women singers?" And he went, "They tart themselves."

Then they went, "All of them?"

And he went, "Yeah."

"Well, what about Joni Mitchell?"

"Oh, Joni, she's like a man." Then he went further though to explain it. "She gets to tell the band what time it is."

So basically I'm like a man because I lead a band. Well, why does that make me like a man? Because I'm not like a man, but I'm a thinking female and I'm not a feminist. So what am I then? A real freak, right? I'm a person outside every box there is, pretty much.

M: Must make you lonely.

J: Sometimes it does. Sometimes I think, "Geez, Joan, you should make an alliance with something. You don't have a church, you don't have a country. You've got an international spirit. You don't have an orthodoxy in terms of . . . you don't stick to one art. You're kind of contemptuous of music tradition for yourself."

I've been excommunicated from every school in music there is. They had excommunicated me from Nashville for bringing a jazz band into the Grand Ole Opry. They thought I was a country singer or a folk singer until I started doing what they called pop music, which is just my music with a band added. Then when I was working with jazz musicians, you were getting kicked out of things for the hybrids. But the only way to anything fresh is to hybrid.

Up until *Court and Spark*, they wouldn't play me on the radio because there was no drums. So I get drums, I get a little airplay and then suddenly it gets too jazzy and

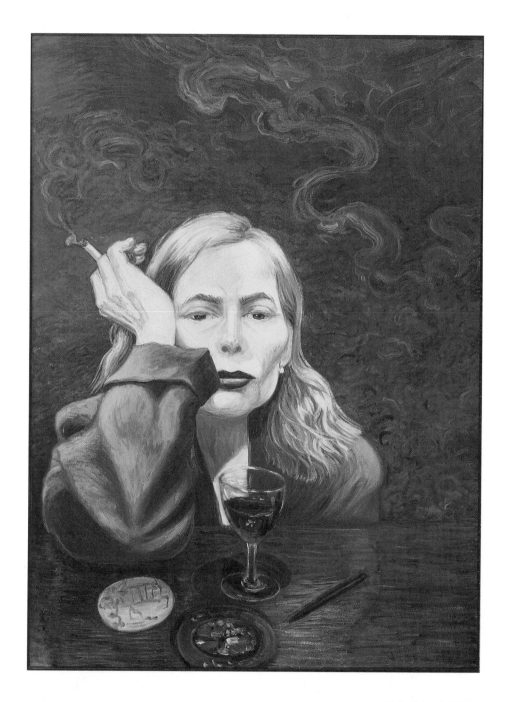

Both Sides 1, 1999

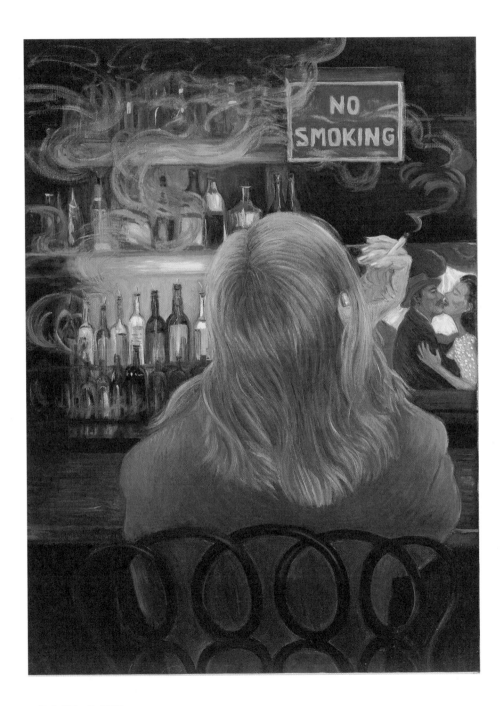

Both Sides 2, 1999
© Joni Mitchell, photo by Sheila Spence

by *Mingus* they said, "If you make this album, they're gonna excommunicate you from the airwaves."

In this society of specialists, I'm going to be treated as a dilettante. As a painter because of my day job [laughs] as a singer/songwriter . . .

There are still some people, they still call me a singer when they write about me or, worse than that, a folk singer.

M: How do you want them to call you?

J: Gershwin was a composer. So am I. I do my own arrangements. I have won awards for arrangements and instrumental music.

M: Do you want to be called a composer? What would you like to be called?

J: I don't know. You'd have to hyphenate, a painter and a poet and a composer. But that leaves out singer. There's a lot of various skills going on, I guess. If you trail too many hyphens . . . I don't know what you'd call it.

It's definitely Renaissance.

M: I heard from survivors that the greatest motivating force in their life was the feeling that you must do something with this life that was saved. Do you think that surviving polio, and other such, spurred you on to venture on this path of doing something with the life that you . . . ?

J: Absolutely.

There's something weird and unique and given to me to be in pain to an abnormal degree, to take it personally . . . it really hurts me personally, more than the loss of a lover, to see a species die.

That's my cross to bear. Not as much as when I was in my twenties, when I would just burst into tears if I'd see a motorboat. But the idea that oil is being hauled around . . . I can't tell you how it pains me whenever I hear of an oil spill. It just tears me up inside.

Why I have to take it so personally, I don't know. I take it physically in my body every time a tanker spills. I see vividly fish gasping for air. I see the atrocities that our ignorant modernity . . . I see the Frankenstein of it all.

My greatest desire is impossible.

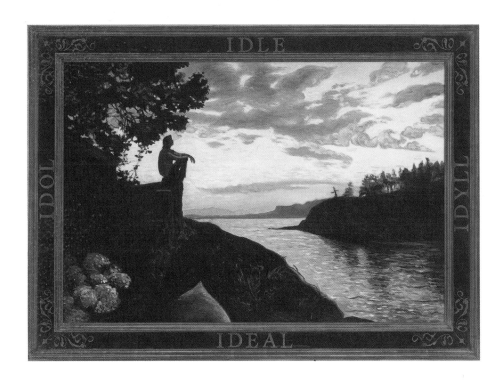

Middle Point, 1995
© Joni Mitchell, photo by Sheila Spence

M: Which is?

J: It's impossible because of the short-sighted stupidity of my species.

Our whole lifestyle is carcinogenic, modernity and technology . . . although I've used it, and I've used the technology to a degree. I'm reluctant to get a cellphone . . . Emily Carr felt like that when she got a radio. It's so funny reading her book.

A radio is in her house. She feels the same way as I do about later gadgetry, but she also, like me, is a visual person canoeing with the Natives and spending days in the bush painting these old villages, so she, like me, is a very earthy woman at heart.

M: Do you think that this particular sensitivity has to do with you growing up as a child in a small town, very close to the earth?

J: Yeah, and my smoking . . . [laughs] When the kids were unreasonable, which they frequently were — jealous, envious, petty, conspiratorial, boring — I would ride my bike out into the country, park it and look for a pretty place. A pretty place was falling water, if it was spring, coming out of a culvert or . . . farmers. Farmers then, they're all gone — it used to be that they would plough in circles around a little grove and in the spring, the birds would be building their nests. I'd sit and smoke and lean against a tree and watch the birds go in and out. And I would just be so . . . happy.

Now most of them, they've got big combines and they've cut the groves down and they go straight across.

M: So this is the sorrow — is it sort of a sense of loss of what you had when you were a child?

J: No. It's a sense of stupidity that people would do the things they've done for a buck. What is your buck gonna buy?

"Don't it always seem to go. You don't know what you've got till it's gone." It's basically that. Because of the short-sighted nature of my species, that deadly combination of not being able to see the consequences into the future of their actions for further generations. No ancestral worship. Me me me me me. The me-ness of my generation. No generation before us could afford to be that selfish.

M: To me — [laughs] sorry for using the me word — to me you are not "only" an artist but a woman that has lived in the arts, with the arts since childhood, and living alone mostly. You don't have anybody supporting you. You're supporting others. To me, you are one of the bravest women I know.

J: I'm good in a crisis. I don't panic.

My karma or my star thing — a pretty girl having fun. I think this is one of the things that had to be done to me to hobble me, to slow me down in a certain way, to get me to fulfill my destiny, to use my depth to do these things — I think it was karmically necessary.

I think that in some cases, destiny has to be run out of you by hardship. If things are going smooth, in the spurts of health that I have, I just go out and enjoy, which is the right thing to do because it's a respite. Little R&R before the next battle.

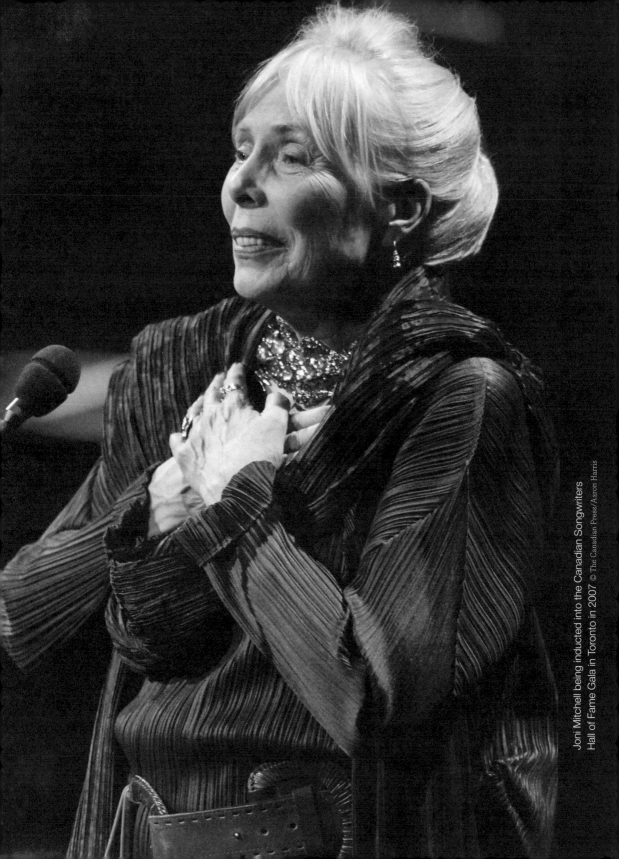

Joni Mitchell being inducted into the Canadian Songwriters Hall of Fame Gala in Toronto in 2007 © The Canadian Press/Aaron Harris

River

It's coming on christmas
They're cutting down trees
They're putting up reindeer
And singing songs of joy and peace
Oh, I wish I had a river
I could skate away on
But it don't snow here
It stays pretty green
I'm going to make a lot of money
Then I'm going to quit this crazy scene
Oh, I wish I had a river
I could skate away on

I wish I had a river
so long
I would teach my feet to fly
Oh I wish I had a river
I made my baby cry.

He tried hard to help me
He put me at ease
He loved me so naughty -
Made me weak in the knees
Oh, I wish I had a river
I could skate away on
But I'm so hard to handle
I'm selfish and I'm sad
Now I've gone and lost the best baby
That I ever had
Oh, I wish I had a river
I could skate away on
I wish I had a river
so long
I would teach these feet to fly
Oh I wish I had a river
I made my good baby say goodbye.

ACKNOWLEDGEMENTS

I'm deeply grateful to Joni Mitchell — for her poetry, her music, her art, and her generosity of heart and spirit.

Heartfelt thanks to Daniel Marom, who first suggested these conversations·be published; to the literary agent Linda McKnight, who took on this book for the sheer love of it; to publisher Jack David, who afforded me that wonderful grace note in life — a second chance; to my editor, Jen Knoch, for being a dream of an editor and a dream to work with; to Crissy Calhoun and the rest of the magicians at ECW Press; to the Ontario Arts Council for their grant; to Leah Lublin, who transcribed all the conversations; to Elliot Roberts, Henry Lewy, Tom Scott, and the musicians of the L.A. Express; to Anne Bayin, for the gift of friendship and wisdom; and to Marv Cohen, for the butterfly dust.

At ECW Press, we want you to enjoy this book in whatever format you like, whenever you like. Leave your print book at home and take the eBook to go! Purchase the print edition and receive the eBook free. Just send an email to ebook@ecwpress.com and include:

- the book title
- the name of the store where you purchased it
- your receipt number
- your preference of file type: PDF or ePub?

A real person will respond to your email with your eBook attached. And thanks for supporting an independently owned Canadian publisher with your purchase!

Get the eBook free!*
*proof of purchase required